Praise for
Inclusive Leader

❚❚ This book is a high impact, practical how-to guide to D&I, drawing on the extensive real-life experience of two master practitioners.
STEPHEN SIDEBOTTOM, GLOBAL HEAD OF HR, CIB, STANDARD CHARTERED BANK

❚❚ This book provides a thorough introduction to D&I with practical and pragmatic advice on how to create a truly inclusive culture. We know that if we get inclusion right, much of our diversity ambitions will follow. Whilst I see compelling research on D&I, there is little advice on how to put this into practice. Fleur and Charlotte have laid out a clear and pragmatic approach that will serve us all well.
PETER DUFF, HEAD OF DIVERSITY AND INCLUSION (EMEA), INTERNAIONAL OIL AND GAS COMPANY

❚❚ In a world of increasing disruption, there has never been a better time for organisations to evaluate where they are on the continuum of inclusive leadership, both internally and externally. This practical book offers insightful stories and guidance to bring to life an effective approach to driving sustainable culture change.
CLAIRE IGHODARO CBE, INDEPENDENT DIRECTOR AND TRUSTEE

❚❚ Finally, a book that can guide both the experienced and inexperienced leaders to implementing diversity and inclusion in their organisations. Moving from 'initiatives' to 'business change' is a challenge for many – Charlotte and Fleur seamlessly walk you through how to do this, sharing examples from their vast experience. A must read for any leader who is serious about attracting the best and getting the best from their people.
SADEQ SAYEED, FORMER CEO, NOMURA INTERNATIONAL

" Admirably qualified to write about the practical challenges, and opportunities, in promoting diversity in business and creating inclusive workplaces. Full of pragmatic ways forward that enable you to convert words into action.

THE RT HON SIR VINCE CABLE, FORMER SECRETARY OF STATE FOR BUSINESS, INNOVATION AND SKILLS

Inclusive Leadership

Inclusive Leadership

The definitive guide to developing and executing an impactful diversity and inclusion strategy – locally and globally

Charlotte Sweeney and Fleur Bothwick

PEARSON

Harlow, England • London • New York • Boston • San Francisco • Toronto • Sydney
Auckland • Singapore • Hong Kong • Tokyo • Seoul • Taipei • New Delhi
Cape Town • São Paulo • Mexico City • Madrid • Amsterdam • Munich • Paris • Milan

PEARSON EDUCATION LIMITED
EDINBURGH GATE
HARLOW CM20 2JE
UNITED KINGDOM
TEL: +44 (0)1279 623623
WEB: WWW.PEARSON.COM/UK

First edition published 2016 (print and electronic)

ISBN: 978-1-292-11272-5 (print)
978-1-292-11274-9 (PDF)
978-1-292-11275-6 (ePub)

British Library Cataloguing-in-Publication Data
A catalogue record for the print edition is available from the British Library

Library of Congress Cataloging-in-Publication Data
Names: Sweeney, Charlotte, author. | Bothwick, Fleur, author.
Title: Inclusive leadership : Inclusive Leadership: the definitiveg uidet od evelopingand executing an impactful diversity and inclusion strategy - locally and globally / Charlotte Sweeney and Fleur Bothwick.
Description: 1 Edition. | New York : Pearson Education, 2016. |rlcludes bibliographical references.
Identifiers:L CCN2 016033806(print)| L CN2 016034392(ebook)| I BN 9781292112725 (pbk.) | ISBN 9781292112749 (PDF) |9BN 9781292112756 (ePub) | ISBN 9781292112756 ()
Subjects: LCSH: Leadership.
Classification:LCCHD57.7.S942016(print)|L CHD57.7(ebook)|D CD 658.4/092--dc23
LC record available at https://lccn.loc.gov/2016033806

Cover design by Two Associates
Print edition typeset in 9.25 pt Frutiger by iEnergizer Aptara®, Ltd.
NOTE THAT ANY PAGE CROSS REFERENCES REFER TO THE PRINT EDITION

Contents

About the authors

Fleur Bothwick OBE

Fleur has worked in the field of diversity and inclusive lead-ership for the past 15 years. She currently leads D&I for the EMEIA Region at EY which is made up of Europe, the Middle East, India and Africa with 99 countries and some 100,000 people. Her role entails developing, driving and embedding an integrated diversity strategy across this large multi-disciplined matrix organisation.

Prior to joining EY, Fleur spent 18 years in the investment banking sector in both talent and D&I roles. A key focus for her current role is stakeholder engagement, specialist consultancy, change management and brand develop-ment in the market.

Fleur is a regular conference speaker and contributor to articles and research in this field. In the Queen's 2013 New Year's Honours List, she was named an Officer of the Order of the British Empire in recognition of her contribution to diversity and inclusion in the workplace.

Charlotte Sweeney

Charlotte has worked in the field of diversity and inclusion for over 15 years and is the driving force behind the programme 'Creating Inclusive Cultures' to drive sustainable change on inclusion across cities. She also has her own boutique consultancy firm that advises companies across many sectors on embedding D&I into their business strategies. She is Deputy Chair of Mid-Yorkshire NHS Trust in the United Kingdom and has led D&I for numerous multinational companies in the retail and investment banking sectors.

She led a high-profile independent review for the then Secretary of State, Dr Vince Cable, as well as co-led the Lord Mayor of London's pioneering programme 'The Power of Diversity'. She has also acted as Vice-Chair of the UK Government Advisory Panel for over six years.

She was recognised by TIAW for advancing the economic empowerment of women and The Global Diversity List/The Economist as a Top 50 Global Diversity Professional. In 2016 she was commended by Northern Power Women as a Transformational Leader and included in The Top 50 Power List.

She's an expert contributor on TV and radio (SkyNews, BBC Radio Five Live, ITV). She is a regular keynote speaker and writes for publications and research in this field.

Publishers's acknowledgements

We are grateful to the following for permission to reproduce copyright material:

Figure 3.1 adapted from 'stages in team development' figure, reproduced courtesy of Alan Richter; figure 13.1 reprinted courtesy of Dr David Matsumoto.

Foreword

Throughout my life I have experienced first-hand, the significance of seeing a spark of talent in someone and nurturing it, regardless of the individual's education or background, their gender, ethnicity or in fact any other factors that make up who they are.

I started my life in a community in West Yorkshire in the United Kingdom, where it would have been easy to get on to the wrong track and have a very different life experience to the one I've had. What changed that for me was the encouragement of my teachers and family who saw potential in me that could be developed further.

In my early life, growing up on the borders of a Protestant and Catholic community, which was also a border between the working and middle class, it became clear to me that diversity was more about a state of mind than something physical. In those days and often still today, people think the road to success in life is through academic achievement. This clearly is part of the answer, but it was in my teenage years that I discovered that the road to true 'mobility' comes from learning about the ways of life of other diverse communities.

Diversity stretches across society. It brings a freshness and selection of perspectives that should be encouraged and welcomed. We are all members of many tribes: wealth, religion, race, sexuality, mental ability, social interests, educational background, to name a few and arguably the two largest tribes relate to our gender.

Personally, it was through my experiences playing semi-professional sport that I really discovered the power of diversity. My sport spanned multiple communities across both geography and social class, I shared a house at University with three guys from the Sudan (one of whom was a direct descendant of al-Mahdi!) and when I started at IBM my boss was the son of an Indian Princess.

I have always sought diversity of thought in addition to the physical and cultural differences that are so often highlighted. We all have potential within us. Unfortunately for some, the opportunities are not obvious and there are often barriers, obstacles and bias, which are not always easy to navigate or overcome. This is not only unfortunate for the individual, but also devastating for the companies and economies that are not getting the best from harnessing the talent available.

This is why throughout my career I have been a huge champion and advocate of diversity and inclusion. For me, this isn't about an initiative, charity or something nice to do – it's a fundamental role of everyone who has management and leadership responsibilities, as well as those who represent the organisation in some way, i.e. it's everyone's responsibility!

I spent a significant amount of my career at IBM. From the very beginning I chose to work for, and with, people based on 'who' they were not 'what' they were. In my experience, teams of diverse personalities work far better together than teams of 'clones'. During my ten years as CEO of IBM UK and Chairman of IBM Europe, Middle East and Africa, I drove our D&I initiatives in an era where this topic received nowhere near the attention in society or business that it does today. There was far more resistance and push-back. However, I was determined to succeed. IBM UK were the original sponsors of the European Women of Achievement awards and the original sponsors of Everywoman some 16 years ago. I am still an ambassador and mentor to the founders of Everywoman today. We were an original sponsor of Stonewall, African Caribbean Network and others.

In terms of what we delivered on the ground at IBM, we stated that all roles in the company could be worked 'flexibly', to try and address the challenges of our people balancing their work hours with the rest of their life. We rewrote our executive competencies to be more gender friendly. I also declared a war on bullying and aggressive management styles. I believe this is the major outlet, both verbally and mentally, for prejudicial thought and behaviour and is a major inhibitor in creating a more inclusive workplace.

In our ever-changing and increasingly connected world it's an absolute business fundamental to seek out diverse talent, to garner different viewpoints and perspectives. It's also fundamental to create an environment where people feel comfortable that they can share their insights and blend them with other people's perspectives without fear of prejudice or bias creeping in. Why would anyone give their best in an organisation that doesn't value their unique views and give them the space and opportunities to use them to the best of their ability?

We have come a long way over the past couple of decades. Now I believe, certainly in some companies, we have reached a milestone in the journey of D&I with more of a focus on the measure of 'who' not 'what'. Yes, we have come a long way but we haven't come far enough and the pace of change should be faster. We need to continually learn and assess what works and what doesn't work, we need to engage and collaborate with our colleagues at all levels of our organisations and we need to convert our fine words into demonstrable, impactful action.

I'm delighted that Charlotte and Fleur have pooled together their significant knowledge and experience to share with you all how we make that change happen in a more sustainable way. One that will also enable you to deliver change in a realistic and reasonable timescale. They have created a definitive guide for people to work through regardless of whether you are the CEO, the D&I practitioner or a colleague at the sharp end delivering to customers and clients.

This book is full of practical tips and insights that you can digest and convert into practical delivery – they move away from purely reminding us that there is a challenge (as so many other books do) to holding your hand through the many steps that you need to take to create a sustainable diverse and inclusive environment that we all aspire to achieve. They seamlessly set out all the elements to consider, regardless of where you are starting on your journey or the size of your organisation – and share some of their own personal stories and experiences along the way.

If you are serious about creating a more diverse and inclusive workplace, if you are serious about embedding change throughout your company from colleagues to clients and from stakeholders to suppliers, if you are serious about being a great business leader of people – and everything else in-between – then this book is the definitive guide for you.

Larry Hirst CBE
Former Chairman IBM EMEA
Senior Independent Director of Mitie Group plc,
Independent Director of ARM Holdings plc,
Ambassador to Everywoman and Black British Business

Introduction

All organisations are perfectly designed to get the results they are now getting. If we want different results, we must change the way we do things. TOM NORTHUP, AUTHOR AND LEADERSHIP GURU

It's over two decades ago since we first started to hear people talk about diversity (usually without mention of inclusion) in relation to talent management. For many diversity and inclusion (D&I) practitioners it was almost by accident that they became involved in what would usually have been part of human resources (HR) or sometimes even corporate responsibility (CR).

Back then, people were far less 'politically correct' and it was not unusual for a manager, when briefing an HR director about an open vacancy, to make a comment such as they didn't want any 'fertile women' applying for the role because they already had two team members on maternity leave.

Recruitment agencies also supported the stereotypes and Fleur remembers being told once by an accountancy specialist that he tended to target Asian candidates because they were more numerate! Charlotte also recalls a conversation with a branch manager who didn't believe that anyone under the age of 35 could bring any value to their customers and that 'you had to earn your stripes over time'.

On the whole, such overtly biased conversations are now history in many geographies, but it doesn't mean that, as individuals, we don't momentarily process similar thoughts in the deep recesses of our minds. In addition, over the years, the reach of D&I has developed beyond talent management to have a significant influence over many aspects of how business operates.

One thing is certain, the term D&I is increasingly one that is part of the everyday business language in large employers and is raising its profile in small- to medium-sized workplaces. Given this, throughout this chapter we will cover what D&I is and articulate a number of reasons why it is important. We will also cover who may benefit from working through this book, as well as why we felt it would be valuable to share our experience.

What is diversity and inclusion?

It is important from the very beginning to outline what we actually mean by D&I as there are so many variations available. We have both experienced examples where the words D&I have been used interchangeably to have the same meaning when, in fact, they are both two very different words which are part of an important jigsaw.

Diversity is about every single person.

Everyone is unique and their perspectives are different, based on lots of influences such as their own life experiences, culture, learning styles, personality type, education; the list could go on. For this reason it is often misleading to stereotype anyone: for example, girls cry easily, boys are better at science, older people can't learn about new technology. Every single one of us makes up the richness of the mix and diversity, by default, is naturally around us.

The real challenge is making that mix work and that's where inclusion comes in.

Inclusion is about creating an environment where everyone can be themselves, feel that they are able to contribute their views and that these will be valued.

An example that is used to bring the above differences to life is a quote by Verna Myers, author and D&I professional based in the United States:[1] 'Diversity is being invited to the party; inclusion is being asked to dance.'

Although we will look at terminology in more detail later in the book, it would be remiss of us at this stage not to share what 'equality' and 'inclusive leadership' are. These are terms that are also used alongside D&I and it is important to understand the differences from the outset.

Prior to the start of the D&I journey, for many organisations the focus was on 'equal opportunities' or 'equality'. This was initially driven by legislative requirements and expectations from laws that were introduced. An example of this is the Sex Discrimination Act that was introduced in the United Kingdom in 1975.

Equal opportunities in the United Kingdom is defined as 'the right to be treated without discrimination' and equality is defined as 'the state of being equal, especially in status, rights or opportunities'.

The other term that is used within the D&I world is 'inclusive leadership'. An inclusive leader is someone who is aware of their own styles and how they view the world who then allows, in fact, invites, others to share their own perspectives and is able to work with many styles that are different from their own. We focus on inclusive leadership in more detail in the chapter on inclusive leadership development (see Chapter 13).

The above terminology can be confusing initially; Charlotte uses the following example to give a simple overview of the differences:

> *Equality is being invited into the room. Diversity is getting a seat at the table. Inclusion is sharing your views and being heard. An inclusive leader enables all of this to happen.*

Why is it important?

There are many reasons to focus on D&I in some way and often there is more than one reason why an organisation starts along this journey. One catalyst is the introduction of new legislation, for example quotas for nationals in the Middle East or the requirement to publish your gender pay gap in the United Kingdom. Another may be a tribunal claim/s made by a member of staff or low engagement scores in your employee survey. You might be prompted to do something to keep up with your competitors or to qualify to pitch for new business. In an ideal situation, the catalyst is when your leadership teams see the value of diverse perspectives and want to see it embedded in to how they do business.

At a high level we know that the world is changing and what we have done in the past is by no means confirmation of success in the future. Who would have thought over a decade ago that today:

- the world's largest taxi company would own no taxis (Uber)
- the largest accommodation provider would own no real estate (Airbnb)
- the largest phone companies would own no telecommunications infrastructure (Skype/WeChat)
- the most popular media owner would create no content (Facebook)
- the world's largest movie house would own no cinemas (Netflix).

When we specifically look at the changes we see in organisations, the case for change is compelling:

- In the United States women account for 85 per cent of all consumer purchases; this is similar in many other countries.[2]
- Research by McKinsey found that workforces that are both diverse and inclusive have 12 per cent higher employee productivity; 19 per cent higher retention; 57 per cent higher team collaboration and 42 per cent higher team commitment.[3]
- Deloitte identified an 80 per cent improvement in business performance when levels of diversity and inclusion were high.[4]
- Grant Thornton estimated the opportunity cost associated with male only boards was approximately US$655 billion for 1,050 companies across three markets (United States, India, United Kingdom).[5]
- In its global study, The Peterson Institute found that 30 per cent female representation on boards can increase company net profits by 6 per cent.[6]
- Ageing demographics show that the average age in many countries is significantly increasing. For example, the average age in the United Kingdom hit a high in 2015 at 40 years.[7]
- In 2015 it was estimated by The World Economic Forum that it would take 118 years to achieve gender pay parity.[8]
- Of the 20 biggest companies in the United States, 14 companies score 100 per cent in the Human Rights Campaign's Corporate Equality Index which rates workplaces based on LGB&T quality.[9]

- Over a billion people live with some form of disability. This corresponds to about 15 per cent of the world's population. Rates of disability are increasing, due to population ageing and the global increase in chronic health conditions.[10]

The following shares more detailed examples of why this is important and some of the different catalysts for change:

THE LAW

At times you will be responding to new legislation, but often with D&I a focus is triggered by an internal grievance which can be time-consuming, or, at worst, a high-profile employment tribunal that has been sensationalised in the press and may have cost the company a lot of money.

An early memory for Fleur is of a senior woman in the United Kingdom who won her case for sex discrimination. Some of the evidence used, and then published in the press, was a string of emails that had been exchanged between her manager and HR, which apart from being derogatory, portrayed the management of the firm as callous and unfeeling. One particularly damming headline taken from an internal email read: 'Had cancer, is a real pain, can we get rid of her?'

When EY initially started their focus on disability in the United Kingdom, some ten years ago, it was driven by the Manager of Employee Relations. He had noticed a trend of complaints from staff with disabilities that were struggling to access reasonable adjustments. The initial focus of the group convened was highly pragmatic and centred on the application process and how this was supported by functions such as information technology and occupational therapy.

In some countries, such as Germany, France and Spain, there are quotas for the number of disabled people a company employs and South Africa has Black Economic Empowerment legislation. In the Middle East, if you don't meet your quotas for the hiring and retention of nationals, the direct business impact means that you will find it harder to obtain work visas for your expat population. In the United States, there is Affirmative Action, and at the time of writing, governments in more than 12 countries had set quotas for the number of women that sit on company boards.

COMPETITOR ACTIVITY

For some organisations the catalyst for a focus on D&I has been seeing what their competitors are doing. Rather than looking internally to find out what the real issues are, they look to see what others within their sector are focused on and aspire to either emulate them or deliver an 'initiative' that is just that little bit better, or have a speaker at a conference that is just a little higher profile. Although we say this light-heartedly, this is a consideration that should be taken seriously. As we mentioned in the key facts previously, if your competitors are making more of a success of D&I, arguably they will have the higher performing teams, produce more innovative products and attract a bigger share of the market.

LEADERSHIP VISION

Ideally, the focus should be on more than legislation or trying to gain a competitive edge; however, these are a starting point. Often a focus on D&I is instigated by either a visionary CEO (as was the original case at Barclays Group) or a talent leader (such as the head of HR). At EY, Fleur was recruited into a newly created D&I function which was part of the talent leader's new strategy. There can be downsides to this if there is just one key sponsor, which include: (i) it's seen as a pet project rather than a business imperative; (ii) the vision is not understood or shared by others; or (iii) commitment can diminish if that person leaves the organisation.

REQUESTS FOR PROCUREMENT (RFPs)

Less common, but not unheard of, is an organisation that has a requirement to be able to tick the right boxes when pitching for business. This is prevalent in South Africa where business can be taken away or awarded to a company based on the number of black Africans leading the organisation. Prior to the recession of 2008, there was a push in the UK private sector to include the topic of diversity in the procurement process.

Fleur remembers attending a conference where she spoke to a man who was looking particularly uncomfortable. He explained that he had been sent to learn more about 'this diversity thing'. He worked for an engineering company and at the time they were bidding for a lot of government business. They had learnt that they would need to show a commitment to the D&I agenda and had worked out that if they couldn't pitch for this business they would potentially lose millions of pounds in business opportunities.

There can also be the need to show diversity in the teams that are pitching for business. A team that is not diverse in some way will often stand out. For example, if you represent your company as five white men to a team of both men and women that includes a black CFO, your lack of obvious diversity will look and feel odd to them. We are not suggesting that you should pull the team together purely based on the level of diversity. The most important consideration is the skills and experience that they each bring to the job and the team that pitches should be the team that is going to deliver the work. However, it is something to consider and that comes up more and more often in some sectors and geographies.

CUSTOMER/CONSUMER REQUIREMENTS

We mentioned competitor activity earlier in this chapter. Another external factor that does gain the focus and attention of organisations when considering why they should do anything on D&I are the expectations of their consumers.

In the United States, for example, women account for 85 per cent of all consumer purchases, including everything from cars to healthcare. It would make sound commercial sense for your organisation to tap into what your consumer demographics look like and what they expect from a company they plan to purchase from or do business with. We look at this in more detail in the chapter on leveraging D&I in the market (see Chapter 19).

As you can see, there are numerous reasons why this is important and any organisation that ignores the impact D&I and the changing world has on their business do so at their peril.

Who is this book for?

As we wrote this book we thought long and hard about who the book was aimed at. Our initial thought was that everyone who works within any type or size of organisation, from a small business to a multinational operating in many countries, should have an understanding of both the impact of D&I as well as how they can create a more diverse and inclusive environment around them.

However, stating that a book is targeted at everyone felt somewhat of a tall order. Therefore, working through this book would specifically benefit the following:

- Leaders and managers at all levels who want to get the best out of their teams, by increasing engagement and recruiting and retaining the best talent.
- HR professionals who are expected to deliver change in some shape or form. They may have been handed the D&I remit in addition to the 'day job' or are interested in how this can impact the work they do now and in the future.
- Existing and new D&I professionals, where this is their day job. They will be at any stage of the journey within their organisation as well as at various stages of their knowledge and experience of D&I.
- Students who are studying for business qualifications.

The book has a global reach, sharing examples from across the world and considering how you deliver D&I across multiple countries and cultures.

Our aspiration is that this book is used as the definitive guide to creating and delivering a diverse and inclusive organisation regardless of your role, seniority or sector. The book has been written in a way that shares practical points sourced from our decades of experience – moving away from the theory of D&I to how you actually make this a reality.

Why us?

The creation of this book was inspired by a conversation we had one evening about the slow pace of change we were seeing with many D&I programmes, the inconsistency of approach across our peer group and, at times, the lack of skills and experience that D&I leaders had. We were both mentoring D&I professionals within industry at the time who each had a desire to make a difference, but just didn't know quite how to do it. It was at this stage that we decided to pool our collective knowledge and hands-on experience of over 30 years: this book is the output.

To share a little more about our backgrounds and how we got to this stage: Charlotte had spent much of her career progressing up the corporate ladder at a global retail bank. She started in the back office, progressing through to sales and then moving on to drive the first culture change programme within the bank. This was both great fun and a terrifying experience as she was asked to lead the cultural shift which touched on most aspects of the talent agenda from annual appraisals to performance management, objective setting and performance-based remuneration. From this, Charlotte's passion for working with leaders at all levels was formed, believing that small changes to behaviour could, and did, have a huge impact on the performance of both the individual and their team.

For Charlotte, the catalyst for focusing on D&I was the arrival of a new group CEO at the retail bank she worked at. He had spent much of his career in Canada and was both shocked and dismayed at the lack of diversity across the head office site when first joining. The CEO took this seriously and Charlotte became one of a 14-strong team leading the charge across all aspects of the business – from management to marketing and from customers to communities. Their global strategy was launched literally to the beating of many drums in their City of London head office and quickly became the blueprint for other companies to emulate.

Fleur had also spent much of her career in banking, latterly working for an American investment bank running HR for the capital markets division. Her key clients were equity and fixed income sales people and traders and she spent a lot of her day on the trading floor with (mostly) testosterone-charged alpha males who had the sole objective of making money. Her HR passion, in addition to effectively running the usual processes such as performance management, recruitment and reward, was to get her managers to understand the value of engaging with their people and the return on investment (ROI) of making sure that everyone could reach their full potential.

In early 2000 Fleur was in a leadership team meeting discussing the concerns of her Head of HR about the level of attention that diversity was being given at head office in New York. As a result Fleur took on diversity in addition to her day job and, working closely with the head of strategy, she spent months scouring the market to better understand what expertise was available externally and where she should start internally. In truth, within six months, she had ground to a halt having become totally overwhelmed with the challenges, a general lack of understanding from others about what diversity meant, inconsistent data available, varying views about what was a priority and a general feeling from HR that they were just too busy for yet another initiative. They did eventually launch a strategy which led to her taking the permanent role of Head of D&I for Europe, but looking back, it would have been so helpful to have had a guide of the dos and don'ts to work through and consider at the outset.

Further thoughts

For some, you may well be wondering where to start on this topic and if it will be a good investment of your time. For others, you may well be some way along your journey and are looking for fresh ideas or ways to take your work to the next level. Wherever you are on this continuum, we hope that with our combined experience of over 30 years, we have produced for you what we believe is the definitive guide to developing and executing a sustainable D&I strategy. Be that in one location, one country or globally.

This of course comes with the caveat that one size *never* fits all.

We hope this book will give you food for thought, light-bulb moments that may change your thinking and lots of pragmatic insights from across the world. However, bear in mind that our thoughts and perspectives will require some customisation to suit different sectors, cultures and geographies as well as where you are on your D&I journey.

In structuring the book, our aim was to accommodate readers with a variety of interests. We have used our own STAR framework as the main structure and have focused on the key issues you may well face as you progress on your D&I journey. We have also included deep dives into particular topics of interest such as networks, new ways of working and the global agenda. Feel free to move around the book as it works for you, read from cover to cover or dip in and out as and when the various topics are of interest to you – either way works!

We hope you enjoy working through this book and we wish you every success in creating more diverse and inclusive cultures.

part one

Starting out

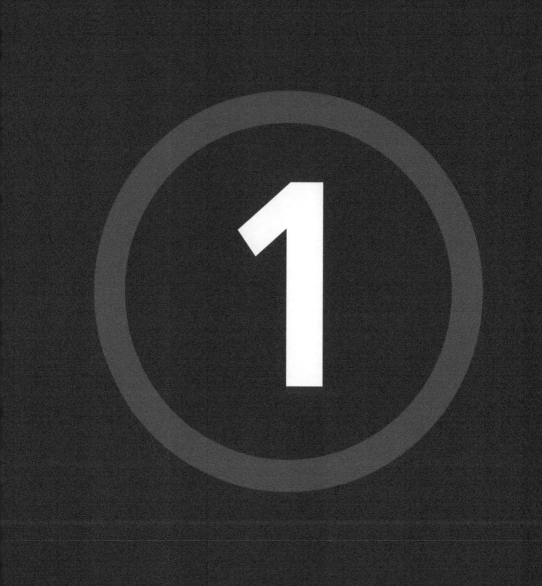

What is 'starting out'?

Change is the only constant. HERACLITUS, GREEK PHILOSOPHER

In this chapter we consider the questions you could ask when starting out. We introduce a framework to help you think about where you are on your D&I journey as well as explain how we use some of the D&I terminology.

Starting out

Creating change is not easy and it is the one aspect in business that can create a level of emotion that is seldom seen in the workplace. Many D&I programmes, although positioned as attempting to change the culture and structures within organisations, actually have no change management principles wrapped around them. The majority of these programmes are focused on initiatives, a number of separate actions and deliverables pulled together on a spreadsheet and presented to the executive committee or diversity steering group in the hope that something will change.

This is one of the reasons why much activity on D&I has not had the desired and anticipated impact on the business or the individuals within it – a lot of undirected or isolated activity will have a very limited impact.

Evidence of this was seen during the creation of The Power of Diversity Programme in London, initiated by Dame Fiona Woolf CBE during her mayoral year of 2013–14, which Charlotte developed and led on Dame Fiona's behalf. A survey was conducted throughout the City of London to identify what impact all the effort and energy around the D&I agenda had made. Over 84 per cent of respondents stated that their companies had commitment from the very top to create a more diverse and inclusive company. However, 87 per cent stated that the work their company had done had *no* impact on them personally and only 15 per cent stated they could see their leaders words translated into their actions.

In 2008 a McKinsey & Company[1] survey of business executives indicated that only 30 per cent of change programmes are successful, exactly the same as the findings identified in John Kotter's[2] research, Professor of Leadership at the Harvard Business School and well-known thought leader in the fields of business, leadership and change.

So, even if you plan to approach D&I in quite a low-key way, we would urge you to position your focus and activity with a change mentality. Not all organisations think of D&I as driving fundamental change that will impact and influence all of the different facets of the business. One Head of Diversity said to Charlotte in a conversation: 'This isn't about change but about creating a lot of great networking events that people can say they have been to.' Fleur remembers a conversation with a D&I lead at a bank in the City of London. He was fairly new in the role and was trying to understand what employee networks the bank had, how active they were and what their key objectives were. He was somewhat dismayed to find that rather than focus on employee development or connecting in the market, their key objective was to host networking drinks – he described their approach as 'too much champagne and no campaign …'.

As an initial starter, regardless of where your starting point is, consider the following questions:

- How is your organisation's brand perceived in the market – are you respected, do you find it easy to attract talent, are the images you use in your adverts diverse, is your website accessible?
- How successful are your recruitment efforts – do you have a high acceptance rate, do new hires settle in well, are they as successful as you had predicted at hire stage?
- Is your performance management process free from bias, are you satisfied that people have smart objectives and are fairly assessed against them?
- Do you know who your high potentials/talented individuals are, are you effectively nurturing them and giving them stretch assignments?
- Do you know if you have a pay gap and if so, what it is and why?
- Are your staff benefits accessible for everyone?
- Is your procurement process free of rules that would deter minority-owned business from tendering?
- Are you developing the most innovative products or solutions – are you aware of the needs and motivation of your entire potential consumer market?

You will be setting yourself up for failure if you try to tackle all of the above at the same time although they are a good initial indicator of where you are starting on this journey.

Introducing the STAR framework

We believe that no matter how small or how large an organisation you are, no matter how much or how little resource you have, there is lots you can do to make sure that your workforce is diverse and your business and people processes are inclusive.

We have developed the STAR framework (Figure 1.1) to help you identify where you are on your journey and also think about where you would like to be. The STAR acronym stands for

    S = Starting out

    T = Taking the leap

    A = Achieving change

    R = Reaping the rewards

Figure 1.1　The STAR framework

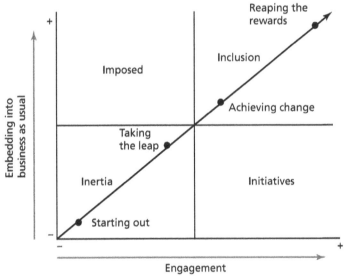

This model plots where each of the stages of the journey fit depending on where your organisation is with their:

- level of engagement with colleagues across the whole organisation – for example, how well the business case is articulated, how much your managers think about D&I in their day-to-day activities
- level of embedding into business as usual – for example, the level of accountability you have established for measures such as good people survey results, or whether this is a consideration in your supply chain.

This will give you a clear focus on how to progress to the next level of your journey to create a more diverse and inclusive organisation as well as articulate your aspiration. You will also see that each quadrant is characterised by the four Is: inertia, initiatives, imposed and inclusion:

Quadrant 1: Low engagement and low embedding results in **inertia** – small pockets of activity that are stand-alone and will cease as soon as the person driving them either leaves the organisation or loses interest. An example of this is where an individual or a small group of individuals sets up an employee network that is purely led by volunteers and doesn't gain any support from the organisation, either financially or otherwise. Those involved can become fatigued and disillusioned by the lack of commitment and stop offering their personal time to drive it forward.

Quadrant 2: High engagement and low embedding – lots of **initiatives** and campaigns that are driven by very engaged and committed individuals may well result in disjointed activity with no real impact for the business. An example of this would be when an organisation becomes a member of a national or global campaign such as #HeforShe (which is a solidarity campaign for gender equality initiated by UN Women[3]). They look as though they are committed to D&I when actually the activity is externally facing to raise their brand profile and is not linked back to anything that is being strategically driven internally. We saw this in is the past when banks in particular were quick to write large sponsorship cheques for D&I activity, but were doing little internally.

Quadrant 3: Low engagement and high embedding will result in **imposed** change – the changes are made by the business, but do not bring their people along with them. This could result in resentment and a feeling that this is being done *to* them and not *with* them. There may also be a feeling that other groups are being favoured without any real understanding of the rationale for this. An example of this can be seen in organisations that impose representational targets such as the number of women in senior positions without sharing the rationale and asking colleagues for their input at any stage of the decisions being made. For many, the first they may actually hear about this is from an external source.

Quadrant 4: High engagement and high embedding – this is **inclusion** where the activity is being embedded into everything the business does and the majority of the employees are engaged and understand why there is a need for change as well as how the change will happen. This creates the sustainable change to the culture that we are ultimately looking for. An example of this is where organisations naturally think about the D&I implications and impact in any new project or process they undertake. It may be that they are creating a new mobility policy and they automatically consider the implications of how the cultures differ and the level of support both the individual and their family may need from the outset.

Where would you place your organisation on the continuum between 'starting out' to 'reaping the rewards'?

Where do you think your organisation currently sits within the four Is? What evidence do you have to support that?

The above can be measured by a set of indicators that can be tailored to the organisation you work within. They will identify where you are and also what you need to do to continue on your journey to ultimately operate within the 'inclusion' quadrant. An example of the measurement tool for the STAR framework can be found in the chapter on measuring impact and realising the benefits (see Chapter 17).

Those of you who are just starting out on this journey may be under-resourced (both in terms of headcount and budget), will likely be overwhelmed with all of the potential areas of focus and may just want to know what the key issues are that you should be focusing on. There will be organisations who just have an appetite to drive a small number of initiatives such as launching a women's network and are more focused on visibly showing that the organisation has

D&I on their radar. Others will see this as an opportunity to fundamentally change the way their organisation delivers their people and business processes and will reap the rewards of harnessing the true power of D&I. Whatever your motivation, there are some basic initial steps that everyone should work through which we will be covering in the coming chapters.

Getting to grips with D&I terminology

It would be worth pausing here to touch on the terminology that is used throughout this book, although we don't want to spend too much time on this. There is often a debate about what to call this specialism – 'diversity and inclusion', 'diversity and inclusiveness', 'inclusion', 'inclusion and diversity', 'equality' and more. We don't think it matters as long as you focus on the mix and how you make the mix work.

This book, at times, refers to certain strands of diversity, for example, women, black people, flexible workers, but we are not implying that the people in each group are the same. As we said earlier, every person is different.

In addition, you may be working globally and we know that certain terminology means different things in different countries. For example, in the United States people reference people of colour, in the United Kingdom people say black or BAME (black and minority ethnic). Describing someone as an ethnic minority in Germany will be different to talking about a minority in India or Africa. In Japan, there isn't a natural translation for the word 'diversity' and in some countries there isn't a word for 'inclusion'.

We don't want to be too politically correct, but we also don't want to offend. This whole topic of political correctness often comes up and can, at times, hinder progress.

At the early stage of their journey, Lehman Brothers had co-sponsored an LGBT (lesbian, gay, bi-sexual, transgender) conference in the United Kingdom and they were given an opportunity for a member of their leadership team to give a keynote speech. He shared the stage with a senior politician and Fleur had thoroughly briefed him on the topic, but was still anxious that he would say the wrong thing. On the day he was word perfect and his speech was well received. That is, until he started to relax and for some reason he went off topic and referred to the 'handicapped' (rather than people with disabilities). After the event Fleur told the organiser that she didn't expect them to be invited to speak again. The organiser replied that it is not the word used, it is the intent behind the use that is important and it was clear that the speaker had every good intent.

For the purposes of this book we talk about minorities and in particular black and minority ethnic (BAME) people. We use the word 'disability' (although handicapped is used in countries such as France), we will talk about LGBT, women, different generations such as Gen Y and Gen X, flexibility (in the broadest sense of the word) and later in the book we look at the difference between targets and quotas and positive discrimination.

We do not intend this book to be an A to Z of all the terminology that may be used when working on D&I. That would be impossible to create given the global context and the continual development of the language used. The main consideration is to know where you can access reliable information sources as well as being clear on the intent of your words – creating change rather than offending.

Five key takeaways from this chapter

- Identify where you are on your journey using the STAR framework and consider where you want to get to.
- One size doesn't fit all – we are sharing our experience and examples of good practice; it will all require customisation for your own use.
- Programmes and initiatives alone will not change the culture.
- Don't get too hung up on the terminology – it's the intent behind the words that matters.
- Even if you decide to start small, do think about what you are doing through a change management lens.

Assessing your current position

The first step toward change is awareness. The second step is acceptance. DR NATHANIEL BRANDEN, AUTHOR AND PSYCHOTHERAPIST

An important step to consider as you start out on your D&I journey is to, literally, take a step back and truly understand the current position within your organisation from a number of different angles. We have seen many examples where organisations venturing out on the journey of creating a D&I programme do not take the time to really understand their starting point and can end up getting pushed down the route of delivering activity quickly, regardless of what that might be.

When starting anything new, there is that general excitement and eagerness to just get started and jump right in. Taking the time to ask questions and to really understand the starting point significantly increases your potential for successful execution and delivery.

Throughout this chapter we cover what you need to be able to take a step back, what information is available and how to analyse your data.

What information is available?

So, how do you really get to assess and understand your current position?

The first important step is to find out (i) what information is currently available and (ii) what additional information you need to have. Accessing both qualitative and quantitative information will help you to build a holistic picture of your current position.

The overall scope of your strategy and activity will dictate what information will be helpful at this stage. Finding out what information is available can be an interesting piece of detective work in itself. Every organisation has a different starting point and some organisations may have a different view of the overall scope of their D&I strategy or activity. For example, some organisations have purely focused their D&I efforts around their employees and their talent management proposition. Others have incorporated a wider focus of including other aspects of their business such as suppliers, clients, shareholders and the wider community.

Here are some examples of key data and information you may want to consider.

EMPLOYEE

1. **Employee demographic data**

   Within your organisation are you able to measure the employee composition at different job levels by different elements such as gender, age, ethnicity and disability? It may be that you are able to gain information about gender and age as these are data points that are more generally required in other elements of the employee relationship such as benefits, pensions and health insurance. However, you may not have considered asking employees about their sexual orientation or their religion or belief, for example.

   If you are working across multiple countries the answer to this question will certainly be different depending on which country you are assessing your current position in. For example, in the majority of countries the only data that is consistently available globally is information about gender. Many countries initially don't want to share sensitive data and will even argue that the privacy laws would not allow it. In some countries being gay is illegal, so collecting and storing this sort of data could put your organisation and the individual at risk. Disability data could be current one day and different the next and there is still a lot of 'discomfort' in some countries, in relation to asking someone the question. With ethnicity, if you are of Indian origin and live in the United Kingdom you might be classed as an ethnic minority for any data-gathering process; however, if you are of Indian origin and live in India you would not.

   Some of these issues are used as a smokescreen because the individual/department you are asking may not be comfortable with the agenda, but most of these issues can be overcome. However, there are genuine challenges in some locations that do prevent you asking your people too much about their diversity and certainly then sharing the answers more broadly.

You also need to access meaningful data. Fleur remembers when she worked for an American organisation and got a call from Human Resources in the New York head office asking for some help identifying the ethnicity of some of her London-based people. At that time they didn't collect their demographic details and she explained that she didn't know. Unconcerned, they suggested that she guess from the person's family name!

Take some time to consider what data is available and acceptable to capture in the different countries and regions in which you operate. Some organisations have attempted to create a list of what you can and can't ask for across the world. This is a good starting point; however, you should be mindful that legislation and what is deemed acceptable culturally can change over time, which means that this is an exercise that should be reviewed on a regular basis. It is also helpful to review this with your legal teams to ensure that any data protection requirements are not compromised.

If you are working across a number of countries this is a good example of considering D&I actions and how they may require adaptation to meet the needs and requirements locally. We cover the practicalities of 'Thinking global, acting local' later in the book.

Figure 2.1 shows some examples of employee demographic data that can be gathered. Take a look to see what you currently have available and what information you would like to be able to monitor in the future.

2. **Employee opinion survey data**

   If your organisation has an employee opinion survey or another way of capturing employee feedback, what information are you able to access about employee perceptions?

   Employee surveys, if used well, are a great source of information for you to understand the current position. There are a number of different ways you can use these:

   ● **The questions you ask:** Many organisations include questions within their surveys that ask about the importance of D&I, what

Figure 2.1 Gathering employee demographic data

THEME	QUESTION	RESPONSE OPTIONS
General Information	Please select which division/ department you work in	List appropriate options for your organisation
	Please select which geographical region you are based in	List appropriate options for your organisation, e.g. United Kingdom Rest of Europe United States Asia Pacific Rest of world
	Please select your level within the organisation	List appropriate options for your organisation, e.g. Trainee Associate Vice president Executive director Managing director Senior managing director
	How long have you worked here?	Less than 1 year 1 to less than 3 years 3 to less than 5 years 5 to less than 10 years 10 years plus
Age	Please indicate the category that includes your current age in years.	16–24 25–34 35–44 45–54 55–64 65+ Prefer not to say
Gender	What is your gender?	Female Male Other Prefer not to say

Disability	In the United Kingdom, the Equality Act 2010 generally defines a disabled person as someone who has a mental or physical impairment that has a substantial and long-term adverse effect on the person's ability to carry out normal day-to-day activities. Do you consider yourself to have a disability according to the definition in the Equality Act?	Yes No Prefer not to say
	Are your day-to-day activities limited because of a health problem or disability that has lasted, or is expected to last, at least 12 months?	Yes, limited a lot Yes, limited a little No Prefer not to say
Race and ethnicity	What is your nationality?	[free format text box] Prefer not to say
	Are you from a majority or minority ethnic group in the country in which you work?	Majority Minority Prefer not to say
	Non-United Kingdom–based employees only: What is your ethnic origin?	[free format text box] Prefer not to say
	United Kingdom–based employees only: What is your ethnic group?	**Asian/Asian British** Chinese, Indian, Pakistani, Bangladeshi, any other Asian background **Black/Black British** African, Caribbean, any other black background **Mixed/Multiple Ethnic Origins** White and Asian, White and Black, any other mixed/multiple ethnicity background

(Continued)

Figure 2.1 *Continued*

THEME	QUESTION	RESPONSE OPTIONS
		White British, English, Welsh, Northern Irish, Scottish, Irish, Gypsy or Irish Traveller, any other white background **Other Ethnic Group** Arab, any other ethnic group **Prefer not to say**
Faith and religion	What is your religion?	No religion or belief/ atheist Buddhist Christian Hindu Jewish Muslim Sikh Any other religion Prefer not to say
Sexual orientation	What is your sexual orientation?	Bisexual Gay man Gay woman/lesbian Heterosexual Other Prefer not so say
Socioeconomic	United Kingdom–based employees only: Did you mainly attend a state or fee-paying school between the ages of 11 and 18?	UK state school UK independent/ fee-paying School Attended school outside the United Kingdom Prefer not to say
	United Kingdom–based employees only: If you went to university (to study a BA, BSc course or higher), were you part of the first generation of your family to do so?	Yes No I did not attend university Prefer not to say

Marital status	What is your marital status?	Single Married/civil partnership Divorced Separated Widowed Prefer not to say
Dependents	Are you a primary carer for a child or children under the age of 18?	Yes No Prefer not to say
	Do you look after, or give any help or support to family members, friends, neighbours or others because of either: long-term physical or mental ill health/disability? Problems related to old age?	No Yes, 1–19 hours per week Yes, 20–49 hours per week Yes, 50 or more hours per week Prefer not to say

the culture is like or if people are treated with dignity and respect. Targeted questions are extremely helpful as they will enable you to not only understand the current position, but also measure the impact of your actions further into your journey, which we will look at in the chapter on measuring impact and realising the benefits.

- **Cutting the data**: Having a section included within your survey that asks employees to share their demographic data should enable you to review all of the question responses by the different characteristics. This will enable you to identify how different groups of employees feel about aspects such as pay and reward, training and development and career aspirations. For example, wouldn't it be helpful to know how people with disabilities feel about their career opportunities compared to others within the organisation? This is generally called the 'perception gap' or the 'inclusion gap' and will be useful to identify where current practices are impacting different employees.

- **Free format comments**: Some organisations include a section within their surveys that enable employees to share their views verbatim. These sections can be targeted at specific topics, for example, what are their thoughts on the business expansion in Europe, or they can be open for any comments from employees about anything that is currently on their mind. This does bring challenges with it: the comments may be quite long and time consuming to work through; however, there will be comments shared that will be helpful and important to include here – both positive and negative.

The following are examples of some of the questions and statements you see organisations specifically asking within their employee opinion survey that can help them understand their current position. Take a look through these and see how this compares to what you currently ask.

- How satisfied are you with your present job?
- How motivated do you feel in your present job?
- How do you feel about the amount of work you do?
- How would you speak about us as an employer to people outside of the company?
- How satisfied are you that we make the best use of your skills and abilities?
- How satisfied are you that there are opportunities to learn what you need to do your job well?
- How satisfied are you with the balance between private/family life and work commitments?
- How satisfied are you with your basic pay?
- How satisfied are you with your bonus?
- How satisfied are you with your total reward package?
- I feel I am valued as an employee.
- I can trust the company to do what it says it will.
- My manager provides the coaching and development I need to improve my performance.
- My manager helps me manage the pressure I come under in my job.
- My manager treats me fairly, with dignity and respect.

- My manager enables me to work in a way that meets business needs whilst taking my personal requirements into account.

- People are open and honest with each other.

- Good performance is fairly rewarded.

- It is safe to speak up and challenge the way things are done.

- This company treats colleagues with dignity and respect.

- I understand the importance of equal opportunities, diversity and inclusion in my workplace.

- This company is committed to improving equal opportunities and diversity and inclusion throughout the business.

3. **Talent management data**

For us, talent management is a holistic view of the entire life cycle of an employee that starts from the moment you are looking to attract individuals into the organisation and continues all the way through their employment until they decide to leave you. Within your organisation what information are you able to access from different parts of the talent management process such as recruitment, promotions and exit interviews that will help you to understand what is happening to your employees at each stage?

If your organisation has the ability to capture demographic information at each stage of the talent management process, it will give you a wealth of knowledge and insights into what is happening within the organisation and where your 'points of pressure' are.

Points of pressure are areas where the data suggests there is something taking place within part of the process that would warrant further investigation. For example, a 'point of pressure' may be that 35 per cent of all people nominated for promotion in one specific year are female; however, only 12 per cent of the promotions are then awarded to women. The significant difference from the start to the end of the process would suggest that there may be more at play than an objective process and would require further investigation to understand why this has happened.

To bring this to life, let's look at an example within the recruitment process and what data you would ideally look for and the types of questions you should ask.

First, identify what you are currently able to collect and store. Second, identify the different stages of the recruitment process where decisions will be made as to whether a candidate progresses to the next stage or not. For example, the process may include the following stages:

- Receive applicant's covering letter and CV via web application
- Complete online psychometrics assessment
- Attend initial telephone interview
- Attend an assessment centre including multiple interviews and exercises
- Confirm application status – accepted or declined.

Once you have broken down the different stages of the process, find out what demographic information you are able to collect at each stage. Increasingly, organisations are capturing this information at the beginning of the application process which enables them to review what is happening at each decision-making stage of the process. However, some organisations may not ask for this level of information until the individual has become a member of staff.

We have focused quite heavily on quantitative data to this point; however, there is also a potential wealth of insights that can be captured via qualitative information. You may already have some of this from your employee opinion survey; there are also other ways of sourcing insights, such as:

- **Employee focus groups:** Some organisations conduct a regular cycle of getting employees together to discuss what is working and what could be improved across the business. Others do this on a more ad-hoc basis when they feel there is a specific issue to address. Creating the opportunity for employees at all levels to share their views and to be heard is hugely important for them and is a mine of information for you – if done well. How you do that depends on what is already available – either tap into a feedback structure that is already established and ask questions about D&I or create your own.

You should always make sure that any focus groups are led by a good facilitator and have a balanced representation from across the company of people at all levels, experience, backgrounds, and so forth. There may well be personal issues and perspectives shared and it is imperative that the individuals that take part feel that they are listened to and their feedback is respected.

Participants may have a history of feeling excluded, unfairly overlooked for promotion or may not feel they are part of the D&I agenda. For example, there can be a backlash from white men in the organisation who feel they are the only people without an employee network. Fleur remembers, some years ago, when her French firm announced their ten-point gender action plan, the male directors expressed a frustration that clearly all the women would now be promoted at the men's expense. It is important to gain views from as many people as possible to ensure you are being as inclusive as possible.

You may also consider conducting 1:1 interviews. In one organisation, the D&I lead for the Middle East conducted a series of interviews with the women in their Saudi offices to better understand the challenges they faced in the workplace and the solutions they had developed. Culturally it was felt that interviews would be more effective which indeed they were. However, in these situations, you are listening to one individual's perception; therefore, any feedback used with your leadership teams should include caveats as to how many people raised the same issue and it should be presented anonymously.

- **Leaders commitment and communication:** It is important to gain a sense of the views and perspectives of your leadership teams on this issue. Much of the information will be gleaned from the above; however, it is also important to understand what your leaders are saying and what they are doing. There are a number of ways of doing this without conducting interviews with your leaders. For example, read through the communications that are sent from your organisation and from its leaders. How is D&I positioned or mentioned? Take a look at the agenda items for senior leaders' meetings. This will give you a clear indication of their level of awareness, commitment and how this is embedded into what they do on a day-to-day basis.

SUPPLIER

The supplier diversity agenda (both the diversity of those companies in your supply chain and what they do to deliver D&I in their businesses) seems to be much more prevalent in the United States than anywhere else, although there is some activity in the United Kingdom and South Africa. The initial key focus tends to be on BAME and female-owned organisations, and for some global companies the whole supplier diversity agenda is being raised within their risk assessments under the human rights agenda. The key areas to consider are:

- **Composition of suppliers**: What does the composition of your supply chain look like? The variety and size of the companies who form your supply chain will vary dramatically depending on the size of your organisation, the sector and the discipline. Do you have an overview of the diversity of business owners within your supply chain? Are you able to gain an overview of the size of the organisations?

- **Activity of supplier**: What are your suppliers doing on D&I? For some organisations, such as the UK Government, there is a requirement for all companies aspiring to be part of the Government-preferred supplier list to articulate what their policy is on D&I as well as the actions they are taking. Is this information that you have available? Is this something you ask all prospective suppliers? Are you comfortable to work with suppliers that may not have the same value set and commitment to D&I as you may have?

Many organisations don't have this information available even if they are some way into their D&I journey, so don't worry at this stage if this is the case. We take a look at supplier diversity in more detail later in the book.

CLIENTS/CUSTOMERS

It is important to have a level of understanding about your clients, their demographics and the level of importance they place on D&I. This helps you to ensure anything you do now or in the future is linked back to the business and how the company performs. The following is important for the clients and customers you already have; however, consideration should be made also for the clients and customers your company aspires to attract in the future.

- **The demographics of clients**: What information do you hold or have access to about your clients? Who are your clients and do you know how your demographic representation across the organisation compares to theirs at different levels? For example, are their senior teams composed of people from varied backgrounds and experiences? Are they more diverse than you?

- **Client sectors and locations**: Clients generally want to work with suppliers and companies that understand their needs and requirements. Wherever the client is located, be that in specific cities, countries or globally, it is important to ensure you are able to understand their requirements, and cultural knowledge will play a part depending on the client locations. Do the clients expect you to comply with a specific piece of legislation or country-wide initiative such as The Scottish Business Pledge?

- **Client activity**: Are you aware of what your clients are doing in the area of D&I and what their expectations of you are? Do they take part in any external benchmarks? Are they profiled in publications? Do their senior leaders talk about D&I? Have they won any accolades or awards? If this is important to your clients, they will naturally want to know where this fits in your company's hierarchy of important issues. They will be going through a similar exercise to yours at some stage, if not already, and will want to know where you fit in, or not!

For many companies, their customers are individuals rather than other companies. Are you aware of any market data that is available within your company outlining the diversity of your customers? Some companies gather this information when creating their marketing strategies, others may have it available via customer incentives such as loyalty schemes. This is covered in more detail in the chapter on leveraging D&I in the market (see Chapter 19).

SHAREHOLDERS

Although this has been a little slower to progress than other elements of D&I, over recent years this has started to increase in some geographies. Especially in the aftermath of the financial services crash of 2008 shareholders are now, more than before, finding their voice on issues such as diversity in the boardroom, the removal of groupthink and diversity in the talent pipeline.

If your organisation has shareholders, who are they? Are they committed to this agenda? What are they doing within their own organisations to create more diverse and inclusive environments? Are they prepared to be more vocal when it comes to the impact of D&I on corporate governance?

Organisations such as Legal & General and Aviva have been increasingly vocal within the United Kingdom on their expectations of the companies they hold shares within. CalPERS, the United States' largest public pension fund also has a clear expectation of the companies they are involved with and regularly ask for examples of what companies are specifically doing, as well as the composition of their employee base.

Just recently, the journalist Jim Armitage, urged shareholders to scrutinise the decision of Schroders to move Michael Dobson from Chief Executive to Chairman.[1] The reason for the move was to provide stability and continuity for the fund managers, but Mr Armitage pointed out that the 'governance rules discouraged CEOs from becoming chairmen to prevent groupthink and bring independent oversight of management. Also, when a long-standing chief executive becomes chairman it can be difficult for his successor – in this case another insider – to be his own man'.

CULTURAL AND COMMUNITY NORMS

Reviewing what is happening in your wider community is dependent on the scale on which your company operates. For some this may be a relatively small area such as a specific city or a region within a country. For others, this may be globally with additional focus within specific countries where you have a significant employee or client base. From a global perspective some of this will be separately discussed in the chapter on thinking global, acting local (see Chapter 16).

There are a number of considerations when looking at the wider community in which your organisation operates, including:

- What are the cultural norms and expectations of that community?
- What are the cultural tensions, if any?
- How prevalent are issues such as gender representation, LGBT or race reported within local press?

- What are the leaders of that region or country saying and doing about D&I? What are their social policies and aspirations?

The above gives a good overview of the information and knowledge you should consider to gain an informed and holistic view of your current position. There may be other sources of information, important to your sector or company, which also require consideration. There may be some gaps in the level of information and data you have available that responds to the above. Once you are aware of where the gaps are, consider if those gaps are significant enough to require plugging at this stage: for example, will the lack of that information hinder the development of a meaningful strategy?

It may be that some valuable information is missing, so finding it becomes one of the initial key deliverables of the strategy action plan. For example, one company Charlotte worked with asked for diversity data during the recruitment process; however, they didn't have the technology internally to be able to hold that data for people once they had become employees. They could see what was happening at the recruitment phase; however, the data was then lost for all other aspects of the employee life cycle. They believed this was important and commissioned a review into updating their internal technology.

Once you are comfortable that you have either sourced the information, have a short-term plan to find the missing information or include that within your longer-term delivery of the strategy, the next stage is to review what the information is actually telling you.

Analysing your data

At this stage you may well have a huge amount of data and insights. Your task is to now sift through all of that knowledge and pull out the key data points that create a picture of what is happening within your organisation. The beauty of this process is that by pulling information from multiple places together, a robust and holistic overview is being created: one that will create a solid foundation for any strategy development and clear data points to articulate why a certain course of action is required.

Ideally this shouldn't be done alone. Charlotte recalls one of the most effective strategies she created was as a result of running a number of meetings with different communities in the organisation, sharing the information that had come out of the initial data-gathering process and asking them for their perspective. Let's remember that this is a D&I strategy: the essence of what we are focusing on is bringing people together from different backgrounds and experiences to create something better than we could alone. Role modelling that behaviour throughout the delivery is critical as it shows people how working in this way can be done, what it can achieve and heightens the level of engagement and commitment from the outset.

If you can access the data, you should try and look at as many aspects of the whole employee life cycle as possible. For example, some progressive organisations report on the demographic splits by rank, retention, recruitment, promotion, engagement scores, scheduling of assignments and performance rankings. In some countries they can also review equal pay and flexible working. Looking over a three- to five-year period can help you identify trends and even predict future numbers and if you have access to an analytics team, then even better. Charlotte has worked in organisations where every element of the employee life cycle has been reviewed from a D&I point of view. This level of analysis gives a wealth of information that can really show what is working and not working, within the company for all employees.

A couple of years ago, Fleur asked her analytics team to use the previous five years' data they had on gender and predict what their numbers would look like eight years from then if they were to carry on doing everything they were currently doing. The findings were startling. Even though they were delivering some great work, particularly around retention and development, the statistics showed that by the end date they would be in roughly the same position. The team then created five different scenarios that could potentially accelerate progress. This was presented to the executive team and a number of robust next steps were agreed. This is the power of the data.

Charlotte remembers working with an organisation that couldn't understand why people over the age of 45 were applying to the company for a job, but didn't get a job offer. After working through the data they found that the majority of people over 45 dropped out of the recruitment process during the second round. They reviewed that part of the process in detail and found that one of the tests they used within the process had some age bias built into it, resulting in the significant drop-out rate. After fixing this issue the drop-out rate of people over the age of 45 significantly reduced. Without the data they wouldn't have been able to get to the root cause of the issue.

The secret is not to get too overwhelmed with the amount of data. Decide what you are trying to achieve and then think about the data that you need. For example, in most professional services firms, to become a partner you need a strong business case and a strong personal case. The business case focuses on your technical skills, your sector experience, the clients that you are working on and your potential in the future to build business. If for some reason, much earlier in your career, you are not assigned to the right clients, it becomes a self-fulfilling prophecy and you are not deemed to be strong enough to be considered for partnership. Therefore, an important aspect for professional services firms is to analyse how assignments are resourced to make sure that everyone gets meaningful experiences. This is also true for many investment banks and will be similar for many sectors and industries.

Finally on this topic, don't forget that there are implications for all of the above activity. The key question is: what are you going to do with what you have found out? If the answer is nothing, then what is the point in mining this information?

Both of us, at one time, were members of an interbank diversity forum which was a group of D&I professionals within investment banks. The US banks, in particular, had a challenge accessing personal data. They felt that sharing this sort of information could raise levels of awareness that hadn't previously been there and could incite action against the firm.

This is a weak argument to not explore your data, but nonetheless carries weight if you have a US headquarters. Our belief is that it is far better to be able to highlight any issues, acknowledge them and focus on improving them, than to put your head in the sand and hope that nothing comes of it. If an employee does end up taking you to court, your case looks far weaker if your defence is that you had no idea these issues existed.

There are also resources available to support you (some at no cost) when you are trying to decide what the information is telling you. Take, for example, the Global Diversity and Inclusion Benchmark: Standards for Organisations Around the World.[2] Led by Julie O'Mara and Alan Richter PhD, the benchmark has been created in collaboration with 80 expert panelists from around the world to help organisations determine their current position and share some examples of good practice in many of the areas mentioned throughout this chapter.

Five key takeaways from this chapter

- Identify what you are trying to understand before you start your data collection.

- Try to align your objectives with your business strategy – for example, are you looking for growth; if so, what is happening in your recruitment function?

- Collating your data is as much a journey as the rest of your strategy – factor any data gaps into your overall strategy and decide how you may want to fill those.

- Qualitative data is just as important as quantitative – consider how you will capture that information.

- One size does not fit all when it comes to data capture – gain consistency where possible; however, this will be limited across countries and jurisdictions.

Creating the case for change

The key to successful leadership today is influence, not authority. KEN BLANCHARD, AUTHOR AND MANAGEMENT EXPERT

Driving change at the best of times is not easy. Driving change without a clear articulation of why the change is necessary, what the driver or 'burning platform' for change is and what the risks of maintaining the status quo are is virtually impossible.

In this chapter we consider how to create the case for change and focus on a number of elements that ensure you will be able to create a robust and holistic case.

How many times have you heard someone question 'Why do we need to change? We have been pretty successful with what we have always done?' This is because the case for change has not been clearly articulated or positioned in the right way for that individual.

Some people do get frustrated with the fact that a case has to be created for D&I and feel that this is about treating people with respect and making sure that you get the best out of the talent you have in the business.

This is a powerful reason and hard for one to argue against, but most people would say that they do treat people with respect already. We don't believe that this is strong enough for an organisation to use to drive sustainable commitment leading to change. It is rare to find people who rally against what D&I professionals are there to achieve, but it is often that people show how little they understand the depth and breadth of the challenge. Be wary of anyone that tells you that they totally support diversity – 'I love women – I'm married to a woman – even my horse is female…'.

All cases for change within organisations are different. However, by considering each of the following elements you are building the foundation for your case for change.

What has worked in the past within your organisation?

This will, undoubtedly, not be the first case for change that your organisation has created. It may be the first from a D&I point of view; however, there will be previous attempts at creating a case for change that you can learn from. Ask your colleagues what they think has been effective in the past. Source that case for change and identify what was important for the organisation. How was it structured and what were the key drivers for change? Was it client service? Employee engagement? Legislative changes or something else? By reviewing this you will be gaining valuable insights into what the important factors are to creating a case that the organisation can acknowledge and buy into.

What's more important – the moral, the legal or the business case?

All organisations are different and what influences and inspires one decision maker will not be the same for the other. Assuming that a committee such as executive committee or the board will make the final decision about the strategy and the level of importance placed on this agenda, all of the following three should be covered to ensure you are engaging with everyone.

- **The moral case**: Simply put, this is the right thing to do!
- **The legal case**: The current requirements from a legal perspective as well as case law and other regulations that will potentially have an impact in the future. These requirements may well be different in various countries and jurisdictions and is important to point that out.
- **The business case**: What positive impact this will have on the business ultimately for the bottom line linking back to employee engagement, brand reputation, shareholder confidence and client/customer loyalty. What impact will this have on supporting and enabling delivery of the existing business strategy?

Creating the burning platform

As you create the case be very clear on 'why this and why now?'. Creating that immediate case for change is critical to gaining the agreement from your organisation and shows a sense of urgency. Leave the decision makers under no illusion about the impact this will have on the business and the potential consequences of not responding to the burning platform.

The most powerful and compelling business case is one that ties in with your business strategy and is based on your internal data. At EY, Fleur pulled on one specific element of the global business strategy called 'Vision 2020'.

To achieve this vision, EY know that they have to field the highest performing teams and they know that high performers are engaged employees. People are engaged when they are doing meaningful work, their work is recognised and they feel included. Many companies take the outputs of their engagement survey very seriously and see a real value in the link with engagement and high performance.

They also know from internal research that the highest performing teams are the most diverse – not more women than men, just a good mix. Of course it's not just about diversity. We know that in the early days of teams forming, a heterogeneous team can often outperform a diverse team – they know each other well and if the ask is a quick solution, there is no time for the classic 'forming, storming, norming and performing' stages of team development. A diverse team does need to be managed well and does need time to get to know each other and work out the most effective ways of working together. Enlightened managers are willing to take that extra time, because as Figure 3.1 shows, in the long term, a diverse and well-managed team is the most productive.

Figure 3.1   Diversity in teams and productivity

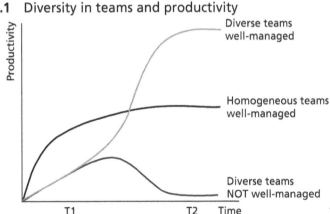

Source: adapted from 'stages in team development', courtesy of Alan Richter.

Do you know your SWOT from your PESTLE?

To truly create your case for change it's important for you to understand and reflect on these two important change tools. The additional information this will create for you during the life of the change programme is invaluable (and important to continue to maintain and keep this up to date)

- **SWOT**: *Strengths, weaknesses, opportunities and threats* – how would you complete this for your organisation? For example, what are the current strengths of the company? It could be that it has a strong brand in the market. How is a strong D&I track record going to support this brand? Ask similar questions for weaknesses, opportunities and threats. Get others involved and ask them what their views are.

- **PESTLE**: *Political, economical, social, technological, legal and environmental* – consider the impact of all of these areas in relation to D&I within your organisation. If you consider this topic from a macro level, there are a number of mega trends that will help underpin a focus on sourcing, engaging and retaining the best talent. All of this information is readily available on the internet; however, the following are recurring trends:

  - **Emerging economies**: The rise of emerging market countries is transforming the world economy and as cross-border investments increase, so will the demand for people with good technical knowledge and the skills and experience to operate cross-culturally.

  - **Demographics**: Despite a growing global population, the availability of skilled workers is actually expected to decline in many countries – not just in developed economies, but also in certain emerging markets, such as China and Russia. A 'demographic divide' will soon arise between countries with younger skilled workers and those that face an ageing, shrinking workforce, increasing the war for talent in certain sectors and the need to attract the best talent.

  - **Technology**: Over the past 30 years, the digital revolution has changed the way we work almost beyond recognition. The number of people accessing the internet has doubled since 2005 to over two billion. Thirty years ago, only one person in 1,000 had a mobile phone. Today, there are five billion mobile phone subscriptions worldwide. Smart mobility is changing the way people interact with each other and we need to learn new skills to effectively collaborate, often virtually.

What impact will the political landscape within your country or the countries that the strategy will have an influence over have? What is the legal framework within those countries? For example, is there any anti-LGBT legislation in any of the countries you operate in? Ask those levels of questions for each of the elements and consider the countries and jurisdictions this will influence and have an impact over.

What's in it for me (WIIFM)?

Many cases for change omit this important element – why should the organisation and the people within it change what they do on a day-to-day basis without understanding what *they* are going to get out of this? Clearly articulate what the benefits will be for people across all levels and disciplines with the organisation.

For example, for an employee at the early stages of their career it may be the knowledge that they will be rewarded fairly against their peers, have the opportunity to share their views on the company and know that their performance will be measured within a transparent and bias-free progression process. For a line manager it may be that they will increase engagement and motivation of their team and they will have a wider talent pool from which to source their employees. For senior leaders it may be knowing they can attract and retain the best people because of the culture created, increased brand reputation in the marketplace, ability to widen service offerings to clients and customers from different cultures and backgrounds and create a positive impact on the bottom line.

Whatever the reasons may be for your organisation, it is important to spend the time articulating the 'WIIFM' factor for people across the firm regardless of their level, discipline or country in which they operate.

Use data that is most relevant for your organisation!

The challenge for creating the case for change with D&I is that often you end up relying on external data points. It can be helpful, but the most impactful business case is built on data from your own organisation, data that people can really relate to.

One well-known global company conducted a piece of research that helped solidify the business case and had the biggest impact. Their global analytics team took one of their business units and analysed 22,000 of their assignments globally. They were able to show that the gender diverse teams (made up of both men and women) were the most profitable whilst retaining a high standard of quality. They were able to prove that this has a positive impact on the bottom line of the business as well as support the delivery of the overarching business strategy.

Charlotte remembers in a previous organisation the senior leaders were lukewarm at best about some external information shared about why change was important. As soon as she was able to articulate that one change, if done properly with a £40,000 up-front investment could save approximately £1 million per annum off the recruiting budget, the senior leaders were fully bought in and fully signed up for the whole programme. Do not underestimate the power of having your own data and creating the case from that.

If you do want to include external research there is a large amount of good, robust work that will help you to enrich your case for change. Organisations that spring to mind include McKinsey, the Centre for Talent Innovation (CfTI) and Open for Business. For example, in 2013, the CfTI published a report showing the link between diverse teams and innovation as a means of driving growth.[1] The Credit Suisse Research Institute has also published a report called 'The CS Gender 3000 Women in Senior Management'[2] showing that greater gender diversity in a company's management coincides with improved corporate financial performance and higher stock market valuations.

Challenging the status quo

This is one of the more challenging but also the more important elements of creating a more diverse and inclusive organisation. Very few people will say that they discriminate or have a bias in any way and will be shocked that their behaviours, individually or collectively, have a negative impact on the organisation. You may well hear the words 'we're a successful company – why do we need to change now?' It's important to clearly articulate the *impact of doing nothing*. Your colleagues may, on the whole, behave in an inclusive way; however, the world is changing and to continue to be successful we all need to adapt, evolve and grow. Some of us may remember the days before computers in the workplace; if we continued to behave now in a way that we did then, we wouldn't be in business.

Let's take a public example of challenging the status quo and projecting future state if the decision is to do nothing. Prime Minister Shinzo Abe of Japan announced that he wanted at least 30 per cent of his leadership positions to be filled with women by 2020. He did this for a number of reasons, the main one being that future projections for the economy of Japan showed that by doing something different, by encouraging more women back into the workplace and by raising the female participation rate to 80 per cent, the country's output could be potentially boosted by 13 per cent.[3]

The golden thread (a thread that links everything together) that comes through on all the above points when pulling the case together is how this will support and enable the delivery of the overarching business strategy. If you can answer that question well, you are onto a winning case.

Once the thread is firmly embedded and people understand the importance of this strategy, it is also important to continue that thread into other strategies and plans that are available across the organisation such as the people/HR strategy, the client proposition and the communications and marketing strategy. By doing this, you are already starting to embed D&I across the organisation.

Five key takeaways from this chapter

- Understand and articulate the key drivers that are fuelling an appetite for a focus on D&I.

- Use your own organisation's data whenever possible to fuel the business case.

- Link this back to the business strategy – respond to the key drivers within the organisation as well as the 'WIIFM' factor.

- Understand what has worked in the past to create a case for change and identify what you can take from that.

- Consider what external sources of information will be influential internally.

Building a strategic plan

To the person who does not know where he wants to go there is no favourable wind. SENECA, ROMAN STATESMAN, PHILOSOPHER

The above quote is as true for an organisation as it is for a person. You have spent time assessing your current position as well as working on the case for change. The vision, a statement or picture of where you want to be is the next important step. If you don't know where you are going, how does anyone know what they should be aspiring to and how do you know when you've got there?

In this chapter we cover how to develop your D&I vision, the components required to create an effective and robust delivery plan as well as including short-term wins into your planning.

Developing your vision

A well-crafted vision statement can help you communicate the D&I inclusion aspirations to employees and management in a single sentence or a few concise paragraphs. This may take some time to create; however, the result will be a tool that helps inspire strategic decision-making, product development and anything else your organisation does.

A vision statement is future-based and is designed to inspire and give direction to the employees of the organisation. It enables people to see and articulate what will be different and helps them to consider the part they may play in this. To create a vision on D&I it's important to understand and articulate how this complements and embeds into the organisation's wider vision.

Creating the vision is another opportunity to engage employees from all levels and backgrounds. Engaging people through the journey and demonstrating this is a collaboration rather than something that is just being done to you will lead to more impact on the overall delivery.

To create the vision ask yourself, and others, the following questions:

- What are we striving to create?
- What will be different? What do we want to be different?
- How will we know when we have got there?
- How will this complement the business vision?
- How does this link to the organisational values? If any?
- What will happen if we don't do this?

The responses to these questions will enable you to draft, re-draft and fine-tune a vision that is inspiring, engaging and clear.

Here are a few examples of vision statements from global companies:

At Oracle we foster an inclusive environment that leverages the diverse backgrounds and perspectives of all our employees, suppliers, customers, and partners to drive a sustainable global competitive advantage. ORACLE

We aspire to build and sustain an environment where our associates are embraced and valued for who they are so that they reach their full potential enabling Hyatt to provide authentic hospitality that is individual and engages each and every guest. HYATT

We aim to maximize the power of Diversity & Inclusion to drive superior business results and sustainable competitive advantage in a dynamic global marketplace. JOHNSON & JOHNSON

Our vision is to become the leading generics company by cultivating an inclusive, high performance environment that values diversity. SANDOZ, A NOVARTIS COMPANY

Consider the above vision statements – what is your immediate reaction to them? Do they engage or inspire you? Do you believe the organisation is committed to their vision? How would you like people to respond to your vision once created?

Once you have created the near final version of the vision, you may want to spend some time creating a 'meta-narrative' for D&I. In literal terms a meta-narrative is an overarching, all-encompassing 'big story'. They tend to be relatively optimistic and create a bigger picture of what will be different in the future.

Spending time creating a 'meta-narrative' whilst finalising the overarching vision will support you in a number of ways. It will:

- enable you to test the vision – is it right? Is it impactful? Is it engaging?
- start the creation of the key messages which will be invaluable for your communications plan
- engage others further in creating the wider story of what D&I will be and will achieve in the organisation
- raise awareness of D&I across employees even before the strategy has been created.

Ideally, the meta-narrative should be no longer than half a page of text or ten bullet points on what will be different by focusing on D&I. Any longer than that means that you haven't yet created a concise and clear message. To help your thought process, here is a meta-narrative Charlotte created with other colleagues across 27 countries for an organisation she worked with (see Figure 4.1).

In summary, the vision and any supporting information such as a meta-narrative are a critical investment for the overall success of the work you are doing. Without a clear vision of what will be different and what D&I is here to achieve, you will be constantly challenged with questions about whether you are focusing on the right areas, if what you are doing is having an impact on the overall business and how you will know when you have got there.

Creating your strategic delivery plan

Once your vision has been created the logical next step is to identify and articulate the critical themes and actions that will bridge the gap between where you are now and where you want to be, taking all elements of the organisation into account and creating a time-bound plan.

Figure 4.1 Vision and meta-narrative

> **Our vision**
> *Inclusion and diversity is simply about the way we do business. It is part of our DNA and embedded into everthing we do*

- Our performance on Inclusion and Diversity is congruent with our performance or aspirations as a top tier global organisation
- An open inclusive environment which is free from bias, prejudice and discrimination
- Inclusion and Diversity is viewed as a business objective
- The divisions take action on Inclusion and Diversity because they recognise the benefits - not because they are told to
- All employees understand our values and support our vision on Inclusion and Diversity
- All leaders actively support our vision and role model the best Inclusion and Diversity behaviours
- There is a consistent global approach to Inclusion and Diversity with local ownership and delivery
- We are seen as a model of good practice that clients want to do business with and investors want to invest in
- The culture of the organisation is enriched making it a vibrant place to work

For some organisations there may already be a set format for designing and presenting delivery plans, for others it may be a case of designing a plan that works for you.

Before jumping in and creating a delivery plan there are a number of strategic questions to consider:

- What are the key themes emerging from analysing your data?
- How big does the plan need to be? Does this plan need to focus on the larger group-wide areas with an expectation of other countries and divisions to create their own plan that sits in line with this?
- What is the appropriate timescale to articulate in the plan – 12 months, two years, five years?

- Who will see the plan? What level of detail will be required?
- How will the themes from the case for change be included into the delivery plan?

Responses to the above will help decide what level of detail is required. Initially, we are creating the strategic plan, the plan that shows how we are going to deliver the vision as articulated. Once this has been created that is when the more detailed delivery plans are developed, whether that is your responsibility or the responsibility of others across the organisation.

There is always the fear that a strategic plan can go into paralysis with the level of detail required. This is where some aspirational change programmes start to flounder as they struggle to maintain a high-level overview of what is required to make the change become a reality.

To create a plan that gives a clear articulation of direction and action to senior leaders, as well as enough information to be able to deliver a more detailed delivery plan, the following elements are required:

- **Focus area/theme**: There will be a number of themes that have emerged from the previous data analysis. The strategic plan will look far more manageable and thought through if these themes are created and presented in a way that both bring a number of overarching actions together and link into the overarching organisational strategic plan. For example, if the organisation is aspiring to become more global in its outlook, or increase operations in different parts of the world, an overarching theme of 'global mindset' may be appropriate. Another theme, for example, may be to 'diversify the talent pipeline' and that may support the business plan to ensure the organisation is effectively scouring the industry for the best talent and may also respond to stakeholder challenges of diversifying the senior talent for the future. In essence, ensure the focus areas and themes are high level enough to show how they fit strategically without going into a huge amount of detail.
- **Actions**: At this stage the actions should go into a little more detail of what the high-level deliverables are that will fit into the above focus areas and themes. Again, this is high level and is a fine balance of

including enough information to give a clear overview of what will be delivered without getting into the detail of a fully blown project plan. For example, if one of the focus areas is to create an agile working organisation, the high-level delivery areas may include: (i) create technology principles and infrastructure that enable agile working; (ii) review all policies, practices and processes to ensure they support agile working; and (iii) develop and articulate the leadership commitment for agile working to ensure global consistency.

- **Owner**: Just as with any other plan, a strategic plan is not effective unless everyone is clear who is responsible for delivery. For this level of plan the 'owner' may be defined as a part of the business, a support function of the business such as HR or a country. It is always wise at this stage to include a named person into the 'owner' element of the plan where possible. This starts to increase the accountability and ensures, further down the line, that there is no confusion as to who is ultimately responsible for the delivery. For example, one of the high-level actions may be assigned to HR for delivery. Rather than purely listing this as 'HR', include the name of the HR director or the leader responsible for that part of the function.

- To create structure some organisations use the 'RACI' principle, which defines the roles and responsibilities within a task or project. The key roles are defined as:

  - *Responsible* (also Recommender) – the people who do the work to achieve the task; they own the project.

  - *Accountable* (also Approver or final approving authority) – the person ultimately accountable for the completion of the task and has to approve any activity before it is effective. The 'R' roles report into the 'A'. There must be only one accountable specified for each task or deliverable.

  - *Consulted* (sometimes Consultant or Counsel) – those whose views and opinions are sought, typically subject matter experts, and with whom there is two-way communication.

  - *Informed* (also Informee) – those who are kept up to date on progress, often only on completion of the task or deliverable, and with whom there is just one-way communication.

In many circumstances the role that is accountable for a task or deliverable may also be responsible for completing it. Outside of this exception, it is generally recommended that each role in the project or process for each task acts, at most, as just one of the participation types. This ensures that all involved in the project or task are clear on their role and removes any confusion.

- **Timescales**: It is as important within the strategic plan to be clear on the timescales for delivery. This area should cover the high-level milestone delivery dates, that is, the key elements of the delivery that are required to take you to the next level. A detailed overview of the timescales is not required here; those timescales will be included in the more detailed project delivery plan where progress will be measured on a regular basis.

- **Impact measures**: Ensuring you are clear on how you are going to measure the impact of the strategic plan is critical. Many plans fall short of this and then find themselves running around later into delivery trying to decide how they can prove their actions are making a difference and delivering towards the vision. To make life much easier, be very clear from the outset how you are going to measure the impact and include this in the plan. When senior leaders and other stakeholders then sign up to the plan they are also signing up to how you are going to measure the success and the impact. Further information as to what will be included is outlined in the chapter on measuring impact and realising the benefits (see Chapter 17).

Figure 4.2 illustrates what such a plan would look like.

Throughout the development of the strategic plan it is critical to consult with your key stakeholders including those who will have responsibility to deliver elements of the plan. The worst thing that could happen at this stage is that you put a huge amount of energy into creating a plan that isn't discussed during development and is then rejected by some of the stakeholders because it doesn't work for them or they haven't been engaged in the process. As mentioned a number of times throughout this book, you can't deliver this alone and because of that, it is imperative you bring people along with you rather than hoping that imposing your strategic plan onto others will be a sustainable solution.

It was also outlined earlier within the book that the overarching vision may cover far more than the people and talent aspect of the organisation. There

Figure 4.2 Example of a D&I action plan with impact measures

Focus area – attract and retain

FOCUS AREA	ACTIONS	OWNER	TIMESCALES	IMPACT MEASURES
Recruitment agencies	**Create and agree our expectations of recruitment agencies** • Work with HR and other interested stakeholders (including some recruiting managers) and create a set of expectations of our agencies • Review any specific considerations across different countries/jurisdictions • Gain final agreement to requirements	AB	Q1	Measures created directly from expectations placed on agencies: • % agencies comply with all measures within D&I requirements document • % non-compliance for diverse shortlist • Number of speculative CVs received per quarter (or other agreed reporting period) • % roles offered to a diverse candidate (gender and other demographic information available) • % roles accepted by a diverse candidate (gender and other demographic information available) • Number of agencies removed from Preferred Supplier List for non-compliance • Quarterly updates from D&I requirements monitoring will be available

| Career development and progression | Develop career development masterclass/modules for managers and all staff

• Identify and agree the key themes for the module
• Create a pilot version of the module and deliver to 12 existing line managers and 12 staff to gain feedback
• Respond to the feedback and create final versions of the workshops and materials
• Commit to all line managers to have completed the module (timescale TBC)
• Commit to 'refresher courses' for all line managers and staff on a biennial basis to ensure skills are kept up to date
• HR (appropriate roles) to also attend 'refresher courses' to have consistent experience as line managers | ZA | Pilot for D&I forum by Q1
Pilot by Q2
Advertise by Q3 | • Feedback from employees on quality of career development conversations
• Feedback from line managers on the impact training has had on their ability to have career development discussions and support the process
• % line managers completing the module and refresher in the appropriate timelines
• I know what I have to do to progress my career (employee survey question)
• My manager takes time to coach me and develop my skills (employee survey question)
• My manager gives me regular feedback on how I am doing (employee survey question) |

may be a requirement to diversify the client base or ensure the services offered cater for the changing demographics. Whatever this may be, it is important to ensure *all* focus areas and themes are included in the strategic plan and cover all the elements mentioned above.

Achieving short-term wins

One of the challenges we do face in creating more diverse and inclusive organisations is that the majority of actions that will have a sustainable and significant impact take time to deliver and even longer to see the benefits. What is really important when embarking on this work is to create meaningful short-term actions, and wins, that maintain interest and momentum without compromising delivery towards the overarching vision.

It is important to get the balance right for your organisation, between short- and longer-term action and focus. If you focus too heavily on short-term wins, you will not create the sustainable and meaningful change you are really looking for. Focusing exclusively on the longer-term wins will potentially reduce the engagement and commitment of some stakeholders when they don't readily see the rewards they expected coming their way. Exactly what that balance will look like will be different for everyone and will depend on aspects such as your organisation, sector, geographic location and level of maturity on D&I.

Charlotte remembers working for a US organisation where a six-month plan was considered long term and asked to reduce this to three-month deliverables. She then moved into a Japanese firm and was told that a seven-year plan was really seen as short to medium term.

The short-term wins must be treated with the same discipline as the longer-term strategic actions. You should ensure:

- there is a clear link back to the overarching vision and business priorities
- the impact of the short-term actions can be measured in some way with a view to how they support the wider impact measures and realising the benefits
- the actions are congruent and complement the longer-term actions, that is, they help to pave the way.

Again, involve as many people as possible in the identification and delivery of the short-term wins. The more that people feel they have a part to play in the change, the more support, influence and impact you will have in the future.

What does this actually look like in practice? Here are two examples:

1. **Longer-term delivery:** Ensure that all companies on our preferred supplier list have (i) commitment from the top for D&I, (ii) have a clear vision, strategy and policy on D&I and (iii) have a clear delivery plan in place by agreed deadline.

Short-term win: Engage with our top five suppliers identified by money spent with them and obtain their buy-in to the longer-term aims of the strategy and ensure all three requirements are in place for an agreed deadline. Communicate the outcome to appropriate stakeholders.

2. **Longer-term delivery:** Ensure at least 40 per cent of roles within the top 1,000 leaders in the organisation are held by women by agreed deadline.

Short-term win: Engage with all recruiters, both internally and externally, to ensure that all future job searches produce a diverse short-list for consideration.

In summary, ensure that short-term wins are factored into your longer-term plans. Create the clear line of sight between the short-term win and the longer-term plan, find ways of measuring the impact and let stakeholders know what you are doing and why you are doing it.

Done in the right way, short-term wins can have a really positive impact on the longer-term success of your strategy and plans.

Five key takeaways from this chapter

- Create a well-crafted vision that supports delivery of your business strategy.
- Change won't happen without challenging the status quo.

- Use every opportunity to role-model inclusive leadership as you work through creating the vision and delivery plan.
- Work closely with others to understand any cultural nuances that will impact the vision.
- Alongside your longer-term vision, make sure that you have identified some short-term wins to celebrate progress on the journey.

Your role as a change agent

Change will not come if we wait for some other person, or if we wait for some other time. We are the ones we've been waiting for. We are the change that we seek. BARACK OBAMA, US PRESIDENT

The role of creating a more diverse and inclusive workplace is certainly one of the more challenging roles that isn't necessarily for the faint hearted. Not only does the role require a good knowledge of how organisations work and an in-depth understanding of D&I, but it also requires the skills of an effective change agent.

Throughout this chapter we review what an effective change agent looks like and share an overview of the skills and competencies required.

What does an effective change agent look like?

In the *Oxford English Dictionary* the definition of a change agent is: 'a person or thing that encourages people to change their behaviour or opinions'.

The role of a change agent is usually a thankless task of encouraging people to embrace and at times enforce the change required.

Although anyone and everyone can effectively be a change agent (which is what we ultimately want within our organisations), there are a number of characteristics that we believe you need to have to be a successful change agent.

- **Resilience**: Effective change agents know there will be days when others just don't understand what they are doing or why they are doing it. They need to find it within themselves to continue and risk being misunderstood and unappreciated, knowing that the real validation of their hard work may be far in the future and may be claimed by someone else.

- **Heightened emotional intelligence**: Change is ultimately about people. Change will really 'stick' when people embrace it, therefore, change is all about the relationships you create with others, the sales pitch, the coaching and the facilitation that bring people along with you. The ability to engage and inspire others is a critical characteristic as well as being able to put yourself in their shoes.

- **Future focused**: Change agents have a vision of what could or should be and use this to mobilise action. They focus on the future, not the present or the past. They are generally dissatisfied with what they see around them and believe there is a better way.

- **Engender trust**: Change agents are able to build strong relationships and maintain trust with their stakeholders and others around them. They show faith in others, behave ethically and display integrity in all dealings. They convert their words into action and share rational reasoning if this isn't going to be possible.

- **Heightened communications skills**: Change agents are able to communicate with people at all levels. They actively listen, involving others in discussions and decision making and are not afraid to tackle conflict directly in a calm and professional manner.

- **Tolerate ambiguity**: Change agents know that ambiguity comes with the role. They are able to commit to moving ahead with the change at the same time as looking around them for evidence that this is either the right or wrong direction of change. They know that ambiguity is part of the process to create change and are comfortable with that.

- **Love of learning**: Effective change agents may be experts in their field, but they know that it is impossible for one person to hold all the knowledge and wisdom. They are keen to learn from others' knowledge and experiences and identify how that may be able to support them or enhance the work they do in some way.

- **Patient yet persistent**: They know that some things are not going to change overnight; however, they know it will change at some stage.

They are comfortable to wait for the right time and be patient and will expect the change to happen at some point.

- **Ask the tough questions**: Change doesn't happen without asking the tough questions and creating some disruption in some shape or form. Effective change agents are not afraid to ask the questions that others may shy away from and are not really concerned about how others perceive them because of that – they would rather be respected than liked.

Being an effective change agent can mean different things to different people and cultures. In China, for example, it may not be seen as acceptable and respectful to ask the tough questions with many people present.

Charlotte remembers her first week at a Japanese firm; she had presented her initial thoughts of how D&I could be delivered within the organisation. There were over 20 colleagues attending this meeting and all seemed to be intrigued and supportive of her views. After the meeting her boss asked her how she thought it went. She replied, 'Very well, they all agreed to the proposal, I'm surprised how easy that was.' Her boss smiled and as he walked away said, 'What you thought was agreement was them confirming they understood you – you certainly have a lot more to do before they are supportive of your proposal.'

The skills and competencies required for a change agent in D&I

At the time of writing this book there are no standards associated with the role of a D&I practitioner that you would usually see with other professions. However, we believe that the previous list of characteristics of an effective change agent is a good foundation, you then need to build on those characteristics with solid experience. To be an expert in this area is just the same as being an expert in any other specialism. To deliver the impact that is truly needed requires a level of knowledge and experience that cannot be gained overnight. If this is really a business imperative, as so many leaders state it is, why would you give that responsibility to someone with limited knowledge and experience? As Charlotte puts it, 'You wouldn't give someone who is passionate about spreadsheets the role of finance director just because of their passion, so why is the bar positioned so low at times when looking for a D&I professional?'

In 2008 The Conference Board published a report called 'Creating a competency model for diversity and inclusion practitioners'.[1] The report was an attempt to create a framework of competencies considered important to drive effective change in D&I, and we believe that there are many synergies with the change agent characteristics that we have just listed. There are seven categories and their related competencies are defined in Figure 5.1.

The report goes on to say that you can't expect to find all of the above competencies within one person; however, a number must be in place and this increases with the level of seniority of the role.

You will of course have the opportunity to gain experience and knowledge on the journey. Charlotte remembers attending her very first meeting when she was responsible for creating the organisation's action plan on sexual orientation in the late 1990s. She sat in a meeting room with five people who wanted to know what she was going to do – she really didn't have a clue as she wasn't, at that stage, fully knowledgeable on the issues and challenges. Instead of bluffing her way through the meeting, she encouraged those attending to work with her to create the plan and share their experiences and challenges with her. The result was a plan that was seen by others as a blueprint for what organisations should have been doing at that time to change the culture on sexual orientation.

Building your skills

Figure 5.1 provides a framework that is an effective tool to use when creating a team around you who should have complementary competencies to you. For example, consider the competencies and skills that are missing when you appoint people to your D&I steering group. You may be looking for someone who has experience of creating a vision, knows how to manage organisational politics or understands how to work across complex group dynamics.

The role of a D&I practitioner has changed and will continue to evolve. More than ever, companies are seeking expertise to help them instil knowledge and skills internally, to forge new competitive ground for their organisations and

Figure 5.1 Diversity and inclusion practitioner competencies

1 CHANGE MANAGEMENT

Organisational development

- Understands and facilitates the change process through completion
- Gains leadership involvement and line ownership

Corporate communication

- Communicates the full spectrum of inclusion
- Utilises multiple communication vehicles such as websites, brochures, talking points and more
- Maintains a balanced global perspective that offers flexibility and variations for use at the local level
- Keeps what is best for the business at the forefront
- Elaborates on benefits of D&I
- Acknowledges and addresses possible unfavourable impact

2 DIVERSITY, INCLUSION AND GLOBAL PERSPECTIVE

Cultural competence

- Understands multiple cultural frameworks, values and norms
- Demonstrates an ability to flex style when faced with myriad dimensions of culture in order to be effective across cultural contexts
- Understands the dynamics of cross-cultural and inclusion-related conflicts, tensions, misunderstandings or opportunities
- Understands the history, context, geography, religions and languages of the regions in which the organisation does business
- Is fluent in more than one, and ideally several, languages

Negotiation and facilitation

- Negotiates and facilitates through cultural differences, conflicts, tensions or misunderstandings

Continuous learning

- Recognises and addresses one's filters, privileges, biases and cultural preferences
- Commits to continuous learning/improvement in diversity, inclusion and cultural competence
- Seeks and utilises feedback from diverse sources

3 BUSINESS ACUMEN

External market knowledge

- Understands and is current on global and local trends/changes and how they inform and influence D&I
- Gathers and uses competitive intelligence
- Understands diverse customer/client needs
- Understands and is current with global socio-political environments
- Understands context and lessons learned

Holistic business knowledge

- Understands the impact of the financial, economic and market drivers on bottom line results
- Understands core business strategies
- Possesses solid financial acumen

(Continued)

Figure 5.1 *Continued*

1 CHANGE MANAGEMENT

- Tracks and communicates strategy progress and setbacks
- Acknowledges and addresses challenges/obstacles/opportunities

Critical interventions

- Offers useful and timely interventions in cases where progress is impeded due to a diversity-related issue

2 DIVERSITY, INCLUSION AND GLOBAL PERSPECTIVE

Complex group dynamics

- Understands and effectively manages complex group dynamics and ambiguity

Judgment

- Is able to discern when to inquire, advocate, drive or resolve more decisively

Subject matter expertise

- Knows and applies best practices in diversity and inclusion practices, strategies, systems, policies, etc.
- Understands subtle and complex diversity and inclusion issues as they relate specifically to marginalised groups (while these vary by region, they often include women, people with disabilities, older people, and racial, ethnic or religious minorities)
- Establishes and manages D&I councils effectively
- Collaborates with other functional teams
- Is a role model for inclusive and culturally competent behavior

3 BUSINESS ACUMEN

- Uses information from multiple disciplines and sources to offer integrated ideas and solutions on issues important to the organisation

Diversity and inclusion ROI (return on investment)

- Determines and communicates how D&I contributes to core business strategy and results
- Creates insights on how D&I contributes both to people and HR strategies as well as business results
- Designs and develops D&I metrics that exhibit the ROI impact

4 STRATEGIC EXTERNAL RELATIONS

Corporate social responsibility/government/regulatory

- Well-informed about external pressure points (e.g. society, work councils, environment, regulatory, government, customers and related trends)
- Effectively anticipates and manages stakeholders (e.g. advocacy, community, non-government organisations)
- Recognises and addresses human rights issues through policy and practice
- Influences media and marketplace via communication and community outreach to competitively position the organisation

Strategic alliances

- Identifies, partners and leverages relationships with key external organisations/leaders to enhance business results

5 INTEGRITY

Ethics

- Acts ethically and with integrity
- Behaves in a way that leads others to trust him/her
- Speaks with candour and tact
- Acts as a voice for perspectives, levels and cultures that are not otherwise represented

Resilience

- Pursues goals with drive and energy; seldom gives up before finishing, especially in the face of resistance
- Maintains positive and constructive outlook

Influence

- Negotiates and persuades effectively at all levels of the organisation
- Navigates corporate landscape and has an impact up, down and sideways
- Listens and adapts approach to fit audience
- Manages and mediates conflict effectively

6 VISIONARY AND STRATEGIC LEADERSHIP

Diversity and inclusion future state

- Collaborates appropriately with others to envision and convey an inspiring, compelling and relevant D&I future state
- Actively seeks new ideas, experiences and thought leaders.
- Is a catalyst for change. Translates/makes connections between new ideas and applications
- Frames new directions in understandable, innovative and inspiring terms

Pragmatism

- Differentiates between strategy and tactics
- Drives alignment with clients, partners and stakeholders
- Is pragmatic regarding working within business realities
- Proactively creates foundation for influence at all levels of the organisation

Political savoir-faire

- Facilitates and manages complex and sensitive matters

7 HR COMPETENCIES

Total rewards/talent management/organisational development/work and life balance/training

- Understands the basic tenets and workings of compensation and benefits programme, policies and best practices
- Provides programme options that ensure equitable treatment and mitigate disparities
- Possesses knowledge of programmes, policies and best practices that ensure equity and achievement of organisational D&I objectives in a variety of HR areas, including but not limited to recruiting and staffing, OD, work and life balance, succession planning, training/development and performance management

Compliance

- Understands applicable laws, regulations and government requirements and their impact on the business
- Ensures compliance through effective programme, policies and practices

(Continued)

Figure 5.1 Continued

4 STRATEGIC EXTERNAL RELATIONS

Diverse markets/supplier

Diversity

- Identifies, partners and leverages relationships with key external diverse suppliers, organisations and customers to:
  - enhance the supply chain
  - increase market share, revenues and loyalty

Brand/reputation management

- Positively influences media and marketplace
- Forges strategic partnerships with internal constituencies through community outreach
- Supports communities in which the organisation operates

5 INTEGRITY

Empathy

- Understands the point of view and emotions of others, in the context of their cultures, including both minority and majority groups
- Acknowledges, in a stated or unstated fashion, others' perspectives
- Understands how to motivate and work with both minority and majority groups

Communication

- Knows where resources are and how to access them
- Communicates effectively
- Engages audience

6 VISIONARY AND STRATEGIC LEADERSHIP

- Knows to whom and where to go to get things done (including working with the Board, CEO and top leaders)
- Collaborates with other functional areas to maximise outcomes for all (especially HR, organisational development, Leadership development)
- Possesses the ability to influence and execute beyond positional power
- Is seen, at all levels, as a trusted source for advice and counsel

7 HR COMPETENCIES

Employee relations

- Works with others appropriate to the situation to resolve individual and group conflict, including the development and delivery of successful interventions
- Sustains and improves the work environment in the face of change and environmental challenges

develop credibility across cultural contexts. There are many ways to build your knowledge. You can attend conferences, panel events, forums, webinars and workshops. You can read thought leadership, complete benchmarking exercises and read books (like this one!). To develop some of your competencies, you can dip in to internal training that your company offers, external courses and D&I-specific training. More subtly, you could think about finding a mentor – either someone more experienced who uses the same competencies in their role or someone working in the world of D&I.

Five key takeaways from this chapter

- As a change agent, your role is to be respected rather than liked.
- It takes more than a passion or a bit of curiosity to make a good D&I leader.
- Start by thinking about the change management competencies that you are strong in and those you need to further develop.
- Consider how you can fill the gaps around your weaker competencies; do other team members or colleagues have complementary skills?
- Create a plan to ensure both yourself and those supporting on the D&I change are developing the right skills and competencies for future success.

Who is there to help? Working with external providers

If you want to go somewhere, it is best to find someone who has already been there. ROBERT KIYOSAKI, INVESTOR AND BUSINESSMAN

Throughout this chapter we will focus on who is there to help and support you on your journey. Although it's impossible for us to list all of the external providers, we do share an overview of what is out there and what we think you should consider as and when you start collaborating. We will look at external benchmarking, charters and kitemarks, various forums and external networks and how to get involved in thought leadership and research.

Something that is quite unique about D&I is the way that people work collaboratively across the profession and beyond to share what has worked for them and their lessons learnt – both the good and the not so good.

Of course, some organisations are in direct business competition with each other and may, at times, feel nervous about sharing 'company secrets'. What is important to remember is that whatever you decide to deliver in this field is totally influenced by your organisation's own specific cultural drivers, business strategy and values. This means that the same activity, if delivered across multiple organisations, will always look and feel different. Or put another way, there is little value in replicating what another organisation has done in the hope that the same results will be achieved, as there are many other factors at play that will influence the outcome. This point is covered in more detail in our chapter on building a strategic plan (Chapter 4).

External benchmarking

In our early days of D&I, we both really valued having the ability to access existing industry benchmarking reports as well as benchmark elements of our activity. The benchmarks we used were created around professionally developed measures that could also show where the organisation stood against others both in a specific sector and much wider. Fleur remembers how time consuming it was to complete the then annual benchmarks on gender, ethnicity and disability, but also how informative the feedback discussions were afterwards. In fact, in the early days of working on her LGBT strategy, the feedback from Stonewall totally drove the thinking and direction of their strategy.

What is really useful about reviewing existing benchmarking reports is that they generally share an overview and trends of what organisations have delivered and the impact those plans have had. When you are starting out you will inevitably be asked: 'What are our competitors doing about D&I?'. The information available within some of the benchmarking reports will help you respond to that type of question.

You may want to consider taking part in a benchmarking exercise as you start out on your journey. This would enable you to very clearly position what your starting point is against a number of external, predetermined, indicators that are recognised and used by others. However, the counter-argument to this is you probably have a good idea what your starting point is from the points discussed in other chapters, and the time required to complete an external benchmark in the early stages may not be an effective use of the resources available.

As you progress and your journey matures, taking part in benchmarks becomes less about informing your strategy and future activity and more about the external recognition that your results or your ranking gives you compared to other companies completing the benchmark. Some benchmarks remain confidential with recognition being driven through awards; in other cases each organisation is ranked – for example, Best Companies to Work For, Times Top 50, Stonewall's Workplace Equality Index and DiversityInc all publicly position the organisations involved by their achievements.

It's a wonderful boost to both you and your organisation to receive external recognition. It's good for your brand and it certainly creates that 'feel good factor' for all of your colleagues working tirelessly to run engaging networks, contribute as forum members and generally support progress. Fleur remembers joining EY in 2007 when they were ranked approximately 97th in the top 100 employers of the Stonewall Workplace Equality Index. Over the following five years, largely due to the amazing contribution of the LGBT network, Unity, EY rose up the rankings to the heady heights of the top position. Each year that they improved their ranking, it was a powerful motivator to help them focus on their next set of objectives.

Although there are many positive aspects of actively being involved in the benchmarks, you do need to think carefully about why you are doing it in the first place, the quality of the results and feedback that will be shared with you – indeed, what will you do with the findings? Our advice is:

- Don't do anything that isn't evidence based. For the benchmark to be credible you should be able to back up your responses with factual data and information. If you find yourself in the top ten of any large public ranking, you should be audited and/or interviewed to confirm your responses.

- Consider the credibility of the benchmarking organisation. Would it be seen as an accolade if they recognised your progress or do they lack true knowledge, credibility and expertise in this area?

- How will getting involved with a particular benchmark support the delivery of your overarching vision, D&I strategy and delivery plan? If there is no real benefit, really consider if you should spend valuable resources (both money and time) doing this.

- Gain clarity into the type of benchmark that would benefit you the most, given where you are in the delivery of your strategy. Would you gain more by completing one that is focused on a specific element of diversity such as ethnicity? Or would you benefit from one that is focused on all diversity elements and is focused more on inclusion?

Before diving in and getting involved with any benchmark, it would be prudent to take a step back and do your homework. If done properly they all take a significant amount of time to complete. It is also imperative that any information shared within the benchmarks is accurate with no exaggerations or elevated responses of what is actually happening. It could be very damaging to your future focus on D&I and the motivation of those around you if the organisation is publicly lauded for a reality that just isn't recognised or experienced internally.

Charters and kitemarks

Over the years charters have become one way for organisations to publicly state their commitment to D&I. Across Europe many organisations have signed up to D&I charters as part of the European Union's Exchange Platform – countries including Poland, France, Spain, Italy, Austria, Germany, Sweden, the Netherlands and Denmark are all involved. The charters are voluntary and are led at national levels, supported by a range of governmental, private and public organisations.

When starting out on your D&I journey, charters or kitemarks do provide you with a clear overview and set of expectations should you decide to become involved. They also give you contact with someone who may be able to share their experience as well as guide you on a route that will both continue to increase your knowledge and support delivery within your organisation. However, it would be helpful to consider whether you would be using this to support you and the organisation to make progress or if you are willing to publicly commit to specific actions.

At a basic level signing up to a charter provides the organisation with a recognised public 'trademark' or 'kitemark' that demonstrates the organisation's commitment to creating and implementing effective D&I strategies to meet their business needs. However, to ensure the charter has some form of positive impact, you need to make sure that your organisation is actually committed to delivering on the terms of the charter. Fleur knows of one global technology charter that has had the great and the good sign up to make their technology accessible in the workplace; however, after the fanfair of signing up, progress initially was slow and very patchy. The key lesson here is that once you have gained the senior leaders' commitment, your immediate next step is to identify and engage the person/people who are going to deliver the expectations.

Areas to take into account when considering your involvement in charters and kitemarks:

- Identify the countries in which you operate that have a charter you may be eligible to sign up to. Understand what the charter expects of your organisation and gauge the level of appetite and commitment from your senior leaders and those around you.

- How does involvement in the charter support the delivery of your vision, D&I strategy and specific delivery plan? How could you leverage your involvement? Could it increase the speed of delivery if public scrutiny is heightened?

- What value will your involvement in the charter bring to your brand? Will you be recognised by the country's government?

- What more will you need to be able to meet their scrutiny and expectations?

- If now isn't the right time on your D&I journey to commit to a charter or kitemark, when would be the right time to review this?

Forums and external networks

There are many forums in the D&I world which take many different formats and, depending on where you are on your journey, will give differing levels of value. They do tend to be very useful networking opportunities and a chance to increase your contacts base as well as find out what others are doing. Through these you get the opportunity to meet peers from other organisations, exchange updates on challenges and successes, explore future trends, share research findings and generally brainstorm ideas. In many geographies there are numerous opportunities to network externally, but for many people this is seen as a 'nice to do' rather than an important element to increasing knowledge, gaining informal development and finding out what is new in the world of D&I. They can, unfortunately, remain an unexplored and under-utilised resource especially for those starting out.

There are a number of different types of forum and it is important from the outset that you consider what you would like to get out of being part of them. There are a number of forums that are managed by third parties, usually charging some form of membership to take part, and they tend to facilitate the meeting and agenda around current issues. Examples of these types of forums include Community Business in Asia, Catalyst in Europe, the United States, Canada and India, and Mercer's Global Diversity and Inclusion Forum. A good example in the United Kingdom is the collaboration of a group of large companies called 'Creating Inclusive Cultures'.[1] The programme was created in

2015 by Charlotte with the aim of bringing companies together in cities across the United Kingdom to focus on creating change in their companies at three levels:

- to connect senior leaders within that city to work collaboratively on D&I issues
- to tackle issues that are consistent for all companies involved and to identify how to deliver and create the change
- to bring employees together at all levels to understand the impact inclusion has on their companies as well as identify the actions they can all take to make their workplaces more inclusive.

What is unique about this forum is that it has been established in a number of cities across the United Kingdom (rather than purely in London), as a reflection that some of the key issues that companies face in their D&I journey should be driven in the local offices rather than directly from head office. The forum commits that all organisations involved will (i) collaborate, (ii) innovate and (iii) create change with organisations involved, signing up to a number of annual commitments as well as access to online resources to drive change for all their employees (see Figure 6.1). At the time of writing, founding members include EY, JLL, Direct Line, Pinsent Masons, DWF, Hays Recruitment, Northern Rail, UBS, The Co-operative Bank and The Institute of Chartered Accountants for England and Wales (ICAEW). Most recently there are plans to expand globally. This is a perfect example of engaging colleagues at all levels to consider D&I within their roles, as well as creating a network of senior leaders outside of the usual head office confines.

There are other forums and networks that are self-managed and usually rely on the goodwill of a small group of people who have a passion for the topic and are keen to spread the experiences and learning. Examples of these include The Network of Networks, which is a body of employee network heads across London and represent gender, BAME and LGBT employees, and Purple Space which is an innovative online platform that brings together disability network leaders to share advice that will drive cultural change on disability in business.

In addition there are special interest groups such as the 30% club, which was originally created in the United Kingdom to engage, and gain the commitment of board chairmen to increase the number of women on their boards.

Figure 6.1 Creating inclusive cultures commitments

Collaborate

Companies and employers will benefit from collaboration at all levels via:

- **Advisory board** where the themes and direction for each city are developed
- **City Leaders Forum** where focus is placed on the strategic diversity and inclusion issues important to each City
- **Events** for people at all levels to raise awareness and connectivity across each City
- **Engage** with existing networks and ensure diversity and inclusion is firmly on their radar

Innovate

Companies and employers will influence the industry by:

- Commissioning new **thought leadership** on issues relating to diversity and inclusion
- Contributing to a **learning network** where ideas will be built upon
- **Challenging current thinking** on how change can be delivered differently

Create change

Companies and employers will create a new way of working by:

- Focusing on specific **corporate issues** influenced by diversity and inclusion which are relevant to the companies and cities
- **Raising the profile** of the companies and leaders striving for change within each City
- **Sharing progress** – the good, the bad and the ugly!

This now operates in many countries including Australia, Canada, Dubai, Hong Kong, Ireland, Italy, Malaysia, South Africa and the United States. For the LGBT agenda there is a group called Out Now Leadership who have a partnership model to connect senior business leaders across sectors through their industry leading global summits in New York, Hong Kong and London. Another example is GIRES, an interest group of trans and non-trans people who provide information and support trans people, their families and other professionals. There are also special interest groups that are created as part of a bigger organisation: for example, the Chartered Institute of Personnel and Development (CIPD) hosts a specific group called the Senior Diversity Network (SDN) aimed at people with a good level of knowledge and experience in this specialism.

We have also come across (in fact at times been members of) cross-sector forums, such as the InterBank Diversity Forum in the United Kingdom which has been established for over a decade. This forum comprises organisations within the investment banking industry and meets regularly to share best practice as well as working together to influence change both across their organisations and across the sector. One of the earliest events the Interbank held was hosted by Goldman Sachs. Each bank sent a group of high-potential women for a day of business and development workshops. Fleur remembers how powerful the event was for the women to be able to network across the sector and to see for themselves how many other great women were working in the city.

Another initiative the Interbank Forum delivered was their annual dinner. This was attended by each Investment Bank CEO and a handful of their senior women to discuss D&I and what they could meaningfully influence as leaders of their organisations. Charlotte remembers attending one of these early dinners with the then CEO of Nomura, EMEA region. This was long before the big drive to engage men in the gender agenda and we both remember the early days when this was a really edgy and quite high-risk event to actually deliver successfully. The CEOs were all male and many were obviously out of their comfort zones with this topic. They were all concerned that they might say the wrong thing and look ill informed, which is a challenge you will often face in the early days of a focus on D&I.

The bottom line is that anyone can convene a meeting for a group of interested parties to share what they are doing and people in the D&I space tend to do this very effectively. About eight years ago we were both having lunch with a small group of speakers at a D&I conference. The issue of the cost of the conference was raised and the fact that when we each spoke at the events we all tended to present the great things that were happening, and what we could really benefit from was talking about what didn't work so well – sharing the pain as well as the pleasure. The head of D&I at Dell at the time suggested we should form our own forum and the rest, as they say, is history. The forum we are referring to is unimaginatively called the EMEA D&I Forum and it is fully self-managed. Existing members propose new members as they meet them on their travels and the only rule to abide by is that the new member has to be working across either the EMEA region or globally (rather than focused in just one country).

Of course, over the years, various members have tried to develop more detailed protocols for this forum, but the light touch means that it is easy to manage and not run by committee. They rotate who hosts the event, who is then responsible for the development of the agenda as well as running it. They tend to meet in person four times a year alternating between the United Kingdom and Europe as well as identifying a number of special interest group meetings inbetween. What's particularly helpful about this forum is that if you have a question, you can send it to the whole group and you will usually receive a response from at least 10 per cent of the members.

There are other external networks that offer personal development to senior level individuals (rather than focusing at the organisational level) such as the City Women's Network in the United Kingdom or the Professional Women's Network who has over 3,500 members across 24 cities globally and run over 600 events each year. Other individual networks such as the Soar Collective Network in Australia and the United Kingdom are designed for entrepreneurs. Networks such as these are a useful resource when identifying any external support required to engage some groups of employees at an individual level.

We are conscious that we haven't mentioned the internal networks you may well have within your organisations within this section – we discuss these in more detail in the chapter on networks. However, what is important to highlight here is that mature internal networks within organisations can have quite an impact and can raise your profile externally as well as support your delivery aims internally.

More mature internal networks host events for clients on business topics such as powering up in Africa, personal development themes such as preparing for a non-executive position, book launches and much more. They may well have the ability to target clients, network with members from other companies, professionals in the field and potential recruits, thus raising your organisation's brand in the countries in which the network is active. These events and connections can also lead to new business relationships, strengthening your organisation's brand when recruiting and even using the events as fund-raising opportunities to give back to the local community.

Finally, pop-up or one-off forums can also be very powerful. In 2014, Fleur convened a three-hour meeting to focus on the LGBT agenda and how it could be progressed globally. Organisations involved in this forum included Barclays, IBM, Thomas Reuter and GSK. The outputs from this meeting informed the content for a powerful piece of thought leadership that was launched through a global webcast which was attended virtually by over 1,000 people.

Areas to take into account when considering your involvement in forums and external networks include:

- There are a wealth of networks and forums that will suit different needs at different times on your D&I journey. Do your homework, find out what is available in the different countries and regions in which your organisation operates and which ones will help you to deliver your vision, D&I strategy and delivery plans.
- When considering your involvement with any forum, check out the quality of the meeting agenda, which other organisations are currently involved and what you will receive for your involvement.
- If there isn't a forum or network that focuses on the areas that are important to you, there is always the potential to convene your own if you identify the right people to be part of it and share the load – good D&I professionals are always keen to share their knowledge and work collaboratively.

Thought leadership and research

This takes us on to the final consideration of who is there to help and the vast amount of thought leadership articles and research that is out there. We have both seen an increase in the number of companies publishing research and general thought leadership covering a variety of D&I topics: for example,

Credit Suisse produced their report 'The CS Gender 3000: Women in Senior Management' which focused on the diversity of management teams.

For many organisations this is an effective way to get their brand associated with a commitment to D&I as well as being seen as enhancing the intelligence available to push the agenda and discussion further externally. When you are further into your D&I journey this may be a consideration for you and your organisation; however, when you are starting out it's important to consider this from a position of what information is already out there that will support and enable you to create the case for change and build your strategic plan.

At the time of writing this book, when we searched the phrase 'diversity and inclusion research' on the internet, 109 million entries emerged. There is a huge amount of information out there and it can be very easy to drown in the quantity of content as well as question some of the quality. It would be impossible for us to list all the credible sources of research and information from around the world, but you will have seen throughout the book that we share examples of thought leadership articles and research that we have used within our work. The following are useful guidelines to help you source the information that would be helpful for you:

- Be clear on what purpose the information will serve – will it be used for general research purposes such as increasing knowledge and understanding in one area or will it be used as a reference within a strategy document?

- Be specific on what information you are looking for – hone your search exactly to your requirements, for example, searching for 'the return on investment of a diverse senior leadership team' will give you more targeted results on the impact on the financial bottom line than searching for 'impact of a diverse senior leadership team'.

- Know who your target audience will consider credible – many organisations have a preference for the business schools and research bodies they perceive to be credible in the work they do: for example, Cranfield University is seen as credible in the research they conduct on gender diversity. This is important to take into account but it must not hinder the opportunity to use and share thought leadership and research from others who are less known if the information is relevant and valuable.

- Ask others what they have used and found helpful or thought provoking – speak to others within your network and find out what data and information they are aware of for the work you are currently doing. Gaining from other people's experiences of what worked for them is hugely valuable, especially when starting out.

This chapter has hopefully given you a good overview of what is out there to help you start out on your journey. Of course, this is an ever-moving feast with new companies, networks and forums being created all the time as well as new topics emerging and coming to the fore. The important message is that you aren't alone. In fact you are spoilt for choice so you just need to identify what you most want to tap in to.

Five key takeaways from this chapter

- Access existing benchmarking reports and review the level of information and quality of insights available to support you.
- Carefully consider which benchmarks and charters, if any, you would take part in and clearly articulate why you are doing them.
- Review the membership and agendas of existing forums and networks and consider how they would support you – attend a couple of the meetings to clarify your thinking.
- Create your own contact list of individuals, organisations and forums who may be able to help you as you progress on your D&I journey – build this from a diverse range of sectors to ensure you are challenging your own thinking.
- Build a resource of thought leadership articles and research that will continue to increase your knowledge and challenge your thinking. Ensure you stay relevant and up to date with new research and thinking.

part two

Taking the leap

Building your team

Nothing is easier than saying words. Nothing is harder than living them day after day. ARTHUR GORDON, AUTHOR

Part Two of the book focuses on the key aspects of progressing your journey on the STAR framework and moving towards 'taking the leap'. Throughout Part Two we look at the elements that will continue to both increase engagement across your organisation as well as embed into business as usual.

In this chapter we consider building a wider team to support and enable delivery of the D&I strategy as well as winning supporters from the board to the shop floor.

Building a broader team

It's important to create the right team and infrastructure to ensure that effective decisions are made throughout your D&I journey. These decisions will include the right reporting mechanisms, the right level of support and the right resources from across the organisation.

At this stage in their journey, many D&I practitioners form D&I steering committees or advisory councils. Fleur is not a great fan of these although this is a personal opinion and she has peers that rely heavily on such bodies. She has worked with two – one in her first D&I role and one in her second. Both times she has found the actual meetings to be uplifting and motivational. Senior leaders from all areas of the business were around the table and willing to give their time to identify the issues and agree a plan of action. However, all too often, at the end of the meeting, they would go back to their day job and leave the D&I professional to execute on their vision.

At one company Charlotte created a 'Diversity Steering Group' which was chaired by the CEO and had representatives from all business areas and functions as active members. It was agreed that their membership of the steering group would be included within their performance management plans and their contribution would be included in their overall performance measurement. This all started well until the CEO started to ask Charlotte to chair the meetings. This gave a small sign to the members that the CEO wasn't 'walking his talk'…They started to procrastinate and the CEO very rarely held them accountable for the deliverables they had publicly committed to so progress was glacial. Very soon the steering group was reformed and reported directly into the Chairman… who, in return, made sure the CEO and their direct reports were ultimately responsible for delivery.

Fleur has found that the most impactful approach is when the CEO and his/her board take ownership of the agenda, rather than relying on a side-bar steering group. At EY, she also asks regions to appoint a D&I partner sponsor (in addition to a key operational stakeholder). Approximately 50 per cent of the regions have done this with varying levels of success. The partner has to want to do the role (i.e. have a genuine interest) and feel that they are accountable for progress to the regional managing partner. They must regularly show their support to the key D&I stakeholder and they must be in a position to influence the partnership. The partner–sponsor role works well in the United Kingdom where every employee network has a sponsor. They act as network chair, but most importantly for the network heads they act as mentors and sponsors. This level of senior exposure is invariably an enormous payback for the individuals running the networks.

What is right for your organisation may depend on the size of the employee base, geographical locations and how other significant programmes such as this are governed. What is important is to go with what works for your organisation and not create an infrastructure because 'everyone else seems to be doing it'.

It is important to create the right structure from the start and also be aware that this may need to change throughout the life of the programme. For example, as the work progresses and becomes embedded into other aspects of the business, there may be a decision to integrate your steering committee into an existing structure further down the line. One critical decision to make at the outset is where the expert and dedicated input will come from to support delivery.

Where's the programme office?

Regardless of the size of the organisation, to make sure any change happens there has to be either a group of people or an individual that has responsibility to make sure delivery of the strategy and the plan actually happen day to day. For some this may be a dedicated D&I team that has the sole responsibility for delivery. For others this may be part of the day job for a number of people. There are pros and cons to each of the above; here are some aspects to consider:

Dedicated D&I team

Pros

- Dedicated resource where delivering the strategic plan is the only priority
- Opportunity to appoint specialists in the field to accelerate the depth, pace and professionalism of change
- External perception that this is taken seriously as the team focusing on the issue are full time.

Cons

- Wider organisational assumption that this is not their responsibility
- Lack of collaboration from other areas of the organisation
- Potential to be siloed from the key business drivers.

Integrated into other roles

Pros

- Increases perception that this is part of other roles and not stand-alone
- Increases the knowledge of others working on the agenda for longer term sustainability across the organisation
- Continually brings different perspectives to the table on how effective delivery and embedding of the agenda can be achieved.

Cons

- The 'day job' may take priority as D&I is seen as a slower burn, resulting in progress being delayed or hindered
- May result in limited 'specialist' knowledge within the organisation, which will hamper quality and speed of delivery or focusing on the wrong priorities
- External perception may be that this isn't being taken seriously by the organisation and purely paying lip service.

Whichever way the organisation decides to structure how the strategy is delivered, what is important is that the responsibilities of a 'programme office' are taken seriously and are positioned somewhere within the organisation.

Here are some further aspects to consider when reviewing and deciding what the right governance structure should be for you:

WHAT'S ALREADY AVAILABLE?

Is there a group that is already available to feed into or do you need to create something new? A word of caution – make sure you do feed into the right existing structure *if* there is one rather than shoehorning into something that may not fit your purpose. For example, if your D&I strategy is going to focus on much more than employees, don't use the HR or workforce governance structure. If you do this, it may well result in aspects of your strategy that are not employee focused losing the appropriate oversight.

THE SIZE OF THE REMIT

If you decide to create a specific steering group, be very clear on the remit of the group. This will depend on the size of the company as well as the overall scope of the programme. Will the group be responsible for the governance of a programme that is based in one, or many, countries? In some organisations with large-scale programmes they create a tiered governance structure with a dedicated steering group at a regional level which then reports into a global steering group. An example of this structure can be seen in Figure 7.1. The size and functions of the steering group will depend upon the vision and the direction of the strategy.

TERMS OF REFERENCE

Be very clear from the start on what the steering group is there to do. All too often it can end up as little more than a talking shop. Is the group there purely as an assurance process to ensure that work is being done and progress is being made, or are they there to pick up on some of the actions and act more like a working group? For some, the steering group may be a hybrid of both of these; however, whatever works for your organisation, make sure this is made very clear in the terms of reference.

Figure 7.1   Governance structure

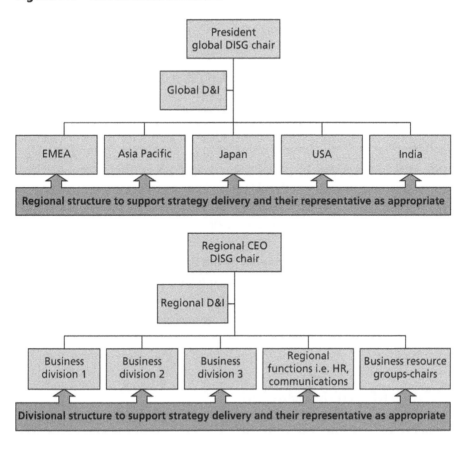

What they are there to do will also have an impact on the frequency of their meetings. A group that is more focused on delivery will naturally meet more regularly to make sure that all is on track, a group that is focused on gaining assurance that progress is being made may not meet as often. In any instance it is important that the momentum doesn't wane and we would suggest that any group, regardless of their responsibilities, should meet every three months as a minimum. For a group that is focused on actions we would recommend meeting once a month as a minimum, certainly for the initial phase of the journey.

The terms of reference should include: (i) overview of what the group is there to do; (ii) what they are accountable and responsible for; (iii) membership and any rules on deputies; (iv) where they report into; (v) frequency of meetings;

and (vi) how long someone will hold that role before membership is rotated to someone else, including how the rotation will be staggered to ensure all new membership across the whole group doesn't happen at the same time.

WHO WILL CHAIR THE COMMITTEE?

For some organisations the natural requirement is that the CEO or board chair person actually chairs the D&I steering group. It undoubtedly raises the profile and importance of the group if either of those people are chairing this. However, who you have chair this steering group depends on what the group is there to do: assurance or action? If the CEO or chairperson chair the group, there is the potential that they may have to cancel at the last minute if other pressing issues arise across the business that require their undivided attention. You may also attract people to attend the meetings if they want to get airtime with the CEO or board chair; however, they may not be the right people for the steering group and they may actually have no impact on the progress of the programme.

Undoubtedly, the steering group should be chaired by a senior leader within the organisation. It may be another executive committee member (a direct report of the CEO), ideally one that is aligned to the business rather than HR.

WHO ARE THE MEMBERS?

The members of the steering group should represent the key areas of the organisation. They should also be people that have an influence over the company and the employees within it. Who the members are will largely depend on the size and scope of the D&I strategy, as you have to make sure that each element within the strategy has some form of representation at the steering group level. For example, if how your organisation is perceived by clients is part of the plan, then the person ultimately responsible for marketing or brand reputation should be a member of the group. Consider the membership of this group very carefully as they have the potential to make the delivery of the strategy a lot easier.

Earlier in this chapter we shared a structure that was created for a client Charlotte worked with that covers both the regional overview for the D&I steering group as well as the global structure that it reported into. This will be a good starter to consider what is required in your organisation (see Figure 7.1).

Unearthing risks

Regardless of what the organisation decides to do on D&I, there will be an element of risk that requires further awareness and understanding – even the decision to 'do nothing' creates an element of risk. Many organisations measure their risk in a number of ways which may also be reported to the board depending on the severity of the risk, the probability of it happening and the control you have over it as an organisation.

There are three key actions that are important for the progression of the D&I strategy:

- Understand how your organisation categorises risk across their geographies.
- Know where they are reported.
- Review your work on D&I and create the appropriate list of risks to discuss with your governing board to agree how to take them forward. For example, within the UK tribunal system there is an expectation that all employees will have completed D&I training in some way, and if the tribunal is linked to equal pay you can be forced to undertake a full, company-wide review. If you do have a discrimination claim that progresses to a tribunal, they may well ask to see the details of the training as well as how many employees have completed it. If the training and monitoring of it doesn't happen in your company, this may well be classed as a risk.

It is also important to consider what the organisation is doing from a wider standpoint and whether D&I contributes to the risks of those strategic decisions. For example, if you are opening offices in a country that treats homosexuality as illegal, how does that sit with your stance on sexual orientation within the workplace and how would you respond to any challenges?

Measuring impact

Measuring the impact of the work that is done on D&I is a critical element of the effective governance of the whole programme. This is covered in more detail in the chapter on measuring impact and realising the benefits (see Chapter 17). What is important to identify here is where the measurement reporting goes and who sees it. What you decide to measure and how you decide to report this will have an impact on the overarching governance and how this feeds into existing reporting methods for the board, executive committee, shareholders and other stakeholders.

Effective governance is much more that creating a steering group and asking the CEO to chair it. It includes delivery and reporting progress, who is responsible for delivery, how risks are escalated, where progress is reported and how you ensure that change is taking place. Get this right and the path to creating a more diverse and inclusive organisation will be far smoother. Deciding to skip this step and dive head first into delivery without having any of the above clarified will potentially be setting you up to fail.

Winning supporters from the board to the shop floor

If you read any case studies and examples of how change is effectively managed, many will say that 'it starts from the top'. That is correct. To ensure that any change is sustainable and committed across an organisation there has to be that visible commitment from the top. The important point to note here is 'visible' commitment. There are few organisations that you will come across that don't have a commitment on their website or corporate literature about how important attracting and retaining the right talent is and how critical it is for their business success.

You will also be hardpressed to find a senior leader that will publicly say that D&I is not good for business and that they do not believe that building a truly meritocratic company is the right approach. All fine words but how does this really translate into 'visible' commitment? You may remember earlier in the book we mentioned the fact that in a survey conducted during the tenure of Dame Fiona Woolf as the Lord Mayor of the City of London, they found that 84 per cent of companies within the city stated they had commitment from the top of the company for D&I. However, only 15 per cent of the employees within those companies said that they saw the words of the senior leaders convert to action, and only 13 per cent stated that the companies' efforts on D&I had had any impact on them personally.

Talent/HR are key stakeholders and are absolutely critical to the success of the D&I strategy as much of it is about your people. However, we have both had experience of finding it difficult to engage them in this agenda for a number of reasons. In Fleur's first D&I role, HR were later to get involved with D&I compared to other business areas (even though she was in HR) and in truth she never really resolved this. One big part of the challenge was that the head of HR just didn't get D&I – she was an exclusive (rather than inclusive) leader, who liked to work with her 'favourites'. She was also disappointed that this was a role created by the CEO as it meant that Fleur had direct access to him and his leadership team and didn't have to work through her.

Fleur's peer group in HR also felt that she got to do the fun side of HR and most of what she was asking them to do created more work for them rather than less. For example, with recruitment, she asked them to source from a broader pool of talent by increasing their demands on their suppliers. They knew that finding a diverse candidate list may take longer and therefore required more engagement with the search firms. She also asked them to run summer intern programmes for disabled students and to go to universities outside of the usual traditional targets to identify more talent from more diverse backgrounds.

For Charlotte, her HR colleagues were a key stakeholder in the work she was commissioned to do by her then CEO and was disappointed they were taking very little responsibility to look at how they could deliver their roles a little differently. Charlotte researched the views of the HR profession across many companies and found that, generally, HR professionals thought they knew what they needed to do within their roles on D&I. However, when it got to the practicalities of delivering it, many didn't understand it and were not comfortable to ask for help as it was assumed by others that they would know everything there is to know about the people agenda. Charlotte then worked closely with the HR team to develop their skills and knowledge in D&I.

Fleur now works in an organisation that, on the whole, has a more naturally supportive talent team. Many of them are always looking for new, better and more effective ways of doing things so she knows that when they are developing a new leadership and development (L&D) programme, by the time they come to her for input, they have done most of the D&I 'proofing' that she would have naturally done. When they review nominations for their talent programmes they automatically ensure that the slates are gender diverse and they actively ask their suppliers to embed D&I into everything that is being developed.

Winning supporters also involves engaging with the people that have the ear of others and are not necessarily identified in a traditional structural chart. Think about those who have different elements of power across the organisation and who may be able to support delivery of the D&I strategy in some way.

Some of the areas of power to consider are:

- Legitimate power comes from the position a person holds. This is related to a person's title and job responsibilities. You may also hear this referred to as positional power.
- Connection power is based upon who you know. This person knows, and has the ear of, other powerful people within the company.
- Expert power comes from a person's expertise. This is commonly a person with an acclaimed skill or accomplishment.
- Information power comes from someone who has access to valuable or important information processes.
- Referent power comes from those who are well liked and respected.
- Reward power is based upon a person's ability to bestow rewards. Those rewards might come in the form of job assignments, schedules, pay or benefits.

When thinking about external stakeholders, who are the people, governing bodies and clients that may well have an influence on your progress, where their commitment and engagement would be beneficial and/or their views and input are respected by the organisation? For example, the governing body for law firms within the United Kingdom, The Law Society, has a clear stance on D&I within the sector and expects all firms to sign up to a number of commitments. How can that be used when thinking about the stakeholders and the commitment you can leverage from others?

To support the creation of a good overview of the internal and external stakeholders, an important step is to create a map. There are a number of ways this can be done. An example of a basic mindmap of key stakeholders for one organisation is included in Figure 7.2.

Figure 7.2 Key stakeholders map

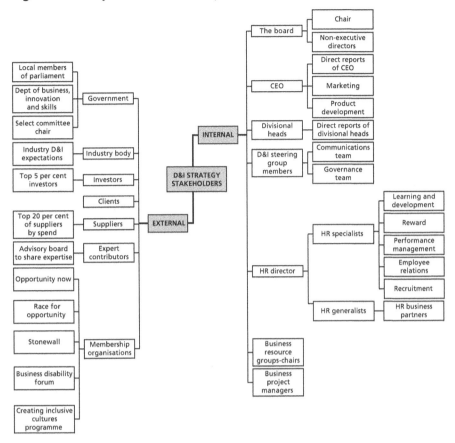

Once a robust overview of the stakeholders has been created, now is the time to think about how you are going to influence them and gain their commitment, as well as how they are going to help you do that with others and truly become part of the team. This won't be done as effectively as it could be without the planning and preparation to really get this right.

Once you are clear on who your stakeholders are, think about the following for each of them:

- What is their level of influence on this agenda?
- Who else do they influence that is important to this agenda? For example, a governing body may have an important relationship with the chair of the company that is important for you to nurture?

- What is their current level of engagement and commitment? What have you heard them say, what have you seen them do to support this agenda?
- What is the level of engagement and commitment you would ideally like from them? What should they be saying, what should they be doing?
- What's in it for them? Why would they do this? Why would this be important to them?
- What might their challenges be in taking this forward and how do you overcome them?

We mentioned in the chapter on creating the case for change (see Chapter 3) that for some organisations either the moral, legal or business case would be the driving force for them; the same is true for individuals. The art of influencing for you is to find out what the key drivers are for each individual and focus your discussions within that area.

Once you have been able to articulate the responses for each of the leaders and stakeholders, create your plan of who you are going to influence to gain their commitment and in what order, for example, is there someone on the list who would be more appropriate to speak to first so that they are able to support you to bring other influencers onboard? For example, someone who has 'referent power' may be able to encourage others to get involved, given they are respected and well liked.

Once the plan has been created it is time for execution. Are there people around you who you may be able to share the plan with and gain their views? Start with a couple of the discussions with key stakeholders, review after each of those meetings and take any learning points from those to fine-tune your future discussions and direction.

Remember, the discussions you have are important for a number of reasons. First, they are an opportunity for you to share your insights and be seen as someone with 'expert power'. Second, it's your opportunity to understand your stakeholder point of view, listen to them and gain insights as to how you can continue to hone your key messages. Finally, this is your opportunity to gain their commitment to supporting the progression of this agenda.

Be very clear on what 'gaining their commitment' actually is. For some that may purely mean mentioning this in a future speech, for others it may be much more hands on or it may be holding their direct reports to account. Be clear on what you want to see as a result of their commitment, be clear what the employees across all levels would be expecting to see and make sure you don't fall into the trap that many others have fallen into where the words and actions of the senior stakeholders just don't match.

Once you have gained their commitment, do not assume that you can put a huge tick in the box for that stakeholder and that relationship. Throughout the programme you must continue to build the relationships with each of your stakeholders, revisit their commitment and ensure that the relationship is two-way – that both of you are reaping benefits from it. As you progress further into the programme the level of commitment from various stakeholders may need to be reviewed and adapted.

Maintaining the appropriate level of professional relationship throughout will ensure that you can have those conversations in the future without compromising their level of commitment and engagement.

A word of warning – not everyone who is a leader or a stakeholder with influence will see the importance of this agenda. Some will continue to wonder why they need to change if they have been successful in the past. Be ready for the fact that you may well not bring everyone along with you; however, do aspire to the fact that those who are not supportive and committed do not actively try and sabotage the work you are doing.

Fleur remembers being told by a peer in the market that her CEO acknowledged the D&I agenda and felt that it was important, but that it wasn't urgent. Making sure that people are either positive about this or neutral is really important as you can end up expending time and energy on those who are not supportive.

Gaining the commitment of your senior leadership team, key internal influencers and external stakeholders is a critical step to progressing the agenda and building your team around you, ensuring what you deliver is sustainable and that you encounter minimal roadblocks along the way. The stakeholder map you create from the start will continue to evolve as stakeholders come and go.

Ensure that you maintain that level of fluidity and identify who your key stakeholders are for each different part of the journey.

Five key takeaways from this chapter

- Invest in good governance at the start as you build your wider team and develop your stakeholder map.

- Establish good team stakeholder engagement – who are you taking on this journey and who is supporting you?

- Consider the different power dynamics and how you can use these to your advantage when identifying who your stakeholders are and how they can influence this agenda.

- Articulate the roles and responsibilities of those involved – who is responsible for what – and continually hold them to account.

- Think carefully about whether you need a D&I steering group. Consider the governance required to deliver the strategy and identify whether there is an existing group this can report into or whether there is an additional requirement.

Communicating the change

To effectively communicate, we must realize that we are all different in the way we perceive the world and use this understanding as a guide to our communication with others. TONY ROBBINS, ENTREPRENEUR AND AUTHOR

How many of us have worked in an organisation where we don't feel that information is cascaded as well as it could be? How many of us have filled the communications void with stories and gossip we have heard from work colleagues? The answer is the majority of us!

Communicating effectively and ensuring it is heard and digested by the majority of your employees is easier said than done. A significant element of any change is how to communicate to everyone throughout the life of the programme and beyond; D&I is no different.

In this chapter we cover creating the right key messages, delivering the right communications plan, using the right media and adapting and embedding D&I into everyday messages, which are all critical for success.

Creating your key messages

There is an old adage with communication that goes: 'Tell them what you're going to tell them, tell them and tell them what you have told them.'

Creating a small number of key messages for your D&I strategy and delivery plan will ensure that all stakeholders are receiving a consistent and well thought through position from your organisation. It is also important to create key messages that reflect the themes the organisation is already talking about, giving the impression that D&I has a clear place in supporting the delivery of the business strategy.

The key messages you create should share enough information that they can stand on their own as a statement. At the same time, they should have a level of flexibility that enables the wording to be used alongside other key points or be tailored to reflect the personality of the person who is delivering them. For example, the style of the message from your CEO may have a different tone to the one from your Head of Marketing. If you created a 'meta-narrative' when creating your overall vision, now would be a good time to take a look at it as this will help you create your key messages.

Examples of key messages may include:

- As a global organisation, it is important that we are attracting, developing and retaining the best people. This means ensuring our culture and values reflect the diversity of our people and the communities in which we operate.
- We know that having a diverse and inclusive workplace will support our strategic vision of expanding into new markets.
- D&I has a positive impact on our ability to attract and retain the best talent by creating a culture that enables people to be themselves at work and makes them want to stay.
- Our D&I strategy has been created to respond directly to our employee feedback, to support the delivery of our business strategy and to take the ever-changing global demographics and expectations into consideration.
- For us, this is not about ticking a box or political correctness. This is a business imperative that will support and enable us to better understand and respond to the increasingly diverse requirements of our clients.

Think about the key messages you would like to ensure are cascaded to your stakeholders at every opportunity. Continually review your key messages as you work through the delivery of your strategic plan. Test them out with others such as your D&I steering group members and other stakeholders to ensure they resonate and portray the right message. As you progress and create change within the organisation, your key messages should reflect that journey, for maximum impact.

Linda Holbeche, Founder and Director, The Holbeche Partnership

'The clearer the links between diversity and inclusion and business, the better. You have to bring the "win-win" to life. For me, the most important group to target is not the very top managers but the layer just below. You need to work with that up-and-coming cadre, so that when they do get to the top they don't just reinforce the status quo.

'I once worked with a family-owned brewing company. It was a great place to work, but people definitely tended to think the same and display the same attitude to change. My way in was via the only board member that wasn't part of the family – he could see that there was a need for change. I worked with the layer of senior managers just below board level. I got them to identify the key issues, and gave them the tools to go off and investigate what other people were doing and establish some benchmarks.

'It was a simple but powerful exercise, because it made people active participants in the process of making the case for change. It took them away from their usual environment and exposed them directly to new ways of thinking and doing things. Plus they had the confidence that came from knowing they were part of a group that would all be advocating for change, rather than being a lone voice. The board got to hear these very consistent, evidence-based arguments, and that convinced them to take some steps towards doing things differently, after a mere 180 years of everything being the same!'

Creating and delivering your plan

The aim of the communications plan is to ensure that you are clear on what you are saying, when you are saying it and to whom you are saying it to. Sounds pretty straightforward, but you shouldn't underestimate how important this is to get your message out there and how difficult it can be at times.

There are a number of ways to create a communications plan and every organisation generally has their own style. Take a look at a number of different styles of plan and find a method that works for you.

Below you will find two examples of what your communications plan might look like and the information required:

Example one – focuses on the key updates to share, if this is to an internal or external audience and when the communication will be distributed.

WHAT	INT	EXT	WHEN	CHANNEL
All Employee Communication Update (you said, we did) ● Message from Executive Committee – the importance of D&I to deliver business plan ● Launch and implementation of revised Equality, Diversity and Inclusion Policy ● 'Creating Inclusive Cultures' Programme involvement across UK cities	X		End Sept	Email Video of CEO Meeting Twitter and Facebook

Example two – focuses on key updates and shares more detail as to who this will be distributed to.

WHAT	GROUP	DIVISION	EMPLOYEE	PRESS/ MEDIA	MP/ GOV	CLIENTS	OTHER
Message from Executive Committee – the importance of D&I to deliver business plan	X	X	X	X	X	X	X
Launch and implementation of revised Equality, Diversity and Inclusion Policy	X	X	X				
'Creating Inclusive Cultures' Programme Involvement across UK cities	X	X	X	X	X	X	X

Regardless of whatever type of communications plan you decide to use, take the following into consideration:

- What do you want to say and when – this should be consistent with your delivery plan as well as taking the overall organisations communications feedback into consideration.
- What messages and updates do you want to share with your different stakeholders and when?
- Who do you want the communication to come from, you, CEO or someone else (this will also be influenced by the audience and the importance of the message)?
- Engage with your internal communications team to ensure the timing and key messages are joined up with other planned communications.

As you create your plan it is also important to consider how you are going to distribute your communications as well as how you will embed into wider organisation communications. To progress this effectively there are three actions to take:

- Build an effective relationship with the communications team.
- Increase your awareness of the key business communications – what will they say and when are they planned?
- Create a number of suggestions for the communications team as to how they can integrate the D&I messages into existing business communications.

MEDIA CHANNELS

The way in which you can share your message has significantly increased over recent years with corporate messages being accessed through social media channels such as Twitter, Facebook and YouTube. As consumers of information, we expect the messages to be given in different ways such as e-newletters, podcasts and video.

Social media gives organisations the great opportunity to create dialogue with their contacts, find out what their thoughts are and create two-way communication rather than purely downloading information. This is a method Charlotte tested when she was challenged to create a campaign called #95inclusivetips via Twitter. This was a way of sourcing input and tips from followers about what their preferred inclusion nudges were to help create inclusive cultures. The project was a success and continues to crowd-source ideas of what individuals can do to influence D&I within their organisations.

Charlotte also recalls working with a firm where they encouraged employees to share their views on D&I via video. They submitted the videos which were then used to influence the future D&I plan and created a video compilation every three months with the best ideas including the organisation's response to those ideas. This ensured that employees were receiving communications from their colleagues, were engaged in the agenda by sharing their views and ideas and it ensured there was two-way communication throughout.

The social 'universe', composed of every single digitally connected person, doubles in size every two years.[1] Social media platforms collectively play a big part in what the data consumers create and share with others. For example, in any one minute there are:

- 31.25 million messages posted on Facebook
- 347,222 new tweets
- 17,361 LinkedIn profile views
- 48,611 photos posted on Instagram
- 300 hours of video uploaded onto YouTube

Given that amount of activity, it stands to reason that organisations should harness the power of social media to engage their employees. The challenge for many organisations, however, is that many of their technology infrastructures are not as up to date as the ones many of us use in our everyday lives. For example, heightened security firewalls can hinder access to many sites, as well as overprotective managers who fear that productive work time could be wasted on accessing social media.

Social media is a great resource to engage people in creating more diverse and inclusive workplaces and a number of campaigns have gone viral. For example:

- Dove created the campaign #SpeakBeautiful to encourage women to realise the role their online words play in impacting their confidence and self-esteem. During the 2015 Academy Awards they posted a video for the campaign; Twitter technology was able to identify negative tweets about beauty and body image and respond in realtime suggesting the users think more positively about what they say.

- #timetotalk raised the profile of mental health on social media encouraging people to blog, video or tweet candid conversations about mental illness. According to a survey by Time to Change, 47 per cent of people aged 21 and under said they find it easiest to talk about their mental health problems online.

One other important consideration is how you engage employees from different generations. As we know, with the ageing demographic in many countries and the desire/necessity to work longer, we are now at a stage where we see five generations in the workplace. How you engage each of those generations is slightly different and worthy of consideration. The following shares a general overview:[2]

Silent Generation: 1920–1946

The Silent Generation is strong, self-sufficient and prefers to work behind the scenes. They are good team players and generally don't ruffle feathers or initiate conflict.

To effectively engage this group:

- Use testimonials and expert endorsements.
- Offer them time with others. This group relies on connectedness and social activities.
- Promote patriotism, teamwork and doing more with less.
- Provide detailed directions on how to do something.

Baby Boomers: 1947–1964

Baby Boomers are the first generation to grow up with TV, audio cassettes, fast food and credit cards. Today, Baby Boomers hold powerful positions in virtually every sector including government, religion, health, education and business.

(Continued)

To effectively engage this group:

- Provide knowledge. This group likes to understand the big picture.
- Offer them a new experience. This group is adventurous and likes to try new things.
- Discuss technology. This group spends the most on technological products.
- Consider communicating via social media. Baby Boomers use Facebook, LinkedIn, have smartphones and tablets. They rarely use these devices for texting.

Generation X: 1965–1982

Generation X grew up in an era of blockbuster movies, popular music on TV, Nintendo, Game Boy Super Mario, Pac-Man, Sony Walkman and cable TV. They are moved by images and graphics rather than written words.

To effectively engage this group:

- Share images and graphics to gain buy-in.
- Deliver what you promise.
- Offer suggestions rather than telling them what to do.
- Approach these individuals from a global point of view rather than a local one.
- Steer away from anything that threatens their lifestyle be it political, social or business.
- Go straight to the point rather than hinting at something.
- Let them get to know you and trust you.

Generation Y: 1983–2001

Generation Y currently makes up the largest group in the workforce. They have an immense impact on consumer trends and markets in North America, Europe and other parts of the world.

To effectively engage this group:

- Consider communicating through instant messaging, text and email, video conferencing, blogs and social networks.

- Give them feedback on their ideas.
- Find a way to get them involved and feeling valued.
- Be transparent.
- Invite groups of friends to get involved.
- Let them communicate with you online for convenience.

Generation Z: 2002 onwards

Generation Z may well emerge to be fastpaced and decisive. They will want their information immediately and will have the tools at their disposal to get it.

To effectively engage this group:

- Communicate through text and instant messaging.
- Realise they are spontaneous and unpredictable. Refrain from formality.
- Get them to feel like they belong.

As you create and deliver your communications plan, consider the different media channels you could use and how you may be able to get your messages to a wider audience in a different, more engaging way.

- What media channels are available for the different stakeholder audiences? How do these differ internally and externally?
- How can the message be delivered differently? 140 characters? Video? Podcast?
- How can you encourage two-way dialogue rather than a monologue?
- How can you make it most accessible and engaging?

ADAPTING AND EMBEDDING INTO EVERYDAY MESSAGES

An important part of any effective communications plan is to ensure the key messages are included in other organisation-wide communications such as messages from the CEO, presentations and external interviews and quotes. The more you can work alongside the communications and PR team as well as leaders who speak both internally and to the outside world the better for your strategy and delivery plan.

Getting people to talk about the importance of D&I and how this links back to their part of the business without it being perceived as a 'D&I communication' is very valuable and can be difficult to find. The more you can make this happen the more it will be seen, over time, as the way that business is done here and part of the fabric of the organisation.

There are a number of points to consider as you adapt and embed D&I into everyday messages and communications; these include:

- **Authenticity:** Whatever the message may be and whoever this may be coming from, it must be authentic and sound like the person or organisation that is speaking. It also has to be backed up with actions. People can tell when the communications are 'corporate babble' rather than the messages that a leader really wants to share.

- **Personal stories:** Support the people who this message is coming from to create the same meaning in their own words and what this means for them and their part of the business. Help them to personalise this with little anecdotes, examples and stories to bring out the meaning and bring it to life, showing that they are human and understand these issues (or want to understand them).

- **Words that you use:** Think about the titles and headings of the communications that are sent out. Ensure the wording is focused on the actions, outcomes and the vision for the organisation rather than about D&I. Charlotte piloted this with a global company she was advising. They tested different communications across the different countries and divisions with headings such as 'Diversity and Inclusion – impact on businesses' and 'The way forward – a message from our CEO'. They found, on average, the communications that did not include the words diversity and inclusion in the title were significantly more likely to be opened and read by employees and other stakeholders. Many people, certainly at the early stages of the D&I journey, who don't feel that it has any link back to them or any benefit to them will generally discard any communications positioned in that way.

Communication is a critical element of the overall delivery of any D&I changes, so consider who may be able to help you. In Charlotte's experience the more successful change programmes have had a communications specialist as part of the D&I steering group, supporting team or acting as a key stakeholder and partner to the D&I professional. Consider how this could work within your organisation.

One way that Charlotte focused on engaging people at all levels with a client was to create awareness events called 'EPIC – Every person influences culture'. Within those events Charlotte shared an overview of what the organisation aspired to achieve and why. She then asked individuals to consider a number of questions, including:

- What does D&I mean for their role in the organisation?
- If they could ask senior leaders a clarifying question, what would it be?
- What does D&I mean for their team and/or the people they worked with?
- What are the three actions they could adopt to enable the organisation to realise its aspirations in being more diverse and inclusive?
- What is the one behaviour they could adapt to enable the organisation to realise its aspirations?
- If there was one piece of advice they would give others to support the delivery of this aspiration, what would it be?
- What one thing would they like the company to do differently?

By doing this, employees at all levels actively felt they had a voice and could influence what was happening and how it would be delivered. They were also personally identifying what part they could actively play in the change.

The responses from each of the events were collated and shared with senior leaders and those coordinating the D&I work. On a regular basis these were consolidated and shared across the organisation to continue to increase engagement and to enable employees to think about the commitments they made in those events as well as consider what their colleagues said. These events were run on an annual basis to ensure that all employees had formal opportunities to share their views and perspectives and continue to feel part of the change.

Five key takeaways from this chapter

- Take communicating the change seriously – create a plan.
- Tailor the communications depending on who they are coming from and, where possible, customise with personal stories; make them sound authentic.
- Review the key messages and how they are communicated on a regular basis.
- Over-communicate and use multiple media channels to attract different audiences.
- Use your words carefully – overuse of D&I within communications may limit who reads the messages.

Bias and unconscious bias training

Everybody is a genius, but if you judge a fish by its ability to climb a tree, it will live its whole life believing that it is stupid. ALBERT EINSTEIN, THEORETICAL PHYSICIST

It is unusual to talk about D&I without the terms 'bias' or 'unconscious bias' being mentioned. In this chapter we look at bias in more detail, the impact of bias and an overview of bias and unconscious bias training.

The impact of bias

We all allow unconscious bias to impact our decisions – it's just a fact of life. Unconsciously, we tend to like people who look like us, act like us and come from similar backgrounds to ours. We all want to think that we are open-minded; however, our personal history heavily influences how we evaluate others. Of course, for survival, often our natural instincts keep us safe – for example, we don't just step in to a busy road to cross over, we don't put our hand on an open, hot grill. However, when we let bias influence our decisions at work, we can end up missing real talent and/or great opportunities.

There are many different types of bias (unconscious or otherwise) which can impact decision making at different points in the employee life cycle: for example, how you evaluate people when going through the assessment process to hire someone, handing out special projects or assigning pay increases and bonuses. For decades now, writers and researchers have been publishing books on unconscious bias and its impact. Academics have developed online bias tests that you can take anonymously, such as the Implicit Association Test from Harvard University,[1] and corporates have spent many millions across the world using consultants to teach their people about the impact of unconscious bias on decision making.

Most often you hear people referring to 'unconscious' bias (rather than bias), which is the term you will usually hear when it comes to training and development. 'Curing' unconscious bias is sometimes perceived as the silver bullet for progressing D&I, which it clearly isn't. The reason people use the term unconscious is usually to try and ensure that an individual doesn't become defensive if you suggest that they are not as openminded as they like to think they are. However, we do wonder if we may have gone too far with the concept of unconscious bias which protects and even forgives the people that should actually be outed for their conscious bias. Some will suggest that for many companies that are new to their D&I journey, they may not be at the 'unconscious' stage, but more at the 'conscious' stage of bias.

A Spanish partner recently shared with Fleur a conversation that she had had with two male partners about a woman's suitability for promotion. The first partner said that she was not a strong performer. The second partner said that this was not his understanding. He had heard that she was an integral part of a recent pitch for new business and had done really well, resulting in them winning the business. The first partner then pointed out that she worked part- time. The three partners discussed this and concluded that there was no policy that said people working part-time couldn't be promoted. As a last attempt, the first partner pointed out that she would be turning 40 the following year, so was too old to be promoted. We are not sure that any of this conversation could be classed as unconscious bias, but there was certainly something going on that was clearly bias.

Fleur was at a conference in Abu Dhabi listening to the EMEA and Latin American head of HR for Roche speaking. She told the story of being in the car when she was young and her mother was driving. Her mother knew she was going to sneeze. She tried to stop it, but eventually she did sneeze and she swerved the car nearly causing an accident. The little girl asked her mother whose fault it was and her mother said it was hers – she knew it was coming, she couldn't stop it, but she was able to correct the impact of the sneeze. This HR specialist suggested that we think about unconscious bias as a form of brain sneeze. We know it's going to happen, we often can't stop it happening, but we can mitigate its impact.

What is bias?

Let's take a step back and look at what unconscious bias actually is. Our brains are processing so much information at any one time that we need a system to work out what is and isn't important. Our brains are hard-wired to make these decisions based on past experience and current perceptions. However, when we are under pressure, for example working on a task or to a deadline, we are most susceptible to the influence of unconscious bias. This can result in, for example, making an unfair judgment about a person's ability which could significantly impact future decisions made about them.

There are many different types of bias. Take for example the impact of affinity bias during recruitment, which is about being 'similar to me'. This can lead us to like people we are interviewing just because they appear to be similar to ourselves. There is confirmatory bias which leads us to look for evidence that confirms our beliefs or judgements about someone and ignores evidence that contradicts those beliefs. If you believe that working mothers are less committed to their career than women with no children, without realising it, you could draw inferences from their comments and actions that back this belief up.

The following is a list of some of the more common biases:

NAME	DESCRIPTION
Ambiguity effect	The tendency to avoid options for which missing information makes the probability seem 'unknown'
Anchoring	The tendency to rely too heavily, or 'anchor', on one trait or piece of information when making decisions (usually the first piece of information that we acquire on that subject)
Bandwagon effect	The tendency to do (or believe) things because many other people do (or believe) the same. Related to *groupthink* and *herd behaviour*
Bias blind spot	The tendency to see oneself as less biased than other people, or to be able to identify more cognitive biases in others than in oneself
Cheerleader effect	The tendency for people to appear more attractive in a group than in isolation
Framing effect	Drawing different conclusions from the same information, depending on how that information is presented
Hindsight bias	Sometimes called the 'I-knew-it-all-along' effect, the tendency to see past events as being predictable at the time those events happened

(Continued)

NAME	DESCRIPTION
Negativity effect	The tendency of people, when evaluating the causes of the behaviours of a person they dislike, to attribute their positive behaviours to the environment and their negative behaviours to the person's inherent nature
Observer-expectancy effect	When a researcher expects a given result and therefore unconsciously manipulates an experiment or misinterprets data in order to find it
Outcome bias	The tendency to judge a decision by its eventual outcome instead of basing it on the quality of the decision at the time it was made
Stereotyping	Expecting a member of a group to have certain characteristics without having actual information about that individual

Consider when any of the above biases have played a part in your decision-making. Were you aware they were having an impact? If so, what did you do to mitigate the impact, if anything?

Pauline Miller, Head of Diversity and Inclusion, Lloyd's of London

'Bias is something that we all have, as the result of our background, environment, personal and work experience and family values. Unconscious bias is what happens when those influences come into play and affect our behaviours and decision making without us being aware of it.

'In the workplace the impact of bias is most often seen when people are making decisions about other people, for example, who to pro-mote, who to send on a long-term assignment, or who to bring into the organisation. These are decisions that affect people's careers.

'At my last company, a global financial services provider, we initiated a programme that aimed to tackle unconscious bias and stop it getting in the way of building a diverse and inclusive culture. We knew there was a strong commitment at the top, among senior leaders, and at the bottom through strong grassroots involvement in employee networks, but it felt like the message was getting a bit lost in that middle layer.

'That was borne out by the results of our employee engagement survey, which highlighted a need to support middle managers in developing the skills they needed to engage with their employees and create more inclusive working environments. We developed two programmes: a basic e-learning session for all employees; and a dedicated programme for middle managers aimed at helping them to understand and recognise bias and develop some techniques for managing it in themselves.

'The training comprised a single 90-minute session. Up to 50 people from across our global offices could take part at any one time, via Webex. Sessions were led by a facilitator and included lots of opportunities for breakouts and discussion between the participants. Embedding bias training was a key objective from the start and so the training became a mandatory module for recruiters, participants of our manager development programme and also for our senior executive promotion committee. Of course, a one-off session isn't enough to change behaviour, so follow-up was really important.

'We developed a range of tools, including a set of video vignettes that proved to be a very powerful resource. They were structured in such a way as to give insights into what was going on in the protagonists' minds and to really highlight the points where bias kicked into the decision-making process. Managers found them really useful as a refresher, for example when they were about to go into an interview situation.

'We also set up an online community, which has thrived. Managers have used it to discuss their experiences and share practical tips. One manager explained how, following the training, he decided to switch to doing all first interviews by phone rather than face-to-face. It made him aware of how his own bias was getting in the way of evaluating candidates in a truly objective way. Speaking on the phone removed some of those barriers, and created a more level playing field.

'Subsequent surveys showed that levels of engagement were higher among those managers that had done the training. They were also

(Continued)

more likely to stay with the company. A year after the training launched, the company introduced three-year goals regarding the number of women in senior roles, so we were able to measure progress against those too and found a significant increase of female representation on management teams and at senior levels within the organisation.

'We realised though that, despite the positive feedback, the pipeline was still not growing as quickly as we would like. The issue was one of accountability: how do you actually make sure that people are demonstrating values and behaviours that create a more inclusive environment? We decided to expand the unconscious bias training to all employees, including those with no line management responsibilities. That way everyone is aware, not only of their own behaviour, but of other people's too. I really feel that if you want to bring about that kind of profound cultural change, you have to make everybody a part of it.'

There are different ways to help people counterbalance their bias, such as:

- Pause and think before making a decision.
- Always review your decisions and those of others for objectivity and stereotyping.
- Know the drivers of your decisions – are you judging someone on style rather than their outputs?

However, it is also important to look at your people processes at each stage of the employee cycle to identify whether there is bias already embedded. For example, a common barrier is often the online graduate recruitment system. In many organisations if you don't have a first or 2.1 degree, you are automatically rejected from the process.

Fleur once worked with a talented chemist who had not been able to complete her degree finals because she had narcolepsy and the stress of exams brought on a life-threatening attack. Her university was happy to say that all of her course work indicated that she could achieve a first, but of course this was of no help with an online application process.

As we have already said, what we know about unconscious bias is that there is no 'cure' for it, but by raising people's awareness about the impact of bias, research shows that if this is front of mind when people are making decisions, the impact can be reduced, although this is not thought to be permanent and is something that has to be continually worked at.

Other examples of bias could include:

- not offering a high-profile project to a team member because it will involve some long days and your star performer is already struggling with childcare and her partner travelling (you may be right and your decision was made with the best of intentions, but it is for the individual to make the choice)

- entering an office where there are three men and a woman and making the assumption that the woman is the junior– we know it sounds like a dated example, but it still happens

- questioning why someone has asked for the assessment centre documents to be produced in Braille because surely they won't be able to do accounting if they can't see

- giving a higher bonus to the man rather than the woman because she won't care as much as her male counterpart as she is not the main breadwinner

- not recruiting a woman to your small team, because she is newly married and you figure that she is likely to want to take maternity leave in the next couple of years

- not wanting to employ someone with a disability because they may have a high level of sickness

- requiring your teams to be in the office, because you are not convinced that they will be working hard if they are at home.

Some years ago, HSBC produced some thought-provoking adverts which beautifully summed up how our own life experience fuels how we look at the world. They were made up of a series of pictures. One example was a picture of a tent with 'holiday' written over it next to a picture of the deck of a cruise ship with 'hell' written over it. They were the flipped around with 'hell' written over the tent and 'holiday' over the cruise ship. Would you find camping fun or would you prefer to be on a cruise? It's the same premise in the workplace: do you put a lot of value on how someone dresses in the office – could you be misled by the calibre of a person because they are smartly dressed in a suit, rather than a casual pair of jeans?

Coca-Cola produced a marketing campaign that showed a picture of the iconic red Coca-Cola can, but there was a difference. They removed the brand. Instead they included the caption 'remove labels'. They focused their campaign on how we naturally want to add labels to everything, including people and wanted to challenge that thinking.

Bias and unconscious bias training

There is value in most training if you can engage with your audience, but in our experience, a lot of unconscious bias (UB) training is fun at the time, but has little lasting impact or any clear impact measures to demonstrate its success. It's great for raising awareness, and research tells us that there is a direct correlation between awareness raising and a decrease in bias, but you have to do this regularly and give reminders at important decision-making stages; otherwise it doesn't stick. Given the opportunity, our brain is quick to revert to whatever is most comfortable – our brains are cognitive misers, finding ways to save on time and effort.

In a webinar that Fleur attended, Dr David Rock, a neuroscientist, pointed out that if you have a brain, you have bias and he suggested that the best you can do is to raise awareness of this, rather than spend a lot of money on training that has little long-term impact. People tend to like UB training – it's intellectually engaging, it's relevant both inside and outside the workplace, it validates the things that we see people do and, by calling it 'unconscious', you are not pointing the blame at anyone. However, the downside of this training can be that, too often, people become aware of everyone else's bias but not their own.

Rock says that there are 50–150 different types of bias and questions how you can possibly start to train everyone in all of them. He suggests the answer is to focus on your people processes and where bias might be impacting rather than trying to train out the individual's bias. That said, we have both seen and experienced some good bias training that at least raises awareness, even if the impact is quite short term.

For example, at EY, they have a web-based learning tool (WBL) that reminds managers about how bias impacts decision making. They are asked to complete it once a year just before the annual performance management cycle. On the whole this had impact, but the real shift in results was seen when this training was accompanied by the use of an excel spreadsheet during the review, nick-named 'Just in time'. The performance rankings were input into the spreadsheet as they were agreed in the meeting, in real time, so there and then the review committee could check the distribution and equity of the ratings by gender.

This WBL itself presents the statistics that show where bias may be impacting, introduces some short exercises with overarching messages such as the fact that we can all be looking at the same thing and seeing something different, gets people to think about language and how easy it is to stereotype – for example, she doesn't say a lot in meetings so may not have leadership quali-ties. It also looks at what can drive bias – for example, working under time pressure and then helps the individual think about how they can challenge themselves and others.

Live workshops can also be fun if they are interactive, and what appeals about this approach is that we are 'all in this together'. It's not about minorities and different groups, it's about how our brain works and the impact this has on our view of the world. The challenge around delivering unconscious bias training and the perceived impact this will create should not be ignored. There have been numerous occasions when Charlotte has heard employees after leaving this type of training joke about the fact that 'as my bias is unconscious there is nothing I can do about it because I don't know I'm doing it'.

In the *Harvard Business Review* article 'What Facebook's anti-bias training pro-gram gets right'[2] it highlights that raising awareness of bias and unconscious bias (as many training programmes do) is not enough to create the desired change and is not the primary answer to enabling change. The article argues that to enable change any interventions should support employees to:

- accept that bias affects them
- enable them to raise their concerns about the consequences and
- ensure they are willing to learn to replace their tendencies to act on bias.

Critical to all of this is enabling employees to discuss and consider when bias has had an impact on their actions and decision making. For example, what does bias mean when thinking about the pay increases in your team or who you decide will get involved in that really exciting project that has just landed on your desk? Without anchoring this back to how people behave and make decisions in everyday aspects of their life, anything you deliver on unconscious bias will be an expense without any significant impact on creating a more inclusive culture.

Five key takeaways from this chapter

- We all have unconscious bias and sometimes it can be helpful.
- Not all bias playing out in the workplace is necessarily unconscious.
- There is no 'cure' for someone's bias and training only raises awareness; it doesn't eradicate the issue.
- The key is to find ways to protect your business and people processes from the impact of UB.
- Awareness raising needs to be repeated and ideally linked back to critical decision-making activities such as promotions and recruitment.

Talent management – recruitment to career development

Employees who believe that management is concerned about them as a whole person – not just an employee – are more productive, more satisfied, more fulfilled. ANNE M. MULCAHY, FORMER CHAIR AND CEO, XEROX CORPORATION

Every stage of the employee life cycle (Figure 10.1) has the potential to be derailed from an equality, diversity and inclusion perspective by either your business or people processes (or at times both): for example, something as basic as your recruitment marketing literature. If the people you feature are all young, white men and women, you are portraying a message to the older generations, the ethnic minority community and others that this isn't a place where they are likely to find many role models or even feel that welcome. Some derailers are easy to solve, such as the example just used, but others are deeply embedded in how your business thinks about and manages its people.

Figure 10.1   Employee life cycle

In the following two chapters we look at the different stages of an employee's life cycle through a D&I lens, to identify where the key challenges are that require consideration and, at times, require change. This chapter focuses on all elements from joining the company to career development.

Fleur remembers in a previous organisation using an external consultant to review their leadership competency model through a diversity lens. The consultant produced two full A4 pages of feedback covering the aspects that would be worthy of change. However, after going through it point by point, the organisation concluded that if you changed too much of the current operating model, it would be so sanitised that no one would relate to it. The art of all of this is finding the right balance.

In addition to this it is critical to make sure that you have identified and engaged the relevant in-house specialist to partner with you on each element of the employee life cycle. For example, you may be working with your communications or marketing teams for external branding or your HR generalists for delivering the performance management process.

Recruitment
PRE-HIRE AND YOUR ORGANISATION'S BRAND

It is easy to be too casual about your external brand and the messaging that you send out to the general public through a number of different ways – through how you promote senior role models, create thought leadership, share news on innovative new benefits and your use of imagery and pictures.

Many organisations now spend a great deal of time and money achieving high rankings as employers of choice with organisations such as Universum, who measure the brand strength of a company on campus with the graduate population. Fleur's talent lead in the United Kingdom tells a great story of a man that had offers from all of the 'big four' to join their graduate scheme. He chose EY, because they were the only one of the accountancy firms that featured in the top three of the Stonewall ranking for gay-friendly employers.

Research shows us that it costs a company more to attract and hire someone if they have a weak employer brand. When positioning your company externally, ensure your images and pictures are as diverse as possible, reflecting the community that you are trying to attract. For example, for some people looking at a picture of a white male rowing team will leave them with the impression of a strong, ambitious, potentially macho culture. For others, it will leave them with the impression that the organisation is not open for business with them.

Senior role models can be incredibly powerful, particularly when they talk about their difference. Think for example of Tidjane Thiam, (former CEO of the Prudential in the United Kingdom and, at the time of writing, CEO at Credit Suisse). He was one of very few BAME executives in the FTSE100 and the first Black CEO of a FTSE100. As described in *The Telegraph*:[1] 'His path to the top has been, in its way, as fascinating as that of his peer Barack Obama, with whom parallels have, inevitably, been drawn. An exotic heritage, stellar academic ability, and ambition have combined to create a leader in whom the expectations of many reside, in the business community, and in Africa. He has often spoken on a personal level about the impact of his ethnicity and the way that can cause people to stereotype him. When he appeared on *Desert Island Discs*, one of his record choices was Stevie Wonder's "Heaven is 10 zillion years away", with the line "why must my colour black make me a lesser man, I thought this world was made for everyman".'

Think of Sheryl Sandberg (whether you agree with her 'Lean In' approach to women, work and the will to lead or not)[2] who has taken the world by storm on the gender debate, and Inga Beale, who became CEO of Lloyd's of London in 2014. She has spearheaded the drive to force the insurance industry to put D&I at the heart of their vision to be a truly global industry. In late 2015, Inga Beale stated at a Business Federation event in Japan: 'An inclusive workplace is the very foundation of what we need for innovation as the world changes like never before. We are facing an economic revolution on a par to the industrial revolution of the 18th Century, but on a greater scale. There is a need to be evermore innovative and evermore inclusive. Diversity in my mind is the very foundation of innovation.'

Of course, not all publicity is good publicity. Marissa Mayer, as CEO of Yahoo, certainly put them on the map for her stance on flexibility when she announced an end to working from home, and many were shocked to read that both Apple and Google offer their employees the benefit of getting their eggs frozen if they are planning to delay starting a family! Hitting the right note or pitching at the right level is not always easy, but for many companies the impact can be expressed in hard currency if they don't get this right. Whether you are going to market to attract the best talent to your organisation, looking to get the highest engagement from them when they are with you, or hoping to capture their spending decisions, you must appreciate the many differences that influence the engagement of different communities and your brand says it all.

The following are some areas to consider in pre-hiring:

- Know your target audience and how to effectively connect with them.
- Review the imagery of your internal and external literature, for example, recruitment, annual business report.
- Identify your brand ambassadors and champions: what are they saying and how are you using them?

ACCESSING THE TALENT POOL

Recruitment is such a powerful route to increase the diversity of your workforce and there are a wealth of ways to access the talent pool, but it can also work against your overarching diversity strategy. We have often come across organisations who are some years in to their D&I journey and are seeing a positive impact on the strength of their leadership pipeline. They are promoting more minorities to senior positions, but they are diluting the diversity of the pool with the non-diverse candidates they are hiring.

Depending on the size of your organisation, there are many different routes to market and it can be difficult to pinpoint where the process is weakest. Where there are budget constraints there is usually a reticence to use third-party providers for attraction and recruitment. This can lead an organisation to consider sourcing their new hires via word of mouth, some calling this the 'friends referral' scheme. If you don't have a diverse workforce to begin with, the likelihood of receiving diverse referrals from this network is minimal.

Many agencies tend to purely act as a conduit for CVs and in the days when discrimination was more overt, many were quite open about deselecting some CVs based on demographics such as gender, nationality or ethnicity. Agencies might be OK for high-volume recruiting, but be mindful of the diversity of the candidates they are putting forward as well as the employer brand they are portraying of your company in the market. You often hear of candidates saying that they just felt processed, and when they weren't successful they were rejected with no relevant feedback – they are likely to associate that experience with your brand rather than directly with the recruiting company.

There is also the headhunting community to consider. Some are genuinely engaged and want to source the most diverse pool of talent for their client; some just want to fill the role and get out with their fee. We have identified two key challenges:

- The business wants the role filled fast so they are not interested in giving the headhunter the extra time to really trawl the broadest talent pool.
- The headhunter is assessing the 'best fit' for the client through their own, potentially biased lens. Often this lens is too narrow and some suitable, less 'traditional' candidates can be overlooked.

Many companies now ask for diverse candidate slates, sometimes by setting a target, but still too often, the overarching policy at the leadership level doesn't translate down to the activity of the hiring manager. The firm is saying how committed they are to receiving a diverse slate of candidates, but the manager just wants to fill the slot – ideally with someone similar to the person they are replacing. This is an example of a real dilemma for organisations to ensure their message and commitment from the top is enacted throughout.

Research by Boris Groysberg[3] actually shows us that senior women moving roles are more successful in their new roles than their male counterparts. Published in the *Harvard Business Review*, it suggests two main reasons for this:

- High-performing women build their success on portable, external relationships – with clients and other outside contacts – unlike men.
- Women considering job changes weigh up more factors than men do, especially cultural fit, values, and managerial style. These strategies enable women to transition more successfully to new companies.

When using third-party providers, consider the following tips:

- Make sure they are aware of your commitment to receiving diverse candidate lists. Discuss with them where they will source their candidates from and how.
- Consider including at least one organisation that specialises in sourcing diverse candidates. In many geographies, this is quite straightforward for gender, but less so for other communities such as disabled people or people wanting to work flexibly.

(Continued)

- Make sure your provider is committed to helping candidates prepare for interview.
- Make sure that they are up to speed with your focus on D&I and can talk to candidates about your progress.

In one organisation that Charlotte worked with she developed a number of expectations for the business to use when working with search firms. The search firms were expected to report back to the organisation on a quarterly basis on how they were performing against their diversity expectations, and there was always a veiled threat to the companies that, if they were unable to perform without a very clear and acceptable reason for a lack of diversity, they would be in fear of losing their business.

An example of the expectations can be found below:

Recruitment agency/search firm – diversity requirements

Our organisation is an equal opportunity employer and strongly believes in the value of a diverse workforce. As one of these trusted partners, we would request that you undertake the following:

- Provide evidence to us that your organisation and those involved in the candidate recruitment process are well trained in the legislation relating to equal opportunities. In addition, provide evidence that your agency considers diversity, inclusion and bias within its training and development processes for its staff and supports the ethical and business case for diversity.
- Regularly assess the diversity composition of candidates on your books and take steps to make your agency more attractive to under-represented groups if necessary.
- Promote diversity and are actively trying to achieve it (e.g. workshops; presentations; forums).

- The shortlist for every role must have a representation of both men and women as well as candidates from diverse backgrounds.
  - If you are unable to comply with the above on a specific role, then we require an explanation as to why.
  - We do not expect the quality of the candidates to be compromised in order to meet the representation.
  - There will be a quarterly review of performance on the above metric, and we expect that you will be able to provide us with statistics for all roles that you have been instructed on.
- If advertising a role on our behalf, ensure that the wording is inclusive and states that we are an equal opportunity employer that values diversity and is committed to creating an inclusive workplace.
- As we look to increase the proportion of women and diverse talent in mid-senior level roles within the organisation, we are open to seeing strong CVs on a speculative basis.
- Agencies that fail to meet with the above requirements on two successive quarters may be terminated.

Another approach is to get the recruiter to conduct a market-mapping exercise to identify what talent is where. It can be quite impactful to show your hiring manager just how rich the pool is, but again you need the commitment of that manager if you are going to turn the names on the list into actual hires. Another positive outcome of doing this is that you are able to start building effective relationships with the identified talent which, in time, may result in a hire. When we talk to headhunters, they always say that, in general, it takes longer to engage with a woman and support her through the hiring process than it does a man.

Targets are also a topic that requires some careful positioning and at times both your business and the headhunter will push back. One well-known global headhunter once pushed back on agreeing to work to gender targets on the grounds that they couldn't guarantee the gender of the candidates even if they said they were female! On the whole, professional and sophisticated providers are happy to agree to a percentage or minimum number of minority candidates on every long list – often varying by geography and sector.

At the time of writing this book, Lloyds Banking Group had announced that they were 'banning all male shortlists'. They instructed their providers that they wanted a minimum of one-third of total submissions to be made up of suitably qualified female candidates and that no shortlist will be progressed until this objective is met, without exception. There was much talk about whether this is legal or not (and of course it will depend on geography), but certainly in the United Kingdom most lawyers believe that it is perfectly legal as long as you are addressing the specific issue of the under-representation of women.

It isn't legal though to ask for all-female shortlists (unless the nature of the role dictates that it can only be done by a woman). This was confirmed in 2014 when Charlotte was asked to conduct an independent review for the UK Government Secretary of State. She was asked to look at the part that executive search firms played in identifying and hiring more women into board positions. During her research she interviewed a number of stakeholders including FTSE 100 chairmen, investors, industry bodies, women who were actively looking for board roles and the search firms themselves.

Her findings led to her making ten recommendations covering the organisations, investors and search firms. One recommendation covered the notion of all-women shortlists and she asked for clarification from the Equality and Human Rights Commission (EHRC). The EHRC said that it was illegal to purposely create an all-female shortlist for a role if there were men qualified and able to do the job. This gave clarity that had been missing for some time.[4]

The following are the ten recommendations from 'Women on boards – voluntary code for executive search firms – taking the next step'. A number of the recommendations are relevant for organisations regardless of the level they are hiring to and should consider how these could be adapted to meet their needs.

1. **Search firms should, in collaboration with their clients, discuss each woman on the long-list and aim to have at least one woman whom they would 'strongly recommend'** the client should meet and put forward onto the shortlist of all executive searches for board positions.

2. The original voluntary code should be considered as the minimum standard and **search firms should create an advanced code including how assessment should be made as to whom should become part of the advanced tier.**

3. Throughout the interviews there were numerous discussions relating to what happens at each stage of the search and hiring process e.g. long-list, short-list and hire. **Search firms should be encouraged to capture this information and to share their statistics with Government as and when requested.**

4. Through the analysis of the search firms' websites only 25% stated their commitment to the voluntary code. Only 12% shared any data to show their success rates of hiring women to board positions.

    a. **Search firms should be more overt on their websites, marketing literature and when talking to clients about their commitment.**

    b. **Search firms should be encouraged to share their hiring data as well as some narrative and case studies of successes.**

5. Search firms are ultimately there to deliver the requirements of their clients. To this end all FTSE 350 companies should challenge the search firms further to deliver against the codes provisions. **Companies should include a statement in all search contracts or agreements clearly articulating they will comply with all aspects of the voluntary code and explain if unable to do so.**

6. Some stakeholders continue to argue there are an insufficient number of 'board ready' women with the required skills for a FTSE 350 role. A database of women with the skills to take a FTSE 350 board position should be created. **The database would be in addition, and complementary, to what is already available with the aim of connecting board chairs with talented women.**

7. Through the interviews a small number of the more enlightened investors were actively asking FTSE organisations what they were doing to create more gender diversity within the board. However, a number of the investors may well have limited knowledge about diversity and what good looks like.

    a. **The investor community should play a more active role on this agenda and challenge businesses further on their plans and actions to create more gender balanced boards**

    b. **Information for the investor community on why gender diversity is important on corporate boards, including the right questions to ask, what they should be looking for and what a good response sounds like should be created.**

(Continued)

8. Throughout the interviews there were a number of discussions regarding the 30% long list and 'women only shortlists'. There have been differing legal opinions as to the ability to request 'women only shortlists' as an appropriate means to redress the balance on boards. **The Equalities and Human Rights Commission (EHRC) should create the appropriate guidance required.**

9. There is limited visibility of the code and those interviewed found it difficult to find the code or details of the signatory search firms. **To ensure this has clear prominence a section within the Government (BIS) website should be created to publish the code, the signatories and case studies of how the code is working in practice.**

10. The FRC UK Corporate Governance Code stipulates 'the search for board candidates should be conducted, and appointments made, on merit, against objective criteria and with due regard for the benefits of diversity on the board, including gender'. **The Voluntary Code for Executive Search should be referenced on the FRC website and within the FRC Guidance on Board Effectiveness when it is next updated.**

It is, however, perfectly legal to partner with organisations that focus on sourcing candidates from specific minority communities. Sponsors for educational opportunities (SEO) in the United States and United Kingdom work with BAME students to secure them internships, ideally leading to a graduate entry offer. Another example is a UK charity called Action on Disability that partners with organisations to secure internships for people with severe learning disabilities.

Martin Swain, former Vice President of Global Employee Relations, Inclusion and Diversity, GSK

'This will be the fourth year that GSK has run Project SEARCH – that's four cohorts of young people whose lives have been changed, and who have made a huge difference to the workplace. It really has exceeded their expectations in every way.

'The idea is very simple: it's to give young people aged 17 to 24 with severe learning disabilities the experience and practical support they need to prepare for work. In this case, GSK take a group of 12 each year, starting in September and finishing in June. GSK provide classroom space, laptops and work experience, while the local college, West Thames, provides a tutor and a London-based charity, Action on Disability, provides a job coach.

'During their time with the company, the young people do three three-month stints in different parts of the business. The focus is on what is called standard repeatable tasks – delivering mail, cleaning, working in the restaurant or staff shop, or updating spreadsheets. There's a lot of variety, and GSK ensure that the roles are visible and involve lots of interaction. This is absolutely not about the jobs other people don't want to do. It's about identifying the strengths and talents these young people have and giving them an opportunity to put them to good use.

'At the end of the year, the company has a graduation ceremony. It's a real celebration. After that, the job coach will carry on working with them to help them find employment. So far, GSK has a success rate of about 70 per cent, which is incredible when you consider that these are young people who would probably never otherwise have found work. Some of them stay with GSK – they have one young man working on reception, one in the hygiene team, two in IT contracts and a young woman working in the gardens.

'Although that's the main point of the programme, there are so many other benefits. The young people grow so much in confidence. They're mainstreamed from the start – so suddenly they have a whole new set of role-models. They are seeing new ways of behaving and interacting with people, and they start to follow suit. They're gaining skills for life as well as job skills.

'Other employees have learned so much too. GSK realised in the first year that they needed to offer more guidance and support, and to help them understand that this programme is about drawing out talent, not philanthropy. They ran a short training session setting out the vision, and explaining the behaviours they needed to demonstrate.

(Continued)

For example it's very important to be absolutely crystal clear and literal in your communication, and to be punctual!

'For GSK, it is a way of really bringing the corporate focus on disability to life. Being truly disability confident means experiencing it, working alongside it and making it part of everyday life. It's spurred the company on to start looking for talent in other places that they would not have looked before. Finding talent isn't just about fitting people into a cookie cutter. Project SEARCH has helped to open their minds.'

There is a small not-for-profit organisation in the United Kingdom called Rare Recruitment that works in the legal sector and focuses on identifying and mentoring students that would not usually secure an offer through more traditional routes. They have developed a really interesting 'contextual recruitment' approach. This means taking a more holistic view of the candidate, in addition to the raw academic scores, looking at the socio-economic challenges of the individual and what they have overcome to achieve their grades.

Specialisterne, was set up in Denmark works across the globe, and originally the majority of their employees had a diagnosis on the autism spectrum. They partner with organisations to recruit people with autism who excel as business consultants on tasks such as software testing, programming and data entry for the public and private sectors. As well as helping source the individual, they will mentor them through the application and induction process and, if needed, come in and train the team they will be working with. In Russia there is a programme called 'Path to Career' which runs an annual competition for young disabled professionals. Finalists take part in a competition and attend training in CV writing, self-presentation and teamwork.

Two approaches that have caught our eye which support engaging with a diverse pool of candidates through a non-traditional route, are 'on-ramping' programmes and 'return to work internships'. On-ramping is where an organisation reaches out to people who have left their profession for a number of years (off-ramped) and are now keen to return (on-ramp). The terminology comes from an early piece of research conducted by the Centre for Talent Innovation[5] that identified how problematic it was for women to get back into the workforce after taking a career break. The concept can be used for any group who find themselves out of employment for various reasons.

In response to that research, in 2005, Lehman Brothers launched a global pro-gramme called Encore. They hosted a day that was a mix of presentations from different areas of the business talking about changes in the last five to ten years, a session on storytelling – helping the attendees to rethink their CVs and the rich experience they had gained during the time that they were out of the workforce and finished with a previous 'on-ramper' sharing her top tips.

Internship programmes for returners are usually for a fixed period, but, if structured properly, they can still give the individuals a rich and rewarding experience. Morgan Stanley recognises that successful careers can be fluid and don't always follow a traditional path. They have created a 'Return to Work' programme that welcomes individuals back who have had a career break. This is a 12-week paid internship where participants are placed in roles based on their skills and interest. At the completion of the programme, some will be offered full-time roles. If this doesn't work out, at least they have gained recent experience to draw from for their next opportunity.

If you are relying solely on direct, online applications, the first rule is to make sure that your website is fully accessible, which you can do using a website such as Berkeley Web Access[6] or contacting the Business Disability Forum.[7] By 'fully accessible 'we mean the content generated, such as PDFs and infographics, are accessible to people with a range of different disabilities. Second, make sure that your job specifications and online selection techniques are appropriate for the role and that people are not rejected for trivial reasons that don't relate to the role. For example, it could be something as basic as the ability to change font size, or something more complicated such as online testing that doesn't take in to account the challenges of dyslexia.

Once you have navigated and accessed the talent pool, the next step is to effectively assess that talent.

EFFECTIVE ASSESSMENT OF YOUR CANDIDATE POOL

In terms of the actual assessment process, make sure that anyone recruiting is aware of the impact of their bias on decision making as well as having undertaken some form of D&I awareness training over the last couple of years. Structure your questioning around competencies (which of course need to be bias free) and regularly track the diversity of your intake so that you can identify where there are potential barriers. Some forward thinking companies have started to move on from competency-based interviews which look at previous experience in certain situations to strength-based interviews to find the most suitable person for a job based on what that person enjoys doing and is therefore good at.

Dan Richards, Head of Recruitment, EY UK & Ireland

'We've been using a strengths-based approach to assessing applications since 2009. All candidates applying for a graduate, undergraduate or school leaver role are assessed against eight strengths: adaptability, analysis, collaboration, drive, growth, pride, managing relationships and work ethic. By focusing on strengths, we get a clearer picture of what people like to do and what motivates them – which tends to go hand in hand with what they are good at.

'We validate the process each year, talking to candidates, partners and key stakeholders, and feeding our learning back into the process. We're constantly monitoring and checking to see that the process is actually delivering the number and calibre of candidates we need. What we've found is that there is a strong correlation between the strengths we're testing and future exam success. We can see that this is working in terms of helping us identify the right people, with the skills, aptitude and temperament to do the job. It's working in terms of giving us access to a wider pool of talent.

'We're now looking to take that a step further, by removing academic criteria for applicants. In the past, we've required candidates to have at least a 2.1 in their degree, or 300 UCAS points – equivalent to three Bs at A-level. Of the 25,000 applicants we receive each year, we estimate that around 4,000 to 5,000 are immediately screened out by that requirement. That's cutting us off from a large group of candidates who may very well have the strengths we need. It's interesting to note that the evidence linking academic performance to subsequent exam success is very weak.

'The academic criteria also has a disproportionate impact on specific groups. For example, research shows that students from Afro-Caribbean backgrounds are more likely to end up with a 2.2. We also know that there's a strong link between socio-economic background and academic achievement. Again, that's narrowing the talent pool, based on criteria that isn't necessarily a strong predictor of future success.

'Universum, an employer branding consultancy that focuses on building strong links between students and companies, did a really interesting piece of research. They asked 42,000 students across Europe, Middle East, India and Africa (EMEIA) about diversity and inclusion in the workplace: What did it mean to them, and what did they expect from an employer of choice? The number one priority issue was ethnicity and the second most important issue the students identified was socio-economic background. I think it's really important that we are seen to be focusing on and taking a lead in this area.

'Getting rid of the academic screening is a big leap forward in terms of further eliminating bias from our recruitment process. It doesn't mean that we won't be looking to attract candidates with a high level of academic attainment, rather it means we will be giving an equal chance to all candidates including those whose strengths may lie in areas other than academia.'

A helpful guide to inclusive questioning and getting the best out of your candidates comes from R.B. Miller and S.E. Heiman's book, *New Conceptual Selling*.[8] They highlight five different types of questioning:

1. To get new information – to force you to listen and accept the reality of current data; it helps you clarify the other person's needs, expectations and desired results
2. To get confirmation – to validate your data or reveal inaccuracies or assumptions about what you thought was true

(Continued)

3. To assess attitude – to identify the other person's values, attitudes and feelings

4. To action commitment – to help you identify your current position in a discussion by identifying what action the other person is willing to take to move things forward

5. To probe basic issues– to help you identify specific concerns that could result in no action being taken.

Open questions require more than a yes/no response and are particularly effective when followed up with probing questions – for example, 'Can you tell me more about?' Or behavioural questions – for example, 'Talk me through how you engaged the team.'

Avoid closed questions (Do you prepare for meetings?)

Avoid leading questions (I assume you would ...)

Avoid multiple questions (How would you deal with ... (a), (b) or (c)?)

In addition to how you structure your questioning, you should also think about the setting the candidates are being assessed in. Some companies, particularly at the graduate level, favour assessment centres. These in themselves can be stressful for some candidates and stop them performing at their best. People with certain social styles, for example, introverts, may end up feeling overwhelmed with the intensity of the activities. However, the structure of an assessment centre can be positive if the exercises are really testing the individual's suitability for the job. As Binna Kandola says, it is important that the candidate doesn't feel that they are being assessed for rejection rather than recruitment.

One example of a sector that went to great lengths to ensure that they were hiring the best talent from the broadest pool is the arts sector. Two professors, Cecilia Rouse and Claudia Goldin, completed a study that confirmed the existence of gender-biased hiring by major symphony orchestras.[9] To counteract this they adopted the 'blind audition' approach. This is when the identity of musician is hidden as they audition behind a curtain. They were even asked to take off their shoes so that the interviewers didn't hear the click of heels.

Blind auditions had a significant impact on the face of symphony orchestras. About 10 per cent of orchestra members were female in 1970, compared to approximately 35 per cent in the mid-1990s. Rouse and Goldin attribute approximately 30 per cent of this gain to the advent of blind auditions.

The following are areas to consider during recruitment:

- Understand the impact of the different routes to market on your talent pipeline.
- Be clear on your asks of your external headhunters and search firms and hold them accountable.
- Ensure the whole interview process and in particular the questions asked are inclusive.

Performance management

We haven't yet come across a performance management process that is entirely bias free and fully effective. However, there is a lot that you can do to counter-balance human influence and subjectivity within the performance management process.

When considering this the first step is to make sure that individuals are clear about what is expected of them in their role. This would include their key objectives, how they will be assessed against them and any areas for development.

The SMART[10] model is a helpful way to develop effective objectives and is used by many organisations. The S usually stands for 'specific' and M stands for 'measurable'. Then depending on who is using it the other three letters can vary.

> - Specific – target a specific area for improvement.
> - Measurable – quantify or at least suggest an indicator of progress.

(Continued)

- Assignable – specify who will do it.
- Realistic – state what results can realistically be achieved, given available resources.
- Time related – specify when the result(s) can be achieved.

Historically, many organisations underpin their process by having a mid-year and year-end review. More recently, this approach is being revisited to reflect the research available on what 'millenials' expect from their employers.[11] Put simply, in addition to flexibility and the ability to work collaboratively, they want much more regular feedback on their performance; they prefer on-the-spot feedback rather than waiting for the usual organisational process. Part of this process should include 360-degree feedback, which can be gathered anonymously if required.

When using 360-degree feedback, you always have to be mindful of the situation that is being commented on. Some people have a limited view of others and their feedback can be impacted by this. Or they might put more or less value on someone's style and experience. To bring this to life, think about the following example.

Jane is relatively quiet during a meeting. Someone observing this could start to add their own meaning – surely she should be saying more as she is a manager. They might make the assumption that she has nothing valuable to say or she is just not assertive enough, which could lead them to conclude that she can't lead a team. On the other hand, with a different frame of reference, the manager could decide that Jane is insightful, is a good listener, has a good understanding of the issues and is an important member of the team.

The observable data is the same; it's purely being assessed with a different frame of reference. The way that someone speaks at meetings can affect the way that their confidence and competence are judged by others, as well as who gets heard and who gets the credit.

Style is something that research shows us can heavily influence the way someone conducts themselves in a performance review and how the assessor draws their conclusions. For example, men and women often show their ambition differently. A manager may conclude that a woman isn't ambitious because she is not displaying the behaviours that they would expect of an ambitious person. The female's behaviour can be more 'low key' and this is translated as the woman having low confidence which equals lower ambition, ability, leadership potential and promotion readiness.

This is often not the case – women express their ambition differently. Women are also prone to using different language to men in their performance reviews. Research conducted in 2011[12] showed that managers tended to think of their male team members' success as being attributable to skill and their failure due to bad luck, whereas for women they tended to attribute their success to luck or the task being easy. The bottom line is that many women are less comfortable than their male counterparts with self-promotion and overtly publicising their achievements. They can be disarmingly honest about their weaknesses and their perceived failures rather than their successes and achievements.

This can also apply to ethnic minority communities. In Sylvia Ann Hewlett's US research, 'Leadership in your midst: Tapping the hidden strengths of minority executives',[13] she highlighted how BAME professionals often hold leadership roles outside of work, serving as pillars of their communities. However, they chose to keep this side of their life invisible from their managers, resulting in employers losing out on a great source of untapped potential.

The following are areas to consider in performance management:

- Ensure everyone has robust, clear and transparent objectives they can be measured against objectively.
- Focus on outcome over style during the discussions and decision-making process.
- Make sure that your current performance management process is future proofed for what most engages and motivates your workforce.

Progression and promotion

In 2012, McKinsey conducted some interesting research into 17 professional services firms.[14] They found that whilst hiring and retention were areas that should be tracked, the key issue in a company for women was career velocity

– for example, the time it took for a woman to be promoted versus the time it took their male counterparts. In law firms, the men were ten times more likely to move from graduate to partner than their female counterparts. In the accountancy firms they were three times more likely.

There will be a number of reasons for this, as with many of the issues we are discussing, but if you couple this with the same research finding that at every level more men than women are leaving, you can see a pattern of committed, loyal, women becoming stuck at one level whilst their male counterparts move up the hierarchy faster. This is something that should be reviewed closely. If you have the data, a good exercise would be to look at how many years it takes on average for each of your people to get promoted to the next level.

Depending on how promotion decisions are made, you should think about the impact of bias, unconscious or otherwise, in the process:

- Is your promotion criteria free from bias?
- How do you define high potential?
- Have all the candidates been given the same feedback? If not, why?
- Have all the candidates had the same level of sponsorship? If not, what as been the impact of that?

We have often heard it said that at times it is easier to move employer to get the next promotion than stay at the same organisation, which just shouldn't be the case.

In one organisation Charlotte was keen to understand what was happening in the promotion decision meetings. The nominations for promotions were generally split 30 per cent female and 70 per cent male; however, the final promotion data showed that 95 per cent of all employees proposed for promotion that specific year were going to be men. She gained agreement from the regional CEO for her to sit in all promotion discussions and even got the opportunity to video one of the them (with the agreement that the video would be erased before leaving the room). Once the decisions had taken place Charlotte asked a number of questions of the attendees about any bias they may have had that would have affected their decisions. They all claimed, of course, that they were making decisions purely linked to the information that was given to them. With this, Charlotte played various elements of the video back to them which showed examples of where bias had played a part in their discussions and, therefore, their decision making. There was one particular example where a senior leader stated that the woman would be 'grateful for the promotion' and 'the man would leave if he didn't see the commitment from us'. A number of those in the meeting were surprised that they had let discussions such as these slip through without challenge and committed to review the decisions made before leaving the room. It was powerful for them to see how they interacted within the meeting, what they said to each other and what influenced their decisions. The review resulted in 25 per cent of those gaining promotion that year being women, a significant increase from the original number of 5 per cent.

Fleur remembers an interesting exercise that a business unit completed at one of their Continental European offices. They asked a third party to sit in and observe the promotion panels. Some of the feedback was fairly predictable, for example, the dangers of how individuals were presented by their sponsors. The challenge being that some sponsors were natural orators, enabling their candidates to be 'sold' more effectively than their peers. The language used throughout the panel was referenced – apparently throughout the course of the discussion, the women were often described as 'girls' whilst the men were described as 'men'. The observers' question to the panel was 'who promotes a girl to MD?'

The following are areas to consider in progression and promotion:

- Review your promotions process to ensure there are no barriers and bias present.
- Ensure that everyone who is part of the process has some form of diversity, inclusion and bias training and awareness in advance.
- Analysis the career velocity of individuals as they progress.

Training and development

We focus on leadership development programmes and inclusive leadership training in the chapter on inclusive leadership development (see Chapter 13); however, on the general topic of training, there are three areas you should consider from a D&I perspective:

- the logistics of training events
- the content of the training
- how you select the people to attend.

LOGISTICS OF TRAINING EVENTS

The logistics of training interventions can be a barrier for some people. Whether its local or global training, you should consider the community you are targeting and whether they can all access the programme(s). For example:

- Is the programme residential which could rule out people with caring responsibilities or some flexible workers?
- Does the timing clash with an important religious holiday such as Eid?
- Does it entail travel on a Friday which might be impractical for a Jewish person who needs to be home before sundown or someone from the Middle East, whose weekend is in fact Friday and Saturday?
- Is the venue and supporting materials for the programme fully accessible for people with any form of disability? Are the supporting materials available in advance?

CONTENT OF TRAINING EVENTS

The next consideration is more about how the content of the training will be delivered and how equalities, diversity and inclusion have been thought through. It is always helpful to walk through the content of a training programme and consider the following:

- Are your organisation's key messages on D&I embedded throughout the training content?
- Are case study content and characters diverse?
- Do the course exercises such as team-building take into account any form of disability, for example dyslexia?
- Are individual style preferences such as introvert or extrovert taken into account when developing the content?

Charlotte remembers working in an organisation where they were keen to include an extreme assault course within their training events as a form of team-building exercise. She kept reminding them that any exercises needed to be inclusive and flexible enough to be adapted for people with different levels of abilities. She continued to outline that team building was about the whole team and not purely for those who were fit and able enough to complete the course. This advice did seem to be ignored until one day the organisers of the event had to significantly change the whole course when a colleague with a prosthetic limb attended the event and was unable to climb a rope ladder! This could have been avoided.

SELECTING THE PEOPLE TO ATTEND

The other factor to consider is who will attend the events. This is highly important when we factor in the importance of training and development for future career progression.

- What is the process to collect nominations – is everyone involved who should be?
- What is the selection criteria – is it consistent and bias free?
- Do you routinely sense check the nominations to ensure they are diverse and reflect the community they are aimed at?

Fleur can remember the launch of her organisation's first global talent programme, and one of the geographies only submitted men to attend the event. The learning and development team reviewing the long list spotted the issue and went back to the country asking them to review their nominations, who in turn resubmitted a more diverse list. This was treated as business as usual – no intervention was needed from the D&I team which is ultimately what you are trying to achieve.

It is important to work closely with the learning and development team to ensure all of the above are embedded into their thinking.

Virtual training

Delivering training virtually is commonly used when people are spread across different offices. It is a form of delivery to consider, but it is not always ideal. It can be a challenge to keep everyone engaged and contributing to the training and too often the individual on mute, if using conference call facilities, is distracted by emails, office conversations or the interesting video on YouTube. Developments in technology and how we communicate have advanced significantly with webinars, Skype and videoconferencing improving the interaction you can have with others when you are not physically with them. However, this can impact the level of engagement you may get in some forms of training and development. It can be effective for things like compliance training, but more difficult to get right for developmental training (but not impossible).

When Fleur first started thinking about rolling out a female-specific leadership programme for her high-potential managers, she piloted a modular programme virtually with a group of women who were spread across geographies. Feedback told her that whilst the women appreciated being targeted for development, they struggled to open up at a personal level with other women that they didn't know and couldn't see.

If you are using virtual training within your organisation, be clear on the type of training you are using it for and gain feedback from attendees as to how inclusive it has been – did they feel engaged and were they able to contribute? Also, make it as interactive as possible to keep people from being distracted.

- Consider the length of the session to maximise the level of concentration throughout.
- Ensure that everyone has a voice, by both inviting verbal and written input and questions.
- Share documents as pre-reads so that people have time to absorb and reflect.

Many organisations conclude training and development events with feedback forms to gain an immediate reaction to the event – some call these 'happy sheets'. As you embed D&I throughout, it is important to reflect on how this is being delivered to employees – do they feel that the training venue was fully accessible? Did they feel they were able to contribute to the discussions throughout the events? Consider how you can factor some of those questions and comments into any feedback opportunities that are available.

The following are areas to consider in training and development:

- Revisit your approach to the design and delivery of your training through an inclusive leadership lens.
- Consider the appropriate use of virtual training.
- Ensure D&I is factored into the evaluation of the training and development.

Five key takeaways from this chapter

- Ensure any third-party providers used to deliver your employee processes are aware of your stance on D&I and are actively supporting and enabling delivery.

- Take a step back – consider how D&I factors into each element of the employee life.

- Start where the energy is within the employee life cycle – for example, if you are in the middle of the performance management cycle identify how you can integrate D&I in to it.

- Ensure D&I messages are factored into all employee communications and all branding is diverse.

- Celebrate and share all good practice across the whole HR community and other important contacts and stakeholders.

Talent management – reward to exit

High performing companies should be striving to create a great place for great people to do great work.

MARILYN CARLSON NELSON, CO-CEO CARLSON HOLDINGS

In this chapter we continue our review of the employee life cycle (Figure 11.1) through a D&I lens, and focus on the elements from reward to finally exiting the company.

Reward – pay and benefits

For many organisations 'reward' is made up of a number of facets. This can well be a combination of basic pay, performance bonuses and benefits. Within all of these elements D&I should be considered. This will mean different things

Figure 11.1 Employee life cycle

to different organisations depending on your policies, practices and processes. The challenge when thinking about this globally is that usually the only demographic data that can be consistently collected is on gender and, at times, age. Therefore different countries will need to develop the breadth of their approach in relation to the data available.

PAY

All organisations will have their own pay structures. Some are bound by legislation and/or negotiated with bodies such as works councils and most are driven internally by the role an individual does and their job grade or rank.

In an ideal world all organisations would agree to the philosophy that men and women doing equal work will get equal pay, and in some countries it is illegal not to pay a woman the same as a man if they are doing the same job. However, in the 2015 Global Gender Gap Report from the World Economic Forum,[1] they projected that it's going to take until 2133 for the gender gap to close. The gender pay gap is the difference in an organisation between men's and women's average salaries.

The gender pay gap can be impacted by a number of factors: for example, the choices that women make in their careers, with a concentration of women in lower-paid occupations; women being less likely to progress to senior roles and a lack of flexibility or access to affordable childcare. The good news is that the gap is narrowing, but it is slow. In the European Commission's 2014 report they found that the gender pay gap had stagnated at 16.4 per cent across Europe.[2]

In what many have called a bold move, the UK government announced in 2015 that by spring 2018, companies with more than 250 workers have to publish their gender pay gaps. At the time of this decision, the gender pay gap in the United Kingdom was 19.2 per cent[3] and woman on average earned around 80p for every £1 earned by a man.

We are yet to find a global organisation that regularly completes a gender pay review consistently in every country that they operate in. It tends to be a topic that organisations turn their attention to when they are some way in to their D&I journey. This is due partly to the complexity of conducting a proper review and partly to the concern of what they might uncover and the obligation to address the situation.

Here are some of the suggested reasons we have seen for pay gaps:

- Women's work is undervalued – jobs requiring similar skills, qualifications or experience tend to be poorly paid and undervalued when they are dominated by women rather than men.
- Performance evaluation which drives pay levels and career progression may also be biased in favour of men – for example, more value can be attached to responsibility for a specific project than to responsibility for good people management.
- Segregation in the market – women and men being predominant in different sectors, some being lower paid than others and women being under-represented in managerial and senior manager positions.
- Traditions and stereotypes – for example, fewer women studying maths, science and technology at university.
- Balancing work and private life – for example, being on a flexible working arrangement, taking maternity/paternity/parental leave.
- Direct discrimination – where an employee or prospective employee is less favourably treated because of their race, sex, marital status (including civil partnerships), religion, sexual orientation, gender reassignment, age, disability, pregnancy or maternity.
- Unconscious bias impacting the evaluation of an individual's performance and the setting of performance ratings.

In addition to the above, there is some interesting research from Linda Babcock and her colleagues.[4] She is a Professor of Economics at Carnegie Mellon and she showed that men's and women's approaches are often different when it comes to opening negotiations. Her research highlighted that women tend to initiate negotiations four times less often than men and ask for about 30 per cent less when they do negotiate.

When it comes to opening negotiations, there are also higher social risks for women than men. Babcock looked at pay rises, resources and promotions and found that men and women got very different responses when they initiated negotiations, based on the perception that women who asked for more were 'less nice'. Babcock went on to do more research with Hannah Riley Bowles and they found that, while both men and women were penalised for negotiating, the negative effect for women was more than twice as large as that for men. This may go some way to explain women's reluctance to negotiate for better pay, and their success rates.

The following gives some top tips that should be considered as part of your checklist when planning a gender pay review:

- Make sure you understand the equalities legislation in relation to terms and conditions of employment in each country.
- Make sure that your pay system is transparent – that everyone under-stands how each element of their pay contributes to their total earnings.
- Try and have one pay system for all your employees.
- Base your pay structure on an objective evaluation of job demands and re-evaluate regularly.
- Limit local managerial total discretion over all elements of the pay package.
- Check salaries on entry to the organisation and on entry to grades. If men are starting on higher salaries than women, then you may be importing pay discrimination.
- Check rates of progression within and through the grades.
- Make sure that you have a range of flexible working options that are accessible to all.
- In countries where there is paternity or shared parental leave, encour-age colleagues to use it.
- Carry out regular checks to ensure that the various elements of your pay package still reward what they are intended to reward.

On this topic to date we have focused on base pay; some organisations also have a performance bonus culture as part of their remuneration offering. At worst this can make the pay landscape less equitable so many of the above principles apply to your bonus process in addition to pay review.

BENEFITS

In addition to core benefits such as annual leave, sickness absence and pension contributions, there are many different options that an organisation can choose to include in their benefits packages such as car allowance, gym membership and critical health cover. We will not go into a long list of benefits in great detail; this is to give you a sense of what should be on your radar from a D&I perspective.

Benefits are rarely consistent across a global organisation because in many cases the starting point is what local legislation states. Take for example the amount of maternity or paternity leave that is available (if in fact you offer paternity leave at all). In the United States you are not necessarily guaranteed maternity pay. In the United Kingdom, with the appropriate length of service you can take up to 52 weeks' maternity leave and some European countries enable you to take up to three years. In some cases, having the right to return to your previous role is part of the legislation.

Of course many organisations will enhance the legal amount for maternity pay and there are several global organisations that are particularly generous because they understand the business case. Vodafone offers all new mothers sixteen weeks' paid maternity leave across the globe and full pay for women working a reduced 30-hour week for the first six months when they return from maternity leave. They took this move after commissioning a survey which showed the cost of doing this far outweighed the cost of losing talented and experienced staff. This shows a clear example of where a company has created their own business case as to why progressing issues such as this will have a positive impact on the business.

That said, even enhanced maternity pay doesn't necessarily work from a retention point of view. Fleur met a lady who enjoyed ten months' maternity leave on full pay at a consultancy, but she always knew that she wouldn't go back after her maternity leave because she did not want to do the travel that her job involved. When it was time to return, she handed in her notice and took a job elsewhere.

Enhanced paternity leave and pay (where applicable) are far less common. This does in itself compound the issue that women are still expected to take the major share of childcare, at least in the early years. In 2015 the UK Government implemented new legislation to enable partners to share their parental leave in the first year of the child's life. This move gives parents choice over how they decide to share the responsibility of caring for their child, as well as balancing their requirements and interests at work.

There has been a mixed response to this legislation. Some organisations have given the absolute minimum benefit required by law and others have used this as an opportunity to mirror the generous benefits they already offer women going on maternity leave. At the time of writing this book, the initial review of the take-up of shared parental leave by men was low, approximately two per cent of those who were eligible. Other countries ahead of the United Kingdom have said it could take up to ten more years to see a shift. Although the law may have changed, there is still some way to go to change organisational and societal cultures to make it second nature that the other parent would be able to take time out from their career to spend more time with their child. Of course, when both parents share the care of their children, this will result in a major mindset shift that will work in favour of women in the workplace.

When reviewing your benefits to make sure that there is no inequity across your employees, also think about how they apply to partners, including same-sex partners. This is particularly important when you look at how you move employees to different countries during the course of their career. Areas to consider include:

- How you support the application for visas/immigration
- What employment support is available, for example, usually in the form of a budget that can be used for integration and job hunting for the partner
- Cost of living benefit
- Flights
- Shipping, for example, furniture and other personal possessions
- Language/cultural awareness training
- Home leave/visiting your country of origin
- Tax preparation assistance

It's also worth checking that an employee can do their own research in to what is available for them and their partner without actually having to share information they may not want to, such as 'outing' themselves as LGBT.

Health insurance is another benefit that can unearth some challenges, for example, in relation to gender reassignment. Most of the insurers we have come across will not offer health insurance that covers gender reassignment. The usual reason they give is that they don't cover 'cosmetic surgery'. A solution one global technology company came up with was to take out a global policy through the United States who do cover this: however, more work needs to be done to establish consistency.

You will have noticed that we have not talked about flexibility/flexible working here because we do not believe that flexibility should be classed as a 'benefit'. We will cover that in more detail in the chapter on new ways of working (see Chapter 14).

The following are areas to consider in reward, pay and benefits:

- Work through the above checklist to scope out conducting an equal pay review.
- Consider the diversity of your employee base – ensure your benefits are equitable, applicable and accessible to all.
- Ensure details of benefits are easily accessible for all staff without needing to ask.

Leaving organisations

Many organisations expect a certain level of turnover and it arguably gives you the opportunity to improve the diversity of your workforce. In our experience, there are many missed opportunities when it comes to how you treat the person leaving the organisation. For example, many don't have a face-to-face exit interview and we've heard of examples of employees being ignored as soon as they hand over their resignation letter.

Some of the poorer practices are driven by the myths and assumptions that managers believe as to why people leave. Take, for example, the myth/assumption that all female leavers do so to start a family. Of course, that will be the reason for some, but for most, it's a combination of reasons. They may have just come back from maternity leave, noticed they have been overlooked for promotion, yet a male peer has progressed and decide they don't trust the firm to deliver a long-term career to them.

If your organisation conducts any form of exit information gathering, it is important to look carefully at your data. Consider the types of questions you may want to ask within this process: for example, 'I felt that I was able to progress my career in the company' and identify whether you are able to analyse the data by different demographic groups. This is a great time to dispel some myths as well as gain valuable insights into what your 'points of pressure' may be. As mentioned earlier in this chapter, when McKinsey conducted their research into the 17 professional services companies, they found that at every level, more men than women left.

Some other examples of good practice we have seen in relation to positive and strategic management of leavers are: (i) alumni networks, (ii) pre-retirement programmes and (iii) training of senior leavers to take up non-executive director positions.

ALUMNI NETWORKS

Some companies think about their leavers very innovatively and develop alumni networks or look for other ways to stay connected. The theory behind creating such a network has a number of possibilities. The individual might decide to rejoin the organisation at some future point in their career – often known as 'boomerangs'. They may now be working for a client or a potential client, they may send their friends your way and, if nothing else, you want them to be good ambassadors in the market for you. The whole boomerang approach is similar to the concepts of on-ramping and internships which have been covered under the recruitment section.

One organisation that has created a global alumni network is Barclays plc. Their network is supported by a team that regularly publishes updates to the network on what is happening within the company as well as profiling what ex-colleagues have gone on to achieve since leaving the company. They also hold a number of events each year where alumni members are invited to talk about their life after Barclays. Although some may be concerned that this may encourage current employees to leave the company and explore other opportunities, it does suggest a pride that Barclays still has for previous employees and an interest in what they have achieved since leaving.

PRE-RETIREMENT PROGRAMMES

Reaching this stage in your career is both exciting and daunting. For many who have worked for the majority of their adult life, considering a time when they suddenly don't have an employer pulling on their time can be a huge cultural shift. Some organisations have recognised this and responded by creating programmes of support to aid the transition.

Some programmes may be a way of giving the employee access to financial advice to consider what they might do with their pension and to continue to be self-sufficient in retirement. For others these can be as advanced as:

- introducing the concept of phased retirement where the employee could consider slowly reducing their hours over a set number of months or years so that they can adjust to the additional personal time they will have
- making personal coaching sessions available for employees to explore what they would like to do in the future, such as finding new hobbies or gaining a non-executive position
- connecting the employees to others who are due to retire over the coming years, enabling them to build a network of contacts and colleagues they can discuss this life transition with.

NON-EXECUTIVE DIRECTOR (NED)

In many countries across the world, we have seen government pressure for organisations to get more women on their boards. Some have set quotas, for example, France, Spain and Norway. Others have raised the profile of this topic, for example, the United Kingdom with the support of organisations such as 30% club[5] and Women on Boards.[6] As individuals start to think about their retirement, forward-thinking organisations are including some information about NED roles in their pre-retirement planning workshops or information packs. A typical workshop would include an overview of board governance, the role of the NED, how you shape your CV for such positions and where to look for them.

Depending on where someone is located, there are various routes to explore – workshops run by third parties (e.g. the FT) or companies (such as Deloittes), headhunters and forums.

Taking a NED role is a good way of phasing into retirement as the roles are usually on a part-time basis, are sometimes paid and have significant authority, which is a consideration for those leaving senior positions in their organisation. This also enables the individual to draw from their skills and knowledge acquired throughout their career.

The following are areas to consider in leaving organisations:

- How can you gather the most insightful information from those leaving the organisation as to why they are leaving? Think creatively as exit interviews may not always be practical.

- Is the exit data giving you some valuable insights? Are certain types of people leaving the company, for example, from a certain age group?

- How can you continue to engage and stay connected to those leaving the organisation? This can have a positive impact on your brand as well as potentially create a pool of people who may decide to come back to work for the organisation in the future.

As you will see from the last two chapters, there are many different touch points in an employee life cycle. Our aim was to signpost a number of 'hot spots' and share some food for thought rather than attempt to focus on any one particular place in great detail.

Five key takeaways from this chapter

- Continuously review and improve your business practices and people processes – continuous improvements will ensure D&I is robustly embedded.

- Capture data and insights across the employee life cycle to continually identify 'points of pressure' and areas of focus.

- Take advantage of external debates and agendas to drive internal progress – for example, the recent pay transparency focus in the United Kingdom, United States and Australia.
- Ensure line managers and leaders are clear on their responsibilities when considering D&I throughout the employee life cycle.
- Continually develop and improve your knowledge – find out what other organisations are doing and what you can learn from their insights.

Networks

Alone we can do so little; together we can do so much.
HELEN KELLER, AUTHOR AND POLITICAL ACTIVIST

It would be impossible to write an essential guide on creating and delivering an impactful D&I strategy without including employee networks. For close to two decades they have been a key part of many organisations' activities, and for most of those organisations they have been positioned as a critical part of the D&I agenda. Take JP Morgan Chase & Co for example, who at one time boasted over two hundred employee network chapters globally, or Accenture with thousands of employee resource groups in 120 offices around the world. Employee networks can be big business.

This chapter works through many of the key areas that should be considered when deciding, regardless of the size of your organisation, if and how to progress down this path, both from a global and local perspective. We focus on what networks are, how to get them up and running and how to measure the impact and return on investment.

Our thoughts and suggestions in this chapter are relevant for those who have created a number of networks in the past and would like to revisit and reflect on how they are progressing. They are also aimed at both an organisation that might want to start a network and a group of employees that want to set something up at a grass-roots level for the first time.

What are networks and why build them?

The *Oxford English Dictionary* defines a network as 'a group or system of interconnected people or things'. On a less formal basis, most of us network daily to do our jobs effectively. What we are talking about here is a more formal approach to gathering people into a community – usually in person, but it can of course be virtually.

Size can vary greatly and can be anything from a handful of people meeting informally to discuss a particular topic, for example, Christianity in the workplace, to a global LGBT network that has the same name wherever you are in the world and the same core principles.

What's in a name?

Throughout this chapter we reference 'employee networks' and appreciate that this may not fully define, in some people's view, what their network actually is, or what they actually want it to be. In the early days of D&I they were called just that, 'employee networks'. However, over time the terminology has changed to – affinity groups, employee resource groups (ERGs) or business resource groups (BRGs).

Although we can, too often, get tied up in the terminology and can be swayed by the trends of where the more recent thinking may be moving, you will be doing your community a disservice if they are not defined properly.

Arguably, employee networks, affinity groups, ERGs and BRGs are all one and the same. However, we thought it would be helpful to define each in a little more detail to help crystallise where you and your organisation are with your thinking:

- **Employee network/Affinity group:** These are groups of employees who join together in their workplace based on shared characteristics or life experiences. They are generally there to (i) provide support, (ii) enhance career development and (iii) increase networking across the organisation.
- **Employee resource group:** These are much the same as employee networks. In addition to the above, they move more towards becoming think-tank type groups that directly impact the organisation and are seen as a resource that can be tapped into in order to influence the 'employee' experience. For example, many organisations encourage their ERG members to become involved in their graduate recruitment activities and profile what it is like to work there.
- **Business resource group:** These are similar to ERGs. In addition, they are a resource for the business to tap into to gain perspectives and

influence what they do for the workforce, clients and consumers. Their different insights, points of view and perspectives can be translated into solutions to meet organisational objectives across channels, brands and business units.

- **Inclusion network:** For organisations that have clearly stated that inclusion is their main priority and don't want a network that is purely focused on one strand/topic. This is a network open and available to all employees, ensuring that different elements of diversity are profiled throughout the calendar of activity. Some would argue that this removes the 'affinity' link to the networks where you are not necessarily networking and connecting with others like you across the organisation and dilutes the link back to individual support and raising the visibility of role models. However, there is some merit in considering this as a viable option especially for organisations who may not have a huge employee base in any one area and numerous networks would not be an option. The additional benefits to creating one 'inclusive' network is that all employees, regardless of their personal characteristics, gain wider knowledge of different aspects around the D&I agenda. They all, collectively, have the opportunity to create the agenda and purpose of the network and have regular opportunities to network and connect with people who are different to them.

As we write, the overall trend is moving more towards creating business resource groups. This is evident in organisations who have had some form of employee networks in place for some time. Rather than following the trend, be clear on what the purpose is of the groups you may be creating. If you are starting out, it may be that employee engagement is the critical driver; for others, it may be the input into the business priorities that is most needed. As with the whole D&I strategy, this is a journey; focus on what is right for your organisation now and this can be adapted over time.

Creating a network and getting it off the ground

One key objective of any employee network is that it is partly about bringing people together to support the overall aim of creating more diverse and inclusive organisations. This can only be done when people feel engaged and feel part of creating and delivering the solution. Don't do this in isolation; include others throughout and make sure that you don't fall into the trap of creating a great launch event and then having little, or no, substance or direction behind it. You will gain immediate publicity and attention, but this could then easily backfire.

Take time to consider:

- **Where the energy from your employees is:** What is it they would like to be part of? Are there already groups of people who get together without the structure of a formal network?

- **What community will the network be targeting:** For example, over the years there has been a lot of discussion about what the most appropriate network is for the transgender community. Many LGB networks include the 'T'. We have heard the argument for and against. In some cases women who have transitioned say this is not about their sexual orientation, but about their identity, so if they want to join a network it will be the woman's network. LGBT networks argue that the transgender community is so small, they could get lost in a women's network and lose their voice.

- **Cultural relevance:** Some employee networks are more culturally or country relevant than others. For example, in the United States, Veteran employee networks are popular; however, you see them less in other geographies.

- **How inclusive do you want the networks to be:** Arguably all networks should be open to all employees who have an interest in that area. On this point it is worth remembering that many in your workplace will have an interest in a number of your networks – a BAME working mother might want to be part of the parents' network, the women's network and the South Asian network.

When you have considered the above and established your position, we would suggest that you do three things:

1. Articulate and clarify the business drivers and the key measures of success.
2. Get sponsorship and senior buy-in.
3. Create robust governance so that you establish ownership and direction.

ARTICULATING AND CLARIFYING THE BUSINESS DRIVERS

Similar to our earlier chapter about creating the overarching business case and strategy for D&I, consider the business drivers for taking the valuable time and resource to create your employee networks. Consider how the employee networks would impact:

- **Retention:** Would the network help employees make a longer-term commitment to the organisation?
- **Engagement:** What are the results of your most recent engagement survey telling you?
- **Culture:** Would the networks help create a more inclusive environment where employees feel more comfortable and willing to share ideas and thoughts, which could ultimately improve the business?
- **Clients/customer brand:** Would it help clients to better relate to the organisation? Could this be a driver for them to want to engage and work with the organisation further?
- **Shaping strategy:** Would the network represent the voice of employees to help shape the future talent and business strategies and ensure the organisation is doing what is right for both the employees and the business?
- **External recognition:** Would the networks enable the organisation to gain positive publicity which may increase the attractiveness of the brand to potential employees and new clients?

As you consider the above questions, it is important to ensure that the business drivers identified are also complementary to the overarching D&I strategy. It is important to create a clear line of sight between the vision for the overarching strategy and how the networks will support the delivery.

SENIOR LEADER BUY-IN

As highlighted earlier on developing the wider D&I strategy, having the senior level buy-in of people who are comfortable and able to talk about the role of the networks can really help to strengthen and galvanise their importance.

Identifying appropriate senior leader sponsorship is an effective way to gain the initial momentum for the networks (and of course, often the budget!). Sometimes senior leaders will offer to play an active part from the outset which can be incredibly helpful from a number of aspects. They can inform the thinking around the governance structure, act as your ambassador across the leadership team, speak at events both internally and externally and get the network aspirations on the business agenda when needed.

Senior leaders involved in the networks should be seen as role models and be willing to be open, transparent and 'be themselves'. By doing this they will naturally encourage others in the business to do the same. This will create a ripple effect across the organisation. Leading by example is key and the importance can be overlooked. Fleur has always favoured having senior leaders as network sponsors and highly recommends its effectiveness. As well as benefitting from the high profile and influence of a senior leader, it's a great developmental opportunity for the network heads to gain exposure to leadership and have the opportunity to receive some informal mentoring.

Charlotte has heard many examples throughout her career where a CEO has suggested a senior leader as the 'executive sponsor' for a specific network because 'they need the development!'

CREATING ROBUST GOVERNANCE TO ESTABLISH OWNERSHIP AND DIRECTION

Creating the right structure and governance from the outset will help to save time and energy further down the line. However, this doesn't mean to say that the structures you create from the start have to be set in stone. It's important to be able to adapt as the network grows in popularity as well as its impact. For example, it may expand across multi sites or go global.

One of the important aspects to consider is 'who is responsible for the network?' Is it something the organisation would like to drive, have control over and dictate what the network is there to do? Or is the best way forward one where the network is employee led, where they propose the focus and priorities of the network and present a business case to the organisation for any resource needs or financial support? Or, should you go with a combination of the two?

Organisations vary in their approach and there are pros and cons for all of the above; some examples can be found below. What is important is to select the right route for your organisation, which includes a framework and approach that could be replicable for other employee networks and other locations both nationally and internationally.

Employee networks led by the organisation

Pros

- Clear line of sight between the vision of the D&I strategy and the activities of the network
- Direction and priorities set by the organisation
- Consistency of brand and governance

Cons

- Creating and leading the networks can be hugely time and resource intensive
- Potentially limited engagement of employees as they perceive they do not 'own' the network
- Disconnect between the objectives of the network and the needs of the targeted community

Employee-led networks

Pros

- Enhanced employee engagement as they see it as their network
- Enables the organisation to identify future talent from those who step up and take a leadership role and responsibility
- Opportunity to identify different and important issues in the workplace that may be shared with 'colleagues' rather than 'the organisation'

Cons

- May find people delivering the activities of the network 'off the side of their desk' which could result in the day job taking priority and the network actions floundering

- Potentially reduced influence by the organisation on the direction of the network
- Limited content for members or benefit for the organisation

A hybrid version of the above would have a combination of both employer and employee input and can be successful as there is a requirement from

Figure 12.1 Example of network structure, roles and responsibilities

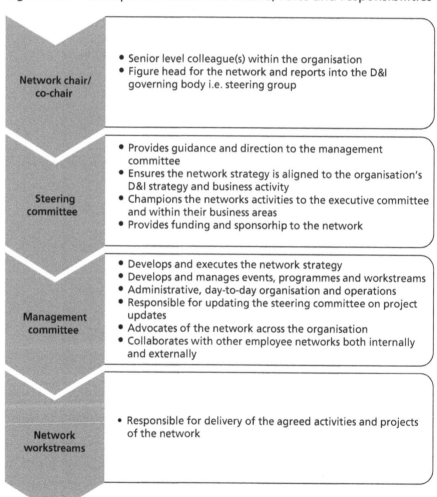

Network chair/ co-chair
- Senior level colleague(s) within the organisation
- Figure head for the network and reports into the D&I governing body i.e. steering group

Steering committee
- Provides guidance and direction to the management committee
- Ensures the network strategy is aligned to the organisation's D&I strategy and business activity
- Champions the networks activities to the executive committee and within their business areas
- Provides funding and sponsorhip to the network

Management committee
- Develops and executes the network strategy
- Develops and manages events, programmes and workstreams
- Administrative, day-to-day organisation and operations
- Responsible for updating the steering committee on project updates
- Advocates of the network across the organisation
- Collaborates with other employee networks both internally and externally

Network workstreams
- Responsible for delivery of the agreed activities and projects of the network

employees who are keen to contribute to the aims of the network and will attend events. At the same time the employer's requirement is to assign budget and time to employees to participate in the network's activity and to hold them accountable for delivery of their objectives.

The other consideration is how the network's internal infrastructure is created and managed. For some smaller networks this level of detail may not be required as long as everyone is aware of the roles and responsibilities each of them have. For others, it may be important to consider the structure and governance from the outset.

Figure 12.1 shows the governance structure and the roles and responsibilities of an employee network that was created within a global organisation headquartered in the United Kingdom. The principles were then replicated for all other networks globally.

Collaboration between networks

The key purpose of employee networks is to help employees feel included in a community and feel that they can contribute to the organisation. Networks should not feel like exclusive 'members only clubs'.

One of the consistent criticisms Charlotte has experienced in her career when talking about employee networks is that they can, too quickly, become exclusive. They can create their own 'in and out' groups and end up discriminating in their own way against other networks or those not in their group. This can become a challenge when your focus is on creating a diverse *and* inclusive organisation.

Some organisations have really focused on tackling these perceptions within the networks and have done some of the following:

- Clearly stated that all networks are open to all employees who have an interest in that area. For example, one organisation clearly stated that the network for people with disabilities was ideal for line managers to get involved as they may currently, or will in the future, have someone in their team that has a disability.

- Changed the name and the focus of the network. For example, one large financial services company changed the name of their women's network to 'Balance' and promoted the fact that the network was about achieving gender balance for both men and women.

- Ensured the chairs of each of the networks (regionally and globally) regularly met with each other to share their plans for the future and plan how they can collaborate on events and projects.

- Encouraged the networks to collaborate with other networks in other organisations across their industry. For example, in the United Kingdom the 'Interbank' network focuses on bringing networks from banks across the City of London together to share examples of their progress as well as ideas and opportunities to work together.

Ideally, the employee networks should not be seen as stand-alone and you will often find people signing up as members of several networks.

Taking your local network regional and/or global?

As the development and delivery of the employee networks progress there may well be a desire to take them out of the head office and either into the regions or globally.

As with all aspects of the D&I strategy and delivery, local considerations should always be taken into account and respected. The way that networks are developed, run and operate will be different in different parts of the world.

Some organisations will want to have one network, with local representatives that report up to a central leadership team. Depending on the size, this can become quite cumbersome and very time consuming. A different approach would be to have one regional/global identity, some overarching objectives and operating principles, for example, having co-heads locally, but then let the local chapter run their network relatively independently with collaboration rather than accountability. This was the approach that EY decided to take when they renamed their LGBT network globally.

Building LGBT networks globally

EY had historically had LGBT networks that had grown organically in different locations across the world, including the United Kingdom, Ireland, America, Australia, Japan, Germany, South Africa, Hong Kong, Taiwan and Singapore. All of these networks operated organically and many had different names, so different branding.

It was agreed that they wanted to develop a more consistent brand globally, so the first challenge was to agree on the one name. This was done through a global campaign that invited network members and interested parties to submit suggestions. A total of 58 were received and each network was asked to select their top five names. These were reviewed by a global panel and the name 'Unity' was chosen. It was also decided to purposefully add the 'A' to the LGBT moniker to make it explicit that allies are a key and integral part of the networks.

Having a single global network is not practical for the size of EY and, therefore, Unity's network of networks operate autonomously at a local level but are able to share the same brand and ethos. All of the networks now communicate more effectively using tools such as Yammer to share best practice and collaborate. Globally, if there is a requirement for all network heads to talk, this is also possible.

This change re-energised the existing networks and now, when a new chapter is set up, there is an immediately available support group that can offer advice and guidance.

As you develop or review the way your employee networks operate, what learning can you take from the EY example?

- How could you engage the majority in the plans for the future and feel that they have a voice?
- How can you use technology to support the connectivity of the networks across offices, countries and different jurisdictions?

- How do you take the considerations of different localities and create a high-level consensus as to the overarching purpose and focus of the network?

We like this approach because although there may be an overarching structure and purpose, it is critical to work through a local point of view, that is, what is appropriate and reasonable within that culture. Charlotte remembers working with a global company based in the United States who wanted to ensure that every single employee network was rolled out in every country they were based in. One of the more successful networks for this company in the United States was the Hispanic network and for a time, they couldn't understand why the 'Hispanic' network was not appropriate or needed in Spain.

Challenges and obstacles

Earlier in this chapter we touched on challenges such as getting senior buy-in and making sure the network is inclusive. Other common challenges include:

- When a network develops an inappropriate or unrealistic set of objectives. A network should not be seen as a substitute for a works council or a union.

- When a network becomes a haven for poor performers. Both Charlotte and Fleur have had the experience of working with network leads who are passionate about D&I, but are poor performers and are struggling with their day job.

- Getting the business to appreciate the benefits – it is always difficult to encourage people to think and act differently and tap into resources that may not have been there in the past. Many networks, even if this is part of their purpose, struggle to be a real partner to the business and to be seen as a resource the business should use when thinking about new products, client services or developing client relationships.

- Consistency – a lot of network activity relies on goodwill and people's personal motivation and passion. Running a network can be time consuming and when others are moaning about something, or don't deliver on a commitment, it can be demotivating. It's important to make sure that the network is not all about one person. When Fleur joined one company, the black employee network was led by a charismatic manager who unfortunately was made redundant. Fleur inherited a frustrated and very cynical group of people who had totally lost direction. We would recommend that you always have co-heads that rotate out of the role after a maximum term of three years. The rotation should be staggered so that both are not moving at the same time and part of their responsibility is to develop their successor.

Measuring business impact and return on investment

Tracking data is crucial to ensuring that you are focusing on the right actions and that they are having the desired impact. We have listed some of the key measures for you to consider for the network:

- **Employee opinion survey:** Are you able to include within your survey a question within the demographics section (if available) for an employee to state whether they are a member of any of the employee networks? If so, would you be able to analyse the data by those who are and those who are not part of a network? Would there be any differences, or any perception gaps, in their responses? Alternatively, could you ask a question within the survey about the networks to gauge employee views: for example, 'I believe the employee networks enable our organisation to be more inclusive'.

- **Attracting new employees:** Do you ask potential job candidates what attracted them to apply for a job in your organisation? Could the employee networks be one of the options they could choose from?

- **Specific surveys:** Does your organisation enable you to conduct additional surveys with your employee base: for example, pulse surveys? Could you conduct one specifically focused on the employee networks and gain the view of both those who are actively involved with the networks and those who are not?

- **Awards:** Although this subject is covered in the chapter on embedding your strategy into the culture (see Chapter 18) – are there specific awards that are available for employee networks? Could the external recognition of the work the network has achieved create a positive impact for the organisation?

- **Interaction with clients/potential clients:** Many networks open their doors to external organisations for events – photograph exhibitions, panel events, book launches, recognising religious festivals. This is a great way of creating opportunities for significant business networking and building client relationships.

There will be many other ways in which you can measure the impact of the employee networks. To support this it is also important to regularly report on the progress the employee networks are making as well as their impact and successes. Where these reports are presented and shared will depend on the governance structures created, as outlined earlier. Some organisations create impressive brochures documenting their employee networks journey, globally. They have shared these with their clients and a wider external audience. Examples of companies who have done this include Morgan Stanley, Air Products and Chemicals Inc.

Networks at one professional services firm

An integral part of our D&I strategy is the role of our networks. Their overall goals are to connect people within the firm, contribute to our recruitment agenda and build our external profile as an inclusive organisation. This case study explores the key elements of a successful network.

Critical success factors for networks

- Bottom up and top down – we believe that networks need to be driven both from the bottom up and from the top down. That means that we don't approve one just because 'management' thinks it would be a good idea – we want to see a groundswell of enthusiasm from the network constituency.

- Business case – the networks need a strong, well-considered business case. If our people are going to devote significant time to network activities, we want to see that there is value in it for them and for the firm. Each network produces an overall business plan with key objectives, performance indicators and budget requirements.

- Co-leadership – all of our networks have co-leaders. A single leader often struggles to maintain momentum – after all, everyone has a day job that they have to deliver as well as their network initiatives.
- Knowledge-sharing – we facilitate knowledge sharing between networks to ensure that good ideas are exchanged, wheels aren't reinvented and joint working happens where relevant. This knowledge sharing can be as simple as forwarding an email round all the networks as well as more formally with a quarterly workshop for all network co-heads.

Outcomes

- External relationships potentially leading to new business
- Improvement in cross-firm networking
- Improvement in our profile in the recruitment market
- Improvement in employee engagement
- Personal development for network members
- Improvement in our external profile
- Improvement in standards for external awards and accreditations.

Five key takeaways from this chapter

- Be very clear from the start on the business case and key objectives for launching a network(s).
- Encourage different regions to consider the impact and support they may bring to the agenda – although there should be a consistent philosophy around networks, there doesn't need to be total conformity in how they are run.

- Consider how people who work remotely can get involved with the networks and feel part of it – for example, rotating the location of a meeting, linking in via webinars, recording/transmitting sessions.

- Outline your expectations of the networks from the outset – agree achievable, measurable objectives – are they there purely to increase engagement or are they there to support the business, for example, giving feedback on new products and services?

- If creating specific networks such as a veterans' network, consider how this can be positioned to support the wider inclusion agenda as it could be perceived as exclusive rather than inclusive.

part three

Achieving change

Inclusive leadership development

Some of the greatest advances happen when people are bold enough to speak their truth and listen to others speak theirs. KENNETH BLANCHARD, AUTHOR AND MANAGEMENT EXPERT

This part of the book focuses on the key aspects of progressing your journey on the STAR framework and moving towards 'achieving change'. Throughout Part Three we focus on elements such as inclusive leadership development as well as removing barriers and obstacles to both increasing engagement and continuing to embed D&I into business as usual.

In this chapter we take a detailed look at inclusive leadership, specific development programmes for different groups of employees and cross-cultural working. We also review the different roles of coaching, mentoring and sponsorship.

What do we mean by inclusive leadership?

An inclusive leader is someone who has a strong self-awareness about their own preferred work style, but is able to flex this style to connect with all of their team, even those who think and work differently and who may have totally different motivators.

When Ann Francke, head of the Chartered Management Institute, was interviewed she said that one of the Institute's aims is to 'eliminate the accidental manager. It's about training and standards. Most people are thrust in to management because they're good at something, usually a tactical or operational role that doesn't have anything to do with management. Often there's no training for these promotions.'[1]

In our experience, too many organisations are full of accidental managers, who are technically strong, but not so effective when it comes to inclusive leadership. The organisation then decides to embark on the D&I journey and somehow expects their managers to shake off the habits they have developed over their working lifetime and become inclusive leaders with little more than the launch of a website and/or a couple of employee networks, a new global D&I policy and a rousing speech from their CEO.

Choosing an approach to D&I and inclusive leadership training

We think about D&I training and inclusive leadership training in two ways.

- D&I training that tends to look and feel a little like compliance training. Usually used to raise awareness of the issues (e.g. too few women in leadership) and to articulate the business case. Organisations tend to roll this all-staff training out at the beginning of their journey. We call it the 'sheep-dip' approach.
- Inclusive leadership training that starts to tackle how you develop and up-skill someone to lead difference, often managing teams that might be dispersed over several buildings, several cities or indeed globally.

D&I training is usually bought off the shelf from a training provider and usually doesn't take the company culture and specific challenges into account. We believe there is some value in doing this as it does increase awareness at some level, as long as you acknowledge that this doesn't lead to any particular culture change or a sustainable shift in behaviours. As a result you will have raised awareness, shared the business case and some examples of what 'good' looks like, but you will not have changed people's behaviours (or at least very few) except for those that will be naturally inclusive without needing training, development and further support.

There is research out in the public domain that suggests that diversity training has 'no positive effects in the average workplace'. In his 2012 *Harvard Business*

Review article, Peter Bregman refers to the research of Frank Dobbin of Harvard, Alexandra Kalev of Berkeley, and Erin Kelly of the University of Minnesota, who concluded that: 'In firms where training is mandatory or emphasizes the threat of lawsuits, training actually has negative effects on management diversity.'[2] They go on to suggest that these sorts of programmes could be counter-productive, for example in 'raising the hackles of white men' and with managers generally, who are left feeling that you are just 'pointing the finger' at them. They do find that they can have a small positive impact in the largest of workplaces, although they have found that having diversity managers focused on the topic, accountable and offering mentoring programmes, are significantly more effective. Both of these points are discussed further in Chapters 5, 7 and 13.

Their research also suggests that having optional (not mandatory) training programmes that focus on cultural awareness (not the threat of the law) can have positive effects. Certainly in our experience, the mandatory tick-box exercise can cost an organisation far more than their annual D&I budget and, less than a year down the line, it's as though it has never happened. The sponsors of the training feel good because they can speak of the high percentage of people that have attended the workshop and they might have examples of positive feedback from a handful of people who have attended, but there is little or no impact on the actual impact measures they are trying to improve.

If you decide to embark on training, you are certainly not short of approaches, both in the type of delivery and the type of providers. There are web-based learning tools (which can be helpful when you have multiple locations or people working shifts), in-house programmes facilitated by an external consultant and/or your learning and development (L&D) professional, external courses and seminars (both virtual and face to face), consultants that use actors to perform vignettes and engage the audience in conversations and many more.

We would suggest that first of all you review your current L&D offerings and identify where you can embed some messaging/learning about D&I – for example, what you do and say at induction, what you offer to new managers, how you prepare people for the performance management season. If you do feel that you need to start with stand-alone training, you should look for something engaging, customised for your business and highly experiential.

At best, you are looking for mindset and behavioural change. If you are developing something that is going to be rolled out globally, do think about the cultural connotations and the fact that with some messaging, one size doesn't fit all. Take for example team-building training that you may have developed initially for Europe. To include D&I you might have a section on collaboration and encouraging diverse perspectives with an element of healthy conflict. In some geographies, for example, the Middle East or Japan, it would be counter-intuitive to be teaching junior team members to publicly challenge their manager.

Whatever you decide to do, we would strongly recommend that you start to embed information about D&I in to all of your L&D offerings as soon as possible. This will ensure that employees see that this is about how you do business, how you behave and how you operate in your organisation. Without that, there is always the potential that this will be seen as something that happens once you have done the day job!

If you do decide to roll out some training, similar to unconscious bias training (outlined in Chapter 10), the benefit of rolling out inclusive leadership training is that you are talking about your whole workforce and not just one strand of diversity. You can of course include a more in-depth section on one area if you feel that there is a significant issue to tackle.

In our experience, the best approach to inclusive leadership training is to focus on engaging the individual's head, heart and hand (the case for change, getting the individual to engage on a personal level with the topic and getting commitment for what they are going to do differently). Budget permitting, we would recommend that you use a third party, who tends to be in a stronger position to challenge the status quo and speak with authority on the topic whilst ignoring inherent organisational politics and hierarchy.

The most impactful training is when the individual is able to go on a journey of discovery around inclusive leadership, rather than feeling that they are being lectured. There are many exercises online that offer great ideas for team games and, depending on the time available, the most sophisticated programmes tend to also cover unconscious bias, in and out groups and micro-inequities (see below) – all very commonplace in the everyday work environment. The time available is, of course, often the issue. In our experience, organisations usually want their training delivered in as short a programme as possible.

We would suggest that you need a minimum of one day, or a similar amount of time delivered over a number of sessions, with some pre-course work (e.g. completing the Harvard implicit association test[3])and some follow up (e.g. 1:1 coaching). Also highly recommended is that, if you are using an external consultant, the workshop has an internal sponsor selected from your senior ranks who will speak to your customised business case and the company data.

For those new to the terminology – below is a quick introduction to 'in and out groups' and 'micro-inequities'.

In and out groups: An in-group is a social group to which a person psychologically identifies as a member. As an example, this could be through race, culture, gender or religion. The in-group is the dominant group and often hold the power base, but they may not be the majority. In contrast, the out group are those people who do not belong, or identify, to a specific in-group.

Micro-inequities: These are subtle, often unconscious messages that devalue, discourage and impair workplace performance. They are conveyed in many ways, for example through facial expressions, gestures, tone of voice or choice of words. These messages can be sent consciously or unconsciously: they could be the way you fold your arms, talk to a colleague when someone else is presenting, check your messages when someone is speaking at a meeting, avoid making eye contact or dismiss someone's idea. Whether conscious or unconscious, they can have a damaging effect on someone's engagement, motivation and productivity in the workplace.

Minority-specific leadership development programmes

This topic often divides opinion, but such programmes can be beneficial when created and delivered in the right way and when there is a very clear rationale of why they are needed. The key is to acknowledge that this is not all about 'fixing' people and is just one of a number of interventions that make up the bigger culture change effort. What we are clear on is that this cannot be delivered in isolation – delivering minority-specific training and believing the job is done is certainly not the answer.

Fleur remembers talking to a well-known provider of women's leadership development who had run several programmes for a high-street bank. They had just completed a review of the impact of the programme and had been surprised to find that 50 per cent of the women who had been on the programme in the last two years had returned to the workplace and within six months had resigned. They shouldn't have been surprised. If you take any high-potential individual out of their workplace and encourage them to open their eyes and think about what they want from their organisation for their career, if they don't see the role models, they don't see the commitment and they don't feel a change in the dominant culture, they will vote with their feet and leave.

Professor Michelle Ryan at Exeter University has been doing some really interesting research which we feel plays in to the debate about what you should be training people about. She has been looking at whether women and men are as ambitious as each other. What she has found is that the women that she surveyed, who were midway through their career, were less willing than men to make sacrifices and to take risks to progress in their career because of the consequences when they tried to 'lean in'. We need to work with our managers and leaders to change those consequences and help them feel that they are working in a meritocracy.

Michelle Ryan, Professor of Social and Organisational Psychology, Exeter University

'Some researchers and commentators argue that women are under-represented in senior roles because of an intrinsic lack of ambition, or because they have a different set of priorities to men.

'The research I've done with my team doesn't bear that out. We've worked with the police force, the Navy, the Royal College of Surgeons and a number of financial services companies, and what we have found is that at the beginning of their training period, men and women show exactly the same levels of ambition. Over time, men's ambition stays the same or even increases; but women's ambition drops off quite dramatically.

'We're talking here about women at very different life stages, from undergraduate science students to surgical trainees in their mid-30s, so it's unlikely to be just about the biological clock. What these women all have in common though is that they've spent time in a very male-dominated environment. To take the surgeons as an example, medical school isn't a male-dominated environment, but surgery as a special-ism is. Suddenly these women are in a place where no one that is suc-cessful looks like them.

'I think what we are seeing is the impact of a lack of structural support for these women to progress their careers, but also a lack of mentors and a lack of role models. One's ambition is very much related to one's expectations of success. Of course there will always be some very strong and determined women who think, "Right, I'm going to make it any-way", but there will be a lot more who think "Well, clearly the top jobs aren't for people like me" and revise their ambitions accordingly.

'In less male-dominated settings, like marketing or publishing, you see more women in senior jobs. What that says to me is that women don't inherently lack the ambition, drive or skills to make it to the top. So it must be something else that's stopping them.

'It becomes self-limiting too. Interview questions often touch on ambi-tion: "Where do you see yourself in ten years' time?" Ask that of a woman who's already given up on the idea of getting to the top and you might well come away with the impression that she doesn't have a clear vision of where she wants to be. She's then less likely to get promoted, and so the cycle continues.

'As part of our work with the Royal College of Surgeons, we developed a vodcast for medical students and surgical trainees. We featured a very diverse range of people in the film itself – a gay man, someone who had been a refugee and people from different socio-economic

(Continued)

backgrounds. The idea was really to show that a good surgeon can come from any background, and that the profession really needs this diverse range of outlooks and perspectives. If you go down the route of showing two or three "superwomen" that can be almost as alienating as not showing any women at all.

'The feedback we've had from that has been very positive. People have told us they found it inspiring. One young woman told us that she saw being the first person in her family to have gone to university as a bigger barrier than being female. Another young man told us how good it was to see a male role model on screen who he felt displayed similar characteristics to him – being gentle, and really caring for people. I guess that reinforces our decision to try to tackle diversity in the widest sense, rather than focusing on just one aspect.'

The bottom line is that in many organisations, the behavioural styles that are most valued in traditionally masculine cultures and are used as indicators of potential, are often unappealing or unnatural for women and high-potential minorities. These specialist programmes aim to provide high-potential individuals with a space to explore their careers to date, how and what they have achieved and what they need to do to get to the next level. In addition to the organisation sending an important message to those invited as part of their commitment to strengthening their leadership pipeline, it's a great way to access organisational learning and to engage and sometimes challenge your business leaders who attend some of the programme as role models and leadership sponsors.

Why are women on minority-specific development programmes, you might still be asking. There is a huge amount of research in this area which suggests that gender-specific training is beneficial:

- It provides a supportive and safe environment in which to challenge.
- Participants realise that they are not alone; there are many similar issues for women from different sectors and geographies.
- Some issues such as organisational politics, being ambitious, self-promotion and work–life integration are particularly challenging for women.

- It provides a 'gender lens' to help reflect on specific work experiences.
- They are able to engage with positive role models.
- It encourages women to support one another and avail themselves of other facilitating structures or opportunities available, such as mentoring.
- It motivates women to become more proactive in managing their careers.
- It increases readiness to step up to a leadership position.
- It creates a rich network of female colleagues across the business.

EY runs three women's leadership programmes in EMEIA targeting women at different stages of their career. Two of the programmes are delivered externally, by a third party and target the senior women. The third programme was developed for women in the middle ranks, the talent pipeline. EY were looking for something that would be suitable for a large number of women spread over 99 countries; they developed a programme that could be used locally without relying on a third party. This programme includes three half-day workshops, (it's recommended that you run one a month) which are presented in a 'toolkit' format so that anyone with good facilitation skills can deliver them. It is highly accessible and is now run in many countries and cities including Pakistan, which was a first for EY.

All three programmes consistently receive positive feedback and when EY conducted a more detailed return on investment exercise on their longest running programme they found that 96 per cent of respondents said the programme was highly impactful or impactful, with comments such as 'best programme I have been on at EY', 'excellent programme' and 'highly valuable' being mentioned multiple times. The alumni also stated they:

- had learnt new career strategies – for example, taking proactive control of their careers
- felt that they had increased their confidence – for example, as a result of the programme, they better understood their own brand and style of leadership
- changed their mindset – for example, realised that barriers to progression can be overcome
- realised that they were not alone – despite differences in business unit, home country and rank, there were many themes that they all identified with.

In the United Kingdom, EY also runs a black and minority ethnic programme and have sent people to a programme run by Stonewall (a UK-based charity supporting employers to promote inclusive leadership for their LGBT employees) and to Chain Reaction, a one-day personal development programme for people with a disability run by Kate Nash (of Kate Nash Associates). This latter programme is designed to help people make sense of disability and develop strategies to manage interactions at work, ask for the workplace adjustments they need and develop tools and techniques to deal with other people's reactions.

Cross-cultural working

Cross-cultural working is a tricky area to get the balance right with training. All too easily you can start to fall into the trap of stereotyping – Americans are this, Japanese people are that. Culture, both national and organisational, influences nearly every interaction that people have on a day-to-day basis. Of course, when working cross-culturally, it is good to understand basic etiquette – issues such as how to present your business card and when not to offer your hand to shake. It's important for developing effective teams and for business relationships as well as when developing and marketing a product or service. One example of this was when Mountain Bell Company tried to promote its telephone services to Saudi. Its advert portrayed an executive talking on the phone with his feet propped up on the desk, showing the soles of his shoes – something an Arab would not do and finds disrespectful.

Culture is multi-layered and you can't teach someone cross-cultural competence in a one-off programme. That said, particularly if someone is new to an international team or about to start an assignment in a different country, they need some guidance.

It is probably most helpful to start by understanding your own preferred work style. Aperian has a global portal called 'GlobeSmart',[4] which allows you to see how your preferred workstyle compares with the average styles of people from other countries. It looks at different dimensions of culture, such as whether you prefer direct or indirect communication, how important hierarchy is, what an acceptable level of ambiguity is, how important a focus on getting a task done is versus building a relationship.

Figure 13.1 Cultural profile comparison

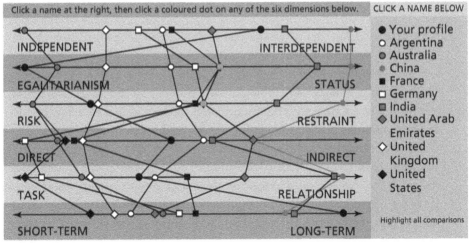

Source: courtesy of Dr David Matsumoto.

Figure 13.1 shows an example of a profile comparison created by Globesmart.

Completing a profile like this prior to attending a workshop or other awareness training could give you a useful framework to start with. Another provider is Tracom who look at social styles and the level of versatility you have to adapt to other people's styles. Again, you complete a profile and ask colleagues to complete a profile on you. Versatility is closely related to the concept of emotional intelligence and is a measure of interpersonal effectiveness. This profile equips you to better understand how you approach your counterparts and could be particularly helpful if you are working cross-culturally because it takes you away from relying on learning about cultural stereotypes. The great news as well is that versatility can be learnt.

Tracom's tool has particularly interested Fleur because Tracom has completed a relatively small piece of research that links someone's level of versatility to their effectiveness as an inclusive leader. They found that managers with high versatility were rated as significantly more effective at promoting D&I than managers with lower versatility scores. Importantly, these evaluations came from the managers' direct reports, those in the best position to determine whether someone is an effective inclusive leader. Managers with high versatility scores were more likely to engage in pro-diversity behaviours, such as actively trying to understand others' experiences and perspectives, recognising employees' contributions, fostering a welcoming environment for the team, and valuing different opinions. Highly versatile managers were rated up to 17 per cent more effective on these behaviours than low versatile managers.[5]

Charlotte used Aperian when she was working for a global investment bank. She found that this tool equipped people to understand different cultures, which helped them work effectively as a team as well as giving a great service to their clients. In parallel to rolling out the Globesmart tool, Charlotte worked with them to create a training programme called 'Cultural Intelligence'. This training module was tailor-made for the company. It focused on the skills and behaviours required for individuals to be able to flex their style and behaviours in different cultures without conforming to cultural stereotypes and losing a sense of their own cultural identity. Over a 12-month period training was delivered across the globe with all attendees then having access to the Globesmart tool which supported them to conduct additional research on different cultures and understand how their personal style compared to others.

A third provider that we thought would be worth mentioning is Knowledge-Workx who are based in Dubai, so arguably provide a more Eastern lens to think about cross-cultural working. They also have a tool to assess your own preferences and focus on inter-cultural intelligence (ICI) which is a combination of knowledge, skills and attitudes. They focus on the relationship between your own culture, someone else's culture, company culture and national culture. Their model looks at how we react to the environment and our orientation to different views of the world. This is the hidden part of the traditional iceberg model you may see when people talk about the visible and invisible aspects of diversity. It's about individual beliefs, norms and values. They focus on three worldviews:

- Guilt versus innocence – where there is no hierarchy and people get straight to the point
- Fear versus power – where there is more indirect communication, and communications are tailored to the seniority of the audience
- Shame versus honour – where communication is indirect and informal with a low tolerance for people who get straight to the point.

Our caution on this topic is to be careful that you don't go down the stereotypical route, but do arm yourself with sufficient knowledge of cultural dos and don'ts. Bear in mind that many global organisations can approach this topic through a 'Western' lens which can often trip them up. For example, it's all very well teaching people that they need to go out, find a mentor and then tell them what you need from them. However, in some cultures it is disrespectful to push your own agenda and/or your own opinions, never mind try and manage upwards. Also bear in mind that the easier part of this is educating people about cultural difference. The key to sustainable success is getting people to act on what they learn and embed it into their everyday behaviours.

In her book, *Growing Global Executives,*[6] Sylvia Ann Hewlett talks about the need for executives to be able to project credibility as they work across the globe and this means different things in different geographies. She suggests they need to adopt a double pivot – demonstrating authority with senior executives in the West (the vertical pivot) and prioritising emotional intelligence with stakeholders in global markets (the horizontal pivot). Pivoting can then be further complicated by cultural expectations around gender. She goes on to suggest that asserting authority and exercising emotional intelligence looks very different for men and women and also across different generations.

One consideration in identifying the right cultural training for your company is to ask people from across the countries that you operate in to be involved in deciding how the training should be delivered, what should be included and what, if any, external provider should be used. By doing that, you are using your own cultural intelligence and putting inclusive leadership into action. You are thinking about the different cultures and what would be most appropriate for all areas of the organisation.

Coaching, mentoring and sponsorship for specific communities

All of us, at some time in our career, need help to understand the unwritten rules of our organisation which can constantly change. Fleur took a call recently from a colleague in Germany who wanted to discuss an issue. They talked it through, confirmed that they were on the same page with the solution, and her colleague then said she would send through an e-mail with the issue, copying in other stakeholders and that she would be grateful if Fleur could respond with what they had just discussed. As she said, 'I've been told that's how we do things around here'. Someone had to tell her how to do that, otherwise she would have just sent the e-mail. There are numerous other rules such as whether it is OK to push back if you don't agree on a point. What's the most impactful way to communicate? How do I get promoted round here? When can I speak up and when do I need to keep my thoughts to myself?

The catalyst report, 'The double-bind dilemma for women In leadership: Damned if you do, doomed if you don't',[7] illustrated that gender stereotypes lead to three main 'double binds' for women:

- Their behaviour, regardless of whether they fit the stereotype, is either seen as 'too soft' or 'too tough', never 'just right' for leadership roles.
- Women are held to higher standards of performance and receive lower rewards than male leaders.
- Women leaders are perceived as either competent or likeable, but rarely both.

In some cultures, these stereotypes are amplified by the patriarchal structure (a system that involves men being an authority over women). The importance of a coach/mentor/sponsor is to help women navigate the fine line between 'lacking presence' and being 'too aggressive'.

It would help at this stage to define what we mean by a coach, a mentor and a sponsor as each of these are very different.

> **A coach:** A coach supports an individual on a specific personal or professional goal. It can be informal; in fact often we can be coached without it being labelled as such if we are lucky enough to have a helpful colleague or effective boss. Usually it's a more formal relationship and often with a third party. You tend to contract on how often you will meet, for how long and what the specific focus is. It will often be for a short period of time – maybe 6 to 12 months.
>
> **A mentor:** This is a development partnership between someone with experience in something and someone who wants to learn from them. It is often about sharing information and the two parties agree on their focus: for example, how can I make my flexible working arrangement work? The mentor can sit at any level of the hierarchy and there are various forms of mentoring – 1:1, peer group, reverse (when the mentor is the more junior person – often successful when trying to educate management about the challenges for a certain strand of diversity such as the younger generations, or perhaps to help senior leadership get up to speed on technology developments).

> **A sponsor:** This is a more senior person in your organisation that has the influence and network to make a meaningful intervention in your career. They are advocates for their protégé's advancement and they are held accountable for achieving the individual's next promotion.

Someone recently described the role of sponsor and mentor beautifully – mentoring is what happens when you are in the room. Sponsorship is what happens when you aren't in the room.

With all of the above roles, we suggest two top tips to ensure they are successful. First of all, both parties must make the commitment to the relationship and follow through with appropriate preparation and allocation of time. Fleur remembers setting up a peer group mentoring programme in the United Kingdom. The model was that each group would be made up of 12 women and they would have two female partners to mentor them. She decided on two partners because she was concerned that as they were so busy, they may not always turn up to the session. Imagine her surprise when in fact it was the mentees that didn't turn up. It turned out to be a real missed opportunity for them as well as a lack of respect for the partner's time.

Secondly, the coach, mentor and, in particular, the sponsor must understand what the real challenges are for the person they are working with. Often the assertive, authoritative, dominant behaviour that people associate with the 'in-group' is just not seen as attractive by the mentee or protégé or is something they would like to emulate. In McKinsey's 2013 study of gender diversity in top management,[8] they confirmed that 73 per cent of the men surveyed agreed or strongly agreed that diverse leadership teams generated better company performance. However, they also showed that on the whole the men did not understand what the challenges were for women.

Charlotte remembers creating a sponsorship programme in a global company which was launched at a dinner with the senior male leaders (the sponsors) and the people being sponsored (the protégés). They got together for the sponsors to hear the challenges that the protégés had experienced, but the programme got off to a rocky start because the male leaders were, initially, quite incredulous to hear these experiences. In fact they just wouldn't believe that the experiences they were hearing about could happen in their company.

It did take some time to get to the stage where the senior male leaders started to understand the real challenges and then started to act and behave as really effective sponsors.

In the *Harvard Business Review* article 'Why men still get more promotions than women',[9] Herminia Ibarra and her colleagues suggest that women are over-mentored and under-sponsored. They conducted in-depth interviews with 40 high-potential men and women. The women confirmed that they gained valuable career advice from their mentors; they explored their preferred styles of operating and what they needed to do to get promoted. The men on the other hand talked about how they planned their next moves, how they could take charge in new roles and how their mentor could advocate for them publicly (really much more of a sponsor's role).

It's really important to keep making the differentiation between coaching, mentoring and sponsorship. Fleur and Charlotte are somewhat divided on the most effective way to set up a sponsorship programme. Fleur tends to favour assigning a sponsor to each protégé based on their experience and business knowledge. Charlotte finds it more effective to gain buy-in and ownership up front from the sponsor (rather than just allocate someone to them). She once worked with an organisation who wanted their top 20 senior women sponsored. However, the executive decided to allocate protégés to the sponsors; the approach didn't work. In Charlotte's opinion sponsorship is more about supporting someone and building trust in them and their skill set so that you are comfortable to promote them to your business contacts and colleagues in a positive way– for example, put your own reputation on the line.

POINTS TO CONSIDER WHEN SELECTING A SPONSOR

As sponsorship is so critical to career progression it is crucial to get the selection right. The following shows what an effective sponsorship programme would involve. It must have:

- A good level of leadership experience to be able to share the 'unwritten rules'
- The personal and organisational authority to intervene when they feel that their protégé is not getting the right development opportunities

- The ability to create a rapport and deep sense of personal engagement with their protégé
- A passion for developing people
- A realistic capacity to commit to the programme

WHAT IS THE ROLE OF THE CAREER SPONSOR?

The sponsor's role is 'low touch but high impact' (Figure 13.2). A sponsor is expected to:

- remove the road blocks; intervene and influence on behalf of the protégé to ensure that the organisation delivers on its promise of realising their unique potential
- leverage their personal and organisational authority to hold line management accountable for retaining, guiding and supporting the protégé to a senior leadership position
- provide anonymous feedback to the D&I steering group or other senior leaders on how the wider organisational system (the hidden barriers) needs to shift to create a more diverse leadership cadre.

WHAT IS THE ROLE OF THE PROTÉGÉ?

- To be open and honest in discussing their career aspirations, performance and development

Figure 13.2 The sponsor's role

| Actively intervene | and | Put their own reputation on the line |

Believe in me and go out on a limb on my behalf	Promotes my visibility
	Gives advice on presentation of self
Advocate for my next promotion	Puts their own political capital on the line
Connects me to senior leaders	Gives honest/critical feedback
Provides air cover	Provides stretch opportunities

- To take the initiative – Sylvia Ann Hewlett[10] suggests that the protégé should be ready to do 70 per cent of the ground work
- To proactively seek feedback
- To do what they say they will do
- To be willing to consider and explore new opportunities
- To listen and reflect.

The role of inclusive leadership and, therefore, the development of inclusive leaders is a core of any robust strategy to create a more diverse and inclusive culture. Many of the focus areas within this book are clearly dependent on each other – ensuring that you are developing and nurturing inclusive leadership skills for now and the future to support long-term, sustainable change.

Five key takeaways from this chapter

- Invest in the awareness and education of your middle managers on this topic, but don't put them through a sheep dip – be creative as to how you can increase their awareness and embed into their everyday behaviours.
- Be clear on the pros and cons of delivering gender- and minority-specific leadership programmes – be clear on what they will deliver for you that integrated training won't.
- Encourage everyone to consider the skills required to be an inclusive leader and how they can develop and enhance them further.
- Ensure cultural nuances are taken into consideration for all training interventions, and cross-cultural training is seen as an imperative for companies who operate in, and with, different cultures.
- Be clear on the differences between coaching, mentoring and sponsorship and use each one as appropriate; don't assume they are all the same and do the same thing.

New ways of working

We like to give people the freedom to work where they want, safe in the knowledge that they have the drive and expertise to perform excellently, whether they [are] at their desk or in their kitchen. Yours truly has never worked out of an office, and never will.

RICHARD BRANSON, ENTREPRENEUR, INVESTOR AND PHILANTHROPIST

In this chapter we delve into thinking about how we can flex the traditional way of working. We will look at the business case for change, the challenges you might encounter and give you some top tips to achieve your vision of creating a more flexible and agile workplace.

What are new ways of working

Doesn't it strike you as odd that, despite the enormous changes we have seen in how work gets done, in particular with the innovations in technology, the way many people think about work continues to be so traditional and, yes, old-fashioned? In the past ten years alone, the number of people with access to the internet has doubled. Thirty years ago, only one person in 1,000 had a mobile phone. Today, there are five billion mobile phone subscriptions worldwide. More and more of us are collaborating across borders as part of our regular daily work and we naturally expect to be provided with the tools and support we need to carry out our work, fulfil our career aspirations and achieve our preferred life style.

New ways of working (NWoW) is not purely about what many refer to as flexible working, or more recently agile working. It also includes:

- Changing the current working model, sometimes including the physical workplace, to empower your people to find ways to work more smartly and innovatively

- A focus on individual well-being and supporting employees to enrich all aspects of their lives, their families and their communities
- A trust-based approach, focusing on employees meeting their objectives – rather than focusing on where they are actually doing the work or even how many hours it takes to complete.

Too many of our workplaces have seen little change in how we actually structure our work and the working day over the past hundred years. In those early days the layout of offices supported factory work – every worker had their own workstation and it was deemed that you were the most efficient at that workstation. Phones and typewriters fixed to the workstation then started to appear, followed by desktop computers.

However, the late twentieth century brought us into the 'era of the knowledge worker', which for the main part is not about working alone, but more about collaboration. As Alison Maitland and Peter Thomson say in their book, *Future Work*,[1] now it is more about 'minimising the constraints and maximising autonomy' of how we work. Today's thinking is moving more towards work being an activity, rather than a certain location where teams come together as a function.

WHY THE FOCUS?

There are numerous reasons for a real focus on new ways of working, both from a business and a talent perspective. Such is the intensity of how many of us are expected to work today, that we need to find ways to balance the many demands on our time and attention, both personally and professionally. Most organisations are constantly trying to do more with less, and the current way of working for many of them just doesn't fit with the expectations of both our people and our clients. A focus on how work can be delivered differently can also be a great way to refresh the culture of your organisation by putting a focus on teamwork and cross-company collaboration.

Productivity

On an individual level, presenteeism doesn't guarantee productivity or quality. Employees can keep showing up at the office, to sit at the same desk for their contractual hours without necessarily feeling engaged or being productive. The reality is that they could be more productive somewhere else. Both academic and organisational research repeatedly show that when someone feels empowered to choose where, when and how they work, they are more engaged; and we know that higher engagement leads to higher productivity and stronger retention. At EY, for example, in 2015 the people who said they could work flexibly were 57 per cent more engaged than people who said they couldn't.

Multi-generational expectations

Earlier in the book we talked about the 'demographic divide' which will soon arise between countries with younger skilled workers and those that face an ageing workforce. Initial research indicates that whilst the younger generation want flexibility from their employer, they don't want to work remotely, or at least, not all of the time. They highly value the opportunity to work as part of a team, but don't want to have to sit at one desk from 9.00am to 5.00pm, just because traditionally that's what everyone has done.

This isn't just about the younger workforce. In many countries people are working longer, and with many different age ranges in the organisation there will be people at different stages of their life with different motivators and challenges. For some, their 30s and 40s can be the most challenging time of their lives as they juggle bringing up a family with caring for elderly and/or sick relatives – you may have heard this described as the 'sandwich years'. To compound the challenge of this situation, unlike maternity leave, caring for the elderly often can't be planned for as you don't know when there will be a problem, or how long you will need the ability to flex how and where you work.

Well-being

One key area of consideration, which in recent years has received more airtime in many geographies, is the health and well-being of employees. In the majority of cases organisations aim to operate at standards above basic health and safety requirements. More sophisticated thinking recognises the real value that supporting health and well-being brings. Many organisations will regularly review and upgrade work environments, such as technology and infrastructure, to promote the physical and psychological well-being of their employees. This could include access to a confidential employee assistance programme, or ensuring there is an accessible online approach for completing ergonomic and work space assessments linked to their specific ways of working.

In a world where mobiles and instant messaging mean we are always accessible, we must remember that 'anytime, anyplace, anywhere' shouldn't mean 'all the time and everywhere'. Organisations should encourage their employees to take control of their own well-being which means taking quality time away from work, taking regular breaks throughout their working time, for example moving away from their computer, both to recharge the mind and to stretch their body. This can be particularly important for people who work alone or remotely. If not managed appropriately, the isolation may lead to feeling separated from the team or not feeling part of it and could impact their psychological well-being.

Of course, organisations with the best of intentions can go too far without realising it (in our opinion). Controversially, a German carmaker announced they would stop their Blackberry servers sending emails to some of its employees when they were formally off-shift. This was in direct response to a number of staff complaints that felt their work and home lives were becoming too blurred. You have to admire the motivation of the organisation for making this move, but for some people the inability to access their emails could cause more stress than it relieves – particularly if someone relies on leaving work early for a personal appointment and chooses to continue working during the evening. Actions such as this are well intended, but can reduce the level of flexibility some people have when deciding how and when they want to work. What would be more impactful is creating a culture where employees feel comfortable, and empowered, to not have to answer emails as soon as they open their email account.

Will Hutton, Chair of the Big Innovation Centre at the Work Foundation in the United Kingdom, said, 'It's bad for the individual worker's performance being online and available 24–7. You do need downtime, you do need periods in which you can actually reflect on something without needing instantaneously to give a reaction. Second it has a poor impact on an individual's well-being. I think that one has to patrol quite carefully the borderline between work and non-work.'[2]

What is flexible working?

When you mention flexibility to many people they generally picture the more traditional flexibility that is usually requested formally and agreed as part of the employment contract. Examples of this include:

- Flexi-time, for example, starting later or finishing earlier
- Job sharing

- Working a reduced number of days in a week, for example, three days a week rather than five
- Compressed working (working contractual hours in fewer but longer days)
- Remote working, for example, working from home
- Term-time working (working weeks mirror school term times).

Your organisation may not be at a place in their journey where they are ready to introduce informal flexibility or you might be in a sector that can't be particularly flexible: for example, an organisation that relies on shift working and assembly lines, such as factories and call centres.

The challenge with formal flexibility can be that the flexible worker can end up being the least flexible within the team in terms of when and where they work. Fleur remembers working with someone who was contracted to work three days a week in the office and an additional day from home. You could have set your clock by her arrival and departure. She would never deviate from those set hours, even if it meant missing deadlines or having others working significantly longer hours to cover. Of course, in some cases, the individual does need the comfort of having set hours to enable them to deal with other demands in their life. For example, they might be pursuing a sport, have an additional job elsewhere, or be in the midst of studying, which will all have an impact on their ability to be flexible.

In some countries everyone has at least the right to ask for a flexible working arrangement (FWA) and good practice would suggest that you start from a position of wanting to agree any requests. Obviously you will need to weigh up the impact on your business, your clients and the others in the team. However, if you start with an open mind you are more likely to grant the request – even if it's purely on a trial basis to begin with.

Some countries have legislation that grants people the right to work flexibly on a temporary basis. The Netherlands, by law, entitles men and women with a child under the age of eight years to temporarily reduce their hours for 26 times their number of working hours per week (per child). This means that if you work 40 hours a week, you are entitled to a maximum of 26 × 40 hours off to use before your child reaches nine years of age. The leave is unpaid; however, some employers do elect to pay an element of the employee's salary.

Figure 14.1 What flexible working is and is not

Flexible working is not	Flexible working is ......
• purely a way to cut costs	• empowering people to have choice in how, when and where they work
• securing a quick win or a short term initiative	• both formal and informal working
• a work agreement that only suits the individual	• future proofing your organisation by investing in infrastructure and technology
• an agreement that is totally inflexible	• finding new and innovative ways to team
• an approach that leaves the main share of work to a handful of team members	• flexible and inflexible arrangements

One effective approach that we have come across in France was an organisation offering women returning from maternity leave a four-day week for the first month whilst paying for the full five days. In another case, in India there was the opportunity to work from home for the first three months of a phased return to work where they would gradually increase their working hours and time in the office.

Having established the basic operating approach for formal flexibility, you should now have a full suite of formal options, a transparent, fair process for people to apply and some form of reporting to regularly track the level of take-up. Once at this stage you can start thinking of how you can progress to the stage of offering a broader range of flexibility.

INFORMAL FLEXIBILITY/AGILE WORKING

On the whole, formal, rigid terms and conditions fly in the face of everything we stated in our opening paragraph. In many cases we are allowing and enabling people to flex from a working construct that is now outdated. Ideally, what we should all be looking for is an approach that empowers everyone to work the hours/days that are required to deliver their objectives and these will vary at any given time. We call this 'informal flexibility'.

Figure 14.2 Activity-based working

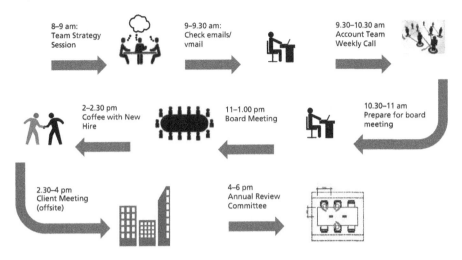

You might also hear organisations who are well on their flexible working journey talk about agility, agile working or smart working. Agile working seems to be used by organisations trying to move away from the stereotype that the description of flexible worker often leaves you with. Some organisations may also refer to 'activity-based working' (see Figure 14.2) which is based on the theory that you don't have one desk; you base yourself in different work areas depending on the work you are doing. For example, you might start your day at a desk in an open-plan office to respond to your emails, you may then go to a breakout area for a quick chat with a colleague and then you may find a private booth to make a call.

Regardless of where you are on the flexible working continuum, it is an incredibly important topic and certainly not something that is going to go away. As we have mentioned before, we do not believe that flexibility should be viewed as a benefit. It's much more than that – it's a cultural approach to the way that work gets done, how effectively you engage with your people and how you support their well-being and performance.

Workplace of the future

Many workplace of the future (WOTF) programmes are initially driven by the real-estate function as a way of streamlining and reducing property costs despite a backdrop of often an increasing headcount. In the flexible working report, 'A study of flexibility in professional services workplaces',[3] Luke Connoley, Head of Knowledge at UnWork, suggests that for organisations with offices in capital cities such as London, the cost of a desk per person, per year, is somewhere between $19,000 and $22,000. This figure is calculated taking rent, rates and service charges into account, but often excludes technology costs. For a professional services firm, the average cost of the workplace real estate is usually between 5 per cent and 6 per cent of profit.

There are enormous savings to be made if you can encourage people to release their offices and dedicated workstations and move to hot-desking and working remotely. This can be a particular driver for an organisation that is running out of office space and purchasing more is not an option. However, the realisation of the real estate savings cannot be achieved in isolation and will fail if the productivity and engagement of the individual's involved decreases. This can happen if the organisation has failed to up-skill and equip both leadership and staff into how they work, manage and lead differently.

In a previous organisation Charlotte played a lead role in a large programme that was commissioned to deliver WOTF to over 67,000 employees. The project was called 'Liberation' and aimed to:

- rationalise the real estate portfolio, release properties and create a minimum annual cost saving of £5 million
- create a culture of flexibility for employees, enabling them to work when, where and how they wanted
- ensure the right technology, great working environments, clear and simple processes, and supportive line management were in place and utilised.

The three elements to the programme that were interdependent and had to be integrated to deliver the overall benefits were (i) the long-term property strategy, (ii) the people strategy and (iii) the IT strategy.

All aspects of HR, IT and property worked closely together throughout the life of the programme and were assigned to deliver the following:

HR

- Develop working styles and behaviour change programme
- Create new contracts of employment or revisions to existing/new policies, for example, expenses
- Clear guidance notes and processes for WOTF.

IT

- Create a simpler process to order IT kit and create the provision of a flexible support service
- Development of wireless technologies
- Maximise use of existing software to enable remote working, for example, collaboration tools.

Property

- Create revised travel strategies
- Develop transition plans to support productive working throughout transition
- Close and dispense with old buildings
- Create updated processes for consumables and procurement.

To help drive the mindset change, a set of 'work styles' were created to house the 67,000 roles across the world. They were defined as:

Fixed office	Flexible office	Mobile office	Home office
Colleagues need to be in the same office to carry out their role for the vast majority of time... with flexibility around when they work	Colleagues spend over 70–80 per cent time working in an organisation's office, but not necessarily the same office	Colleagues have a nominated work base (office or home) but generally spend less than 30 per cent time there... majority of time spent at other offices customer/ client sites	Colleagues whose home is their contractual work base, visiting organisation offices occasionally for team or other specific meetings

Each work style clearly defined (i) the technology required to work in that way, (ii) appropriate office facilities such as space allocation or hot desks and (iii) leadership development support such as the need for a robust performance management process and training for leading remote teams.

The programme was phased into the organisation over a number of years to ensure that it was appropriately embedded in each business area before moving on to the next. At the time of the Liberation project being rolled out, it was ahead of its time and would still be considered as leading edge a decade later.

Challenges to progressing a culture of flexibility

There is often resistance on multiple levels to creating real, sustainable change. Some of it is well grounded, but often the issues being raised are not insurmountable. The three challenges that seem to come up consistently are technology, legislation and mindset/behaviours.

Depending on where in the world you are operating, there are a number of areas for you to consider:

- **Local legislation:** You need to understand the local legislation and what this means for your organisation. It may be in the way contracts are written and any changes will require careful negotiation with local works councils to gain their buy-in. For example, in Italy, there is legislation that protects an individual if they work remotely. Should they become injured, the law looks to the organisation and a named member of the senior leadership team to take responsibility, which at worst could lead to prosecution and jail. There are countries in the Middle East that have legislation preventing you from reducing someone's contractual hours. Most recently Fleur was talking to a colleague in Japan who was struggling with the concept of remote working. The business was most concerned about the client's reaction if an employee lost their laptop and its confidential contents. In some cases they could face prosecution and most likely they would lose the client.

- **Technology:** Technology is often cited as a challenge, particularly when flexibility involves working remotely. IT solutions can be expensive and globally may be beyond your control. For example, in parts of Asia the internet can be unreliable, slow and expensive, but having the right technology strategy to support your vision and objectives is both an imperative and an obvious investment. Identify whether you have the infrastructure to support flexibility. Some organisations still think of Blackberrys and iPhones as a 'luxury' or 'perk' of the job and have policies that only allow certain grades or roles to have one.

- **Mindsets and behaviours:** The way individuals think and act plays a significant role in progressing this agenda and can be the most challenging to overcome, in particular the thinking of managers. They may have concerns which include:

  - How do I know my team is working if I can't see them?
  - How can I create a sense of community?
  - How can we effectively collaborate if not physically together?
  - How can I develop my people if they aren't near me?
  - How can I keep them engaged?

For many, they are asked to be more flexible in their thinking, be more proactive and to change their habits, such as micro-managing. Many of these habits have developed over a long period of time and may well have seemed effective in the past.

In addition, on an individual basis, not everyone wants to work flexibly; some people prefer to come in to an office to work. They may prefer having specific boundaries between work and home. They may live in a city such as Paris or Hong Kong where property prices are expensive and they may not have a home big enough to create a specific office or work space. They may live in a country that routinely has multiple generations living together or they may be a millennial with research suggesting that they want flexibility, but don't want to work alone and would prefer to work in an office environment and collaborate with their colleagues.

Very few organisations consider the influence of personality types such as Myers Briggs Type Indicators (MBTI)[3] on how people feel they are most effective at work. For example, people who have a preference for introversion (that doesn't mean they are shy, but rather that they restore their personal energy from within) generally find that a quiet space allows them to be the most productive. On the other hand, extroverts draw their energy from collaboration and brainstorming and will prefer to be around other people in the office. Both are effective styles, but both want different things of both the available workspace and how they are able to flex their work.

From a cultural perspective, the *Harvard Business Review*, 'Balancing "We" and "Me"' by Christine Congdon, Donna Flynn and Melanie Redman,[5] shared some interesting insights about people's attitudes towards personal space across a variety of cultures. They found that German offices allocate an average of 320 square feet per employee, American offices allocate an average of 190 square feet. For workers in India and China, the figures are 70 and 50 square feet respectively. Yet despite their relatively dense workspaces, both Indian and Chinese workers rated their work environments highly in terms of their ability to concentrate and work without disruption.

Some solutions to overcome the challenges

Professor Lynda Gratton is spot on when she says that the early frays into 'untethered' work can go through a rough patch.[6] As the mindset often has to change, so too does the behaviour. It's the same when creating a diverse team. At the beginning, the level of dissent can be challenging, but with effective inclusive leadership we know that these teams will ultimately be the most successful.

FIND WAYS FOR TEAMS TO BUILD TRUST WITH MANAGERS AND COLLEAGUES

Fundamental to the success is the ability to establish trust, both in one-to-one relationships and across teams. A significant amount has been written about trust with a number of definitions of what it means in relation to the workplace.

Think of trust as the foundation for effective collaboration, particularly when you are working across geographies. What most writers and researchers agree on is that trust is the number one driver of engagement and productivity – teams that trust each other outperform teams that don't.

In his book, *The Speed of Trust,* Stephen Covey[7] argues that employees will stay at an organisation longer, and will be more engaged, when there is a high degree of trust. In her work, Suzanne Jacobs of The Positive Group, developed the Jacobs Model[8] of trust which identified eight intrinsic drivers (such as choice and autonomy, fairness and purpose) and three external factors (flexible working, workload and work–life integration) that were critical to creating trust. She refers to trust as the 'performance currency'.

Building trust in the workplace is challenging enough when working face to face; when it comes to virtual teamwork, everyone needs to work harder at building it. To enable trust to grow there is a reliance on reading and understanding non-verbal cues; depending on who you are working with, cultural influences will also play a part. For example, when working with colleagues in Asia and particularly in Japan, there is a much stronger hierarchical leadership style which means that a more junior employee will not want to be seen to contradict or disrespect someone senior to them by talking over them.

If a manager is really nervous about a team or team member changing their hours of work or where they are working, a suggestion is to set delivery goals for the short term with more regular reviews to ensure both the team member and manager are comfortable with what is being delivered and how the different ways of working are impacting this. Regular reviews and check-ins could take place as often as needed. Start with a focus on weekly or monthly outputs and you can extend timescales as confidence with the arrangement grows.

It's worth remembering here that the average contract of employment will specify an amount of pay for a number of hours to be worked; it rarely specifies the actual productivity expected. As we have mentioned earlier, someone can be sitting at either their desk or in a meeting and not really be productive. What you are ultimately looking to achieve is an engaged, motivated workforce that is operating to their highest potential to deliver their objectives. The bottom line is that a manager should trust their team until they become untrustworthy and not start from the other way round in a position of automatic distrust. It is human nature that if you know someone trusts you and shows that in their actions, there is a much higher possibility that you will trust them in return.

BE CLEAR ON OBJECTIVES, DELIVERABLES AND TIME FRAMES

A lot of what we have discussed in this chapter, and the rest of the book, comes back to strong and effective leadership. We have never seen successful and sustainable culture change occur without the full sponsorship of the leaders. This means people who understand and buy in to the business case, who 'walk the talk' and who inspire and enable others to think differently. In terms of walking the talk, they might for example: openly say that they don't respond to email over a weekend; set SMART objectives and regularly review them with their team; challenge themselves to make sure that they include people who work flexibly in high-profile projects; and avoid micro-managing their people once their goals have been agreed and signed off.

WORK HARD ON IDENTIFYING EFFECTIVE COMMUNICATION CHANNELS

An important aspect of strong and effective leadership is good communication, and this is just as important for new ways of working as it is for wider culture change. From a leadership perspective, it is helpful to consider and agree how and when regular updates are going to take place. Where possible, adopt an open diary approach. Arrange regular virtual updates as well as aim to meet in person as often as needs be. Plan contingency time in the diary for the unexpected deadlines or challenges that will invariably come your way.

ADOPT SMART WORK PRACTICES THAT LEVERAGE WHAT IS ALREADY AVAILABLE

Each individual also has a responsibility to make working flexibly a success. Given the level of technology available, there are so many more ways to communicate and stay in touch – instant messaging, teleconferencing and Skype all make new ways of working far more effective. It is important that individuals set their own boundaries, know their limits in terms of where and when not to work and ensure that they do have quality down time during the week. Most important is that they must schedule holidays which should be a break from work, not purely a different place to work.

Another important factor that we have both seen fall by the wayside when people reduce their working hours is factoring in the time they should be spending on their own development. For example, often when someone reduces their working time from five to four days a week, they retain the same level of work and drop anything that is not obviously seen as 'work', such as attending training, having coaching sessions or coaching and mentoring others.

Jane Ayaduray, Manager, Group Diversity and Inclusion, Standard Chartered

'We need to move away from the idea that flexibility somehow matters more to our female employees – it's something that matters to everyone. We also need to stop thinking of it as a benefit, or something we do for people as a favour, and start recognising it as a real business driver.

'As a global business spanning 69 different countries, we depend on our employees being flexible. We require people to do things outside their working day as a matter of course, and we need to acknowledge that cuts both ways. We also need to make sure that we're not putting unnecessary barriers in the way of recruiting the best talent: we should be looking for the best person for the job, not the best person that can work in a certain place between certain hours.

'It's not easy to change the culture, though. When I came into this job two-and-a-half years ago, we had rolled out flexible working arrangements in 13 countries. People said they were interested, but very few were actually doing it. Part of the problem was the bureaucracy – you had to fill in a form, get it signed off, and so on. There was also an underlying assumption on the part of both employees and managers that in order to be doing the job properly you needed to be putting in long hours in the office.

'What we set out to do was to get people focused on outcomes rather than process: on what people achieve, rather than how they achieve it. We also asked managers to make a public commitment to supporting flexible working, by signing up to our Flexibility Charter. The Charter states that work should be treated as an action not a place,

(Continued)

puts the emphasis on adding value to the organisation, and calls on managers to model good time management and work–life balance.

'At the same time, we tried to overcome some of the specific barriers. For example, some managers were worried that team members might not be getting the job done if they were working remotely. Equally, employees worried about managing their time and staying focused. The solution to both concerns was the same: set clear objectives, and agree to review the situation after a certain period of time, and, of course, constant communication.

'People also worried that they may not be seen to be sufficiently dedicated and committed if they initiated a conversation about flexibility, and that they may not get the same opportunities as their peers who were in the office. Again, that comes down to making sure managers are really committed to the goals of the Charter and also making them aware of the potential for bias to creep in.

'We know from both our own analysis and external research that distance has an impact on performance rating. Someone sitting near their manager will be rated differently to someone sitting in an office elsewhere. It comes back to really focusing on what adds value to the business. Actually, where someone sits should have no impact whatsoever – it's what they deliver that counts.

'In a business like ours, people will always have to work long hours at times, but there should be flexibility around that. They need to know it's not going to happen every day. Or that if they've been working really hard on a deal they'll be able to take some time off to relax and reflect.

We want to create a safe space for those kinds of conversations to happen and for both managers and team members to take a broad view of flexibility as a tool for enabling people to be more effective in all areas of their life.'

Tips to achieving your NWoW vision

To achieve a change in mindset and behaviours for an organisation to successfully move to new ways of working can be significant if the deeply ingrained norm within the organisation is that managers need to be able to physically see their team around them. Achieving real change requires a systematic approach and we would recommend the following steps:

- **Create your vision for new ways of working:** What are you trying to achieve and what will success look like? When EY started their journey in EMEIA, their first milestone was to get each region to have a set of formal flexible working policies that were open to all ranks and both genders (yes, initially one region thought flexibility was a benefit for working mothers only). Their long-term goal included a number of key performance indicators (KPIs or, as we talk about in this book, 'impact measures'), including the consistent approach that applications for flexible working would be 'reason neutral' and everyone would be working in an environment that supports their current activity – that is, activity-based working. Alongside the vision, a customised case for change for your own organisation is essential to gain the buy-in of your most senior sponsors.

- **Create a change management group:** Sometimes known as a steering group or innovation group who will act as catalysts for change and ambassadors within the business. This group should include representation from different areas of the business, different ranks and different functions and, as a minimum, IT, communications, property and HR. It is important to also identify people who will lead the change – including ideally someone with change management experience. One of their first jobs should be to source any data that is available to understand the size of the challenge. This could be in the form of people survey results, number of people on formal flexible working, outputs from focus groups or people who already access the organisation's IT infrastructure remotely, for example, email or intranet access.

- **Assess how well the current technology is enabling flexibility:** When Fleur first started working in this field, she found that a Blackberry was only given to people at certain ranks and the rules varied by business units meaning that two people of the same rank could be at the client site, one with a Blackberry and one without. Technology is often used as the reason that flexible working can't work. There may be geographic challenges, potential security concerns and interesting rules set within organisational technology firewalls, but on the whole these can largely be an excuse put forward from the resistors. We acknowledge investment in technology that enables remote communication and collaboration may well be required; however, this sort of investment can be justified by increased productivity through increased engagement and, in some cases, reduction in real estate costs.

- **Complete a skills gap analysis:** Create a plan with detailed deliverables, timelines, milestones and impact measures (or KPIs). The plan should reflect the outputs of a training needs analysis and include how you intend to approach behaviour change and up-skilling your people to think and act differently; therefore working with relevant functions such as learning and development are important. The training element may well cover a number of facets including: (i) use of any new technology; (ii) getting the best out of collaboration platforms; (iii) effective virtual working (setting of objectives, performance management, communication, teamworking); and (iv) effective paper management.

- **Share the training with your steering group/innovation group:** This will equip them with the knowledge and skills to help them think about the different ways to influence and engage other stakeholders as well as how to manage resistance to change. An added bonus is that their level of engagement and commitment to the change may well increase, giving you more committed and well-informed 'ambassadors' for the change throughout the organisation.

- **Create and deliver an effective communications plan:** At times of change there is no such thing as over-communicating. As mentioned previously, finding ways to engage people with the change that is two-way, listening as well as telling, so that they feel that they are part of the change rather than something being done 'to' them, is really important. It is also important to recognise within the communications plan that the level of change required in many organisations on this topic will take time. When we say time, we don't mean weeks or months but years, and during that time the pace of change will not be consistent.

- **Share success:** Report on progress regularly with a compelling story and this will increase your chances of engaging those who remain sitting on the sidelines waiting to see what happens. This will also give you the opportunity to identify and celebrate good role models and share good practice from different parts of the organisation. Fleur remembers working in an office that moved from structural offices to an open-plan working space. The sceptical leader found it challenging to have to relinquish his own private office space and go and seek space for private and confidential calls; however, he found that the benefits of collaboration far outweighed these challenges and he took every opportunity to talk about the benefits. As a result they found that:

- work flow increased because people didn't have to wait for formal meetings to gain a decision
- communication flow improved with a more seamless transfer of knowledge across the team
- junior members of staff really valued the improved access to leadership whom they felt that they could learn from.

Five key takeaways from this chapter

- Too many of us expect our people to work to an outdated work model – there has never been a better time to think about working differently.
- There will be lots of challenges from people resistant to change, for example, technology, legislation, but it's rare that they cannot be overcome.
- To create effective and sustainable change requires a collaboration across the whole organisation; as a minimum, HR, property and IT must work together.
- Working flexibly doesn't automatically mean working fewer hours, just often more productively.
- A change in mindset is critical to success, which also drives a change in behaviours.

Removing barriers and obstacles

If you can't fly then run, if you can't run then walk, if you can't walk then crawl, but whatever you do, you have to keep moving forward. MARTIN LUTHER KING, JR, CIVIL RIGHTS ACTIVIST

Before change is embraced by employees there will be some form of rejection and pushback during the process. In this chapter we focus on why some D&I strategies fail, identify what the barriers and obstacles may be and how to reduce their impact.

Why some D&I strategies fail

Over the years we have both seen a number of organisations throw themselves into the D&I arena – spending a lot of money externally on sponsorships, pitching for awards and rolling out firm-wide training. This has all been at a high cost of both budget and resource – only to then reduce or close the function when the business priorities changed or the sponsorship moved on and often disappeared off the radar for several years.

Ideally, failure is not an option; however, this is not unique to delivering a more diverse and inclusive workplace. John Kotter, who we mentioned earlier in the book, found that approximately 70 per cent of change programmes do not deliver the aims and outputs they were originally designed to do. He found a number of reasons why change generally fails:

- *Allowing too much complexity* – falling into the detail rather than focusing on the bigger picture

- *Failing to build a sustainable coalition* – failing to create momentum through teams that can drive the change

- *Not understanding the need for a clear vision* – if you don't know where you are going, how do you know how to get there?

- *Failing to clearly communicate the vision* – no clarity on the future goal to drive towards

- *Permitting roadblocks* – not understanding or acting upon potential roadblocks

- *Failing to create short-term wins* – these build morale and motivation; long-term change will suffer if the impact, in some way, cannot be seen

- *Declaring victory too soon* – it's a long process; celebrate successes but continue to keep the foot on the pedal

- *Not anchoring changes into corporate culture* – the lack of reinforcing the change and the lack of transition plans can set the sustainable change up for certain failure.

Change is difficult; however, the level of difficultly is compounded if appropriate thought, governance and structure is not created around the programme to support both the delivery of the change and those delivering it.

How to identify barriers and obstacles

Creating change, getting people to think differently and do things in ways that they may never have done in the past, will not come without its challenges. In fact, if you don't encounter barriers and obstacles whilst doing this work, you should really be asking yourself whether you are doing it right in the first place and whether you are pushing far enough.

Regardless of how supportive and committed the senior team are, regardless of how passionate your employee networks are and regardless of how 'bias blind' your organisation says they are, there will be barriers, obstacles and challenges to overcome through the life of creating the change.

There are a number of different types of barriers and obstacles that you may well need to navigate. The different types of barriers do not work in isolation and you may be faced with more than one of the following:

- **Structural:** This could be, for example, a physical obstacle such as a building that has access issues for people in wheelchairs and, as you don't own the building, you are told that you can't change the layout. Or it could be a hierarchy within an organisation, such as the management structure that has D&I reporting in to HR who then report in to the chief of administration (COA) who only has an interest in cost cutting and headcount control.

- **Procedural:** This is where a current process or procedure is causing a challenge. This could be an HR process: for example, the IT system used as the first stage of the recruitment process that automatically rejects applicants that don't have a 2.1 degree. Or, for example, the way that headcount is tracked and reported. Fleur once worked at an organisation that reported on the number of people rather than overall payroll costs. Where there was a need to reduce numbers, people who were in a job share arrangement (i.e. two people sharing one role by sharing the working hours of a full-time contract) were disproportionally penalised.

- **Attitudinal:** For many this will be the biggest barrier or obstacle as well as one of the more challenging to tackle because, quite often, people can mask what they really think. This will include bias, stereotypes, beliefs and perceptions as well as the motivation to change. It isn't enough to just understand why the change is required if the individual doesn't believe it is important. 'If it's not broken, why fix it?' is at the back of many people's minds when we talk about the business benefits of introducing more diverse thought and perspectives to a team. For all of your great policies, it's the people bringing them to life that you most rely on.

- **Skills and knowledge:** Where individuals have limited or no skills or knowledge around the specific topic and are unaware of how this may be progressed or do not understand the importance. D&I can be such a broad agenda that some people may have extensive experience in one area and know very little about another. For example, if you have little emotional intelligence or versatility of style, you are going to struggle more when navigating the challenges of working differently and working with difference.

Overcoming barriers and obstacles and reducing their impact

When tackling a barrier or an obstacle it is important to understand which of the above are hindering progress, as this will help you identify how to address it and the actions required.

At this stage it is also important to consider whether the barrier or obstacle you are encountering is the 'root cause' or the 'symptom' of something else.

The root cause is defined as 'a key issue or reason why a symptom is evident' whilst the symptom is defined as 'an indicator that a problem exists'. Therefore, identifying and tackling the root cause will have a better chance of stopping the symptoms from emerging in the future.

Tackling the symptom will have no impact in the longer term and could result in other symptoms emerging over time. Many D&I action plans, unfortunately, focus on the symptoms and not on the root cause.

This may sound confusing and can be difficult at first to really define what a symptom is and what the root cause behind it is. A simple and effective way to do this is to use 'the five whys'[1] technique. This is a technique that is used within Six Sigma which is a disciplined methodology for eliminating defects in any process. The technique can help you delve past the different layers of symptoms and get to the root cause of a problem. This usually presents itself as a statement that you can then take action upon. Although called 'the five whys', it may take fewer or more times to ensure the root cause is identified. Let's give you an example:

Point: The data shows that people with disabilities don't progress in the organisation past associate level.

Question: Why don't people with disabilities progress?

Point: Some decide to leave the organisation. The ones that stay with us usually stay in the same job.

Question: Why do some decide to leave the organisation?

> **Point:** The exit interviews don't share a lot of information; however, a couple have suggested a lack of support for the individual.
>
> **Question:** Why do they suggest a lack of support? What could that refer to?
>
> **Point:** We may not be aware of the level of support employees with disabilities need and we may not make it easy for them to ask.
>
> **Question:** Why aren't we aware of the level of support employees need?
>
> **Point:** We don't make it clear to line managers how to give the appropriate support to employees with disabilities of where they can go for help.

In the example above, the symptom is that people with disabilities are not progressing through the organisation. The root cause of this is that the organisation is not providing the support and help to the line managers who have a disabled person in their team, which in turn is limiting the support available for the individual.

For sustainable change to take place, this organisation should focus on changing the root cause issue rather than delivering an action that will respond purely to the symptom. In this case, responding to the root cause may be adding specific awareness events for people with disabilities and their line managers to outline the support and tools, such as appropriate reasonable adjustments, available to them.

One final consideration to take into account is that you may well not be aware of all the different barriers and obstacles that are within your organisation. Ensure that you engage and involve individuals from across the organisation, at different levels and different backgrounds to consider what the challenges are, where they are and what they can do to ultimately remove them.

Five key takeaways from this chapter

- Seventy per cent of change programmes do not deliver the aims and outputs they were originally designed for.
- Continually sense check your plans against the key reasons why change fails.

- For sustainable change, focus your energy and activity on tackling the root cause rather than symptom.
- It is likely that there are a number of different barriers and many are inter-related.
- This is a long process, so don't celebrate victory too soon.

Thinking global, acting local

Globalisation means we have to re-examine some of our ideas, and look at ideas from other countries, from other cultures, and open ourselves to them. That's not comfortable for the average person. HERBIE HANCOCK, PIANIST AND COMPOSER

In this chapter we consider how to create a global ethos and translate that into local delivery. We also review the part that local leaders and employees play to help deliver their plan.

Glocal – think global, act local

Regardless of whether your company is truly global with locations in many countries or you are an organisation based in one country with a number of sites in different regions, your vision and strategy needs to be meaningful on a global level and resonate locally.

For every size of organisation it is absolutely right to have a global, overarching ethos and vision. However, it is also important to have the flexibility to enable local areas to define what that actually means for them, what their priorities are within that and what is right for them. For example, in South Africa their focus is directed by Black Economic Empowerment (BEE) which is a programme launched by the government to redress the inequalities of apartheid by giving certain previously disadvantaged groups (Blacks, Coloureds, Indians and Chinese people) of South African citizenship economic privileges previously not available to them.

We have both seen examples where the global strategy and expectations of how this will be delivered have been so restrictive or inappropriate, that it has been difficult and close to impossible for the local locations to do what works for them – which is ironic given that this is what D&I is all about. Think, for example, about the sensitivities of trying to set up an LGBT network in some African countries. In fact, in some countries it would be illegal. An example that often comes up relates to people's focus on ethnicity and nationality. In the United States, many companies have networks for their Hispanic employees and will ask about activity in Europe where being Hispanic is viewed differently.

Creating a global ethos

To do this effectively from the outset there are a number of elements to consider. Fundamentally, your D&I strategy should underpin your business strategy, as we have highlighted in earlier chapters. Ideally it shouldn't be purely driven by 'Western' values if you are an organisation operating across the world. This is a common complaint that we hear from our emerging markets as we roll out cross-cultural training which is stereotypically based on nationality through a Western lens. The framework that contains what you are planning to achieve must be globally applicable along with many of the tools and resources. To get this right, there are a number of additional considerations including:

- Engaging people from across the different parts of your organisation, giving different countries and jurisdictions the opportunity to input into the overarching global direction
- Thinking about the use of vocabulary – for example, 'people of colour' can be offensive in some locations and yet used in others
- Ensuring all governance structures such as D&I steering groups have appropriate representation from across all global or regional sites
- Factoring in enough flexibility for all regions, jurisdictions, countries and sites to have the space to translate what the global direction means for them – for example, ethnicity will mean different things in different countries
- Enabling and supporting, where needed, for different locations to create a number of actions and impact measures that are right for them, whilst aligning with the global vision and direction – for

example, in some countries in the Middle East, they have to comply with quotas for the retention of nationals

- Considering and discussing with colleagues from across the regions, jurisdictions, countries and sites what, within the strategy, should and could be globally consistent – for example, a focus on strengthening the leadership pipeline from a gender perspective

- Identifying how you work across the different areas to ensure that whatever is delivered takes into account important differences such as cultural norms, regional customs and legislative requirements

- Customising centrally created tools to show respect for local colleagues – for example, Fleur worked with a company that ran training using actors and vignettes. As they travelled round Europe, they made sure that at least one of the actors spoke the local language in each country.

Translating a global aspiration to local delivery

When Charlotte created a strategy for a global financial services firm, she knew that the cultures across the many international offices were vastly different and one approach would certainly not fit all. To respond to this she created an overarching D&I vision and four themes which were an enabler for the wider business plan. The vision and the four themes were discussed and agreed across all of the business areas globally.

The overarching vision for the organisation was: 'Inclusion and diversity is simply about the way we are and the way we do business here. It is part of our DNA and embedded into everything we do'.

The themes of the strategy were created into a 'strategy pyramid' articulating the four themes as well as the supporting actions required to enable sustainable change (see Figure 16.1).

Each of the countries were then tasked with creating their own plans, articulating what the above meant for them, what their challenges were, three actions within each theme they were going to deliver and how they were going to measure the impact.

Figure 16.1 Strategy pyramid – global D&I

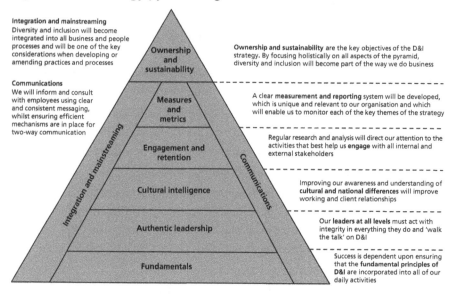

Integration and mainstreaming
Diversity and inclusion will become integrated into all business and people processes and will be one of the key considerations when developing or amending practices and processes

Ownership and sustainability are the key objectives of the D&I strategy. By focusing holistically on all aspects of the pyramid, diversity and inclusion will become part of the way we do business

Communications
We will inform and consult with employees using clear and consistent messaging, whilst ensuring efficient mechanisms are in place for two-way communication

A clear **measurement and reporting** system will be developed, which is unique and relevant to our organisation and which will enable us to monitor each of the key themes of the strategy

Regular research and analysis will direct our attention to the activities that best help us **engage** with all internal and external stakeholders

Improving our awareness and understanding of **cultural and national differences** will improve working and client relationships

Our **leaders at all levels** must act with integrity in everything they do and 'walk the talk' on D&I

Success is dependent upon ensuring that the **fundamental principles of D&I** are incorporated into all of our daily activities

Pyramid levels (top to bottom): Ownership and sustainability · Measures and metrics · Engagement and retention · Cultural intelligence · Authentic leadership · Fundamentals

Pyramid sides: Integration and mainstreaming · Communications

As you can imagine, the action plans had very different starting points and each had prioritised different actions depending on their own set of circumstances in their part of the organisation, country or region. For example, within the theme of 'Engagement and retention' the focus in Botswana was to increase the percentage of senior positions held by locals rather than ex-pats, and in Japan it was to increase the percentage of women in the workplace. Another example within the theme of 'Fundamentals' was the focus in Germany of creating an initial agreement with the work councils of what flexibility meant for them, whilst in the United States the focus was to equip the individuals with the technology and support to work in other locations such as home and not have to commute in to the office every day.

Don't underestimate the complexity of working globally or across multiple sites. You will have multiple plans in place and feel that you are juggling a number of balls at any given time. The art here is to ensure that you bring people along with you, enable others to create the plans with your support, give them a level of ownership and accountability for their part of the organisation and, importantly, look for progress, not perfection. There is no point in having a perfectly created action plan if it is not being delivered.

Rohini Anand, Senior Vice President, Corporate Responsibility and Global Chief Diversity Officer, Sodexo

Sodexo is a large global organisation with a geographically dispersed footprint. We have 420,000 employees from 130 different nationalities, working in 80 countries in 35,000 locations and we are the 18th largest employer in the world. Given the diversity of our employee base and that of the 75 million customers we touch every day, it is no surprise that Diversity and Inclusion (D&I) are an inherent part of our culture and our business growth strategy.

Our global D&I strategy encompasses four key strategic focus areas – workforce, workplace, marketplace and communities. The success of each of these focus areas is dependent on our ability to create value through tailoring strategies and interventions to local and national needs that serve to develop culturally agile leaders. We empower regions to prioritise their focus based on their local context, recognising the need for customisation to accommodate regional cultural differences. For example, France and Brazil prioritise disabilities as their diversity focus, while developing local nationals is a key focus in many of our Asian, Middle Eastern and African locations, and in China generational issues and retention of talent are focus areas.

While gender is a focus in every region, the approach is nuanced and can take disparate forms as countries ensure relevance and success. An illustration of this is within our Indian market, where initially we were leveraging mentoring and leadership development for mid-level managers to advance gender representation. However, the importance of listening to the local workforce became evident as women in India shared their experiences and unique challenges. They shared that often they live with their in-laws as part of a larger joint family and when they worked late, they were often chastised as dinner would be rushed or delayed. Consequently, a recognition day for women was initiated, which entailed extended families

(Continued)

being invited to the workplace where the women were honoured with awards to acknowledge their contributions. Following the celebrations, the women reported a shifting dynamic of greater acceptance. In fact when the women had to work late the family was willing to prepare meals rather than be dependent on the working women, enabling them to more fully engaged and commit to their careers.

As with any new strategy, the articulation of a strong business case is crucial to develop buy-in. To that end, Sodexo conducted an internal study to demonstrate the correlation between gender-balanced management teams and performance. Each of the six key performance indicators which were studied (employee engagement, brand image, client retention, organic growth, gross profit and operating profit) increased with a gender-balanced management group. Ultimately, the study revealed that gender-balanced teams generate positive outcomes, which are more sustainable and predicable. As a result, this study was instrumental in neutralising resistance and enabling our gender diversity initiatives to progress. Additionally, buy-in has been enhanced through training such as Sodexo's Spirit of Inclusion training that raises awareness and provides managers with robust tools to advance our diversity and inclusion culture. Thinking globally and acting locally is integral to the roll out process of this successful initiative. The training program has global objectives, as well as a consistent framework and message. However, in order to ensure relevance and resonance in different countries we adapted the details, including local challenges and case studies to suit local needs. As we cascade the training in various countries, we collaborate with the local teams at the very outset to gain their input, resulting in greater ownership. Senior executives serve as champions and the training is delivered in the local language. Taking a cascading approach, the training, which includes the business case for D&I, is first delivered to the executive committee. These leaders then endorse further roll out through a train the trainer certification process for designated internal facilitators. While time consuming, this process has proven successful and has resulted in an expanded roll out, made possible by a global network of ambassadors. Over the past 10 years we estimate that 37,000 Sodexo employees based in 28 countries in 4 continents have participated in the programme. We will continue the process of tailoring our Spirit of Inclusion training to local needs, with anticipated roll outs planned in Asia, North Africa and Eastern Europe.

Remaining open to new perspectives and adapting initiatives will create synergies that drive business success. As evidenced, the key is to understand the importance of the local context and gain the input of regional stakeholders to successfully execute local D&I strategies within a global framework. This has proven integral to achieving Sodexo's Quality of Life mission.

Empowering local employees to deliver their plan

At EY, Fleur covers 99 countries in EMEIA clustered into 12 regions with over 100,000 people. At an area level she is one half of a team of two; she is totally reliant on her colleagues working locally. She tends to think of her role as that of an internal consultant with the business as her clients. The approach she has taken is to have at least one dedicated D&I lead in each region (see Table 16.1 for job description), who feeds in to the EMEIA strategy and then translates it to be relevant locally. Most regions also have a D&I partner sponsor who is responsible for maintaining the profile of the leadership team's agenda.

Fleur calls this her core stakeholder group. Her extended group is then made up of anyone who has expressed an interest in driving progress through their functional roles: for example, recruitment leads, leadership and development managers, HR business partners and internal communications specialists. The D&I lead role can be hard to fill. It needs to be someone that usually has little direct resource, but is skilled at working across a matrix with many different stakeholders and can engage others to help deliver their priorities.

Table 16.1 Role description for a senior D&I manager

Purpose	Accountabilities
Responsible for developing and driving the diversity and inclusion agenda across the region. The strategy will vary by region, but will include: 1. Engaging our stakeholders – to build buy-in so that they understand the organisational and commercial benefits of investing in D&I 2. Educating our people – increase stakeholder understanding and appreciation of how to leverage difference effectively. 3. Integrating D&I into our processes – embed D&I in to our business systems, policies and practices.	Typical areas of responsibility could include: • Engagement with our key internal stakeholders on how to integrate D&I into everyday activity • Project management – such as benchmarking and initiatives • Data analysis, tracking the impact of the D&I strategy, reporting and action planning • Provision of consultancy and support to the business • Representing the firm externally on D&I • Working in partnership with external interest groups to support our D&I strategy • Representing the region as part of the area D&I stakeholder group. This role could also contribute to: • Corporate communications – monitoring and ongoing development of internal and external communication plans • Working with our functional partners (e.g. recruitment, supplier diversity, L&D) to embed D&I into their business systems • Network management – key partner for network leaders as they develop and drive their network plans • Governance – budget management, coordination of sub-area and network plans.

It can be quite a lonely role, but the stakeholders have a formal call once a month where they share updates on what they are doing, what has proved successful and how they plan to tackle any challenges they face. Over the years it has been an inspirational source of good practice sharing and, despite being a virtual team, the group members, many of whom haven't met each other, are a great support for one another. For example, Fleur developed a programme for high-potential female managers that could be customised and delivered locally. The Middle East had done a fantastic job of rolling this out and the Central and Southern Europe (CSE) region were keen to follow suit. So the D&I leads in the Middle East ran a 'train the trainer' programme (virtually) for the HR team in CSE.

Most recently Fleur has hosted a series of webinars about change management for her core stakeholder group, which focus on topics such as managing resistance and leveraging your network. She talks with each of them individually and visits them as often as she can. Her most important lesson learned over time is that key to success is to make sure that your stakeholder group know that your number one priority is to support what they are aiming to achieve.

Five key takeaways from this chapter

- Make sure from the outset that you include local stakeholders in the development of your D&I strategy.
- Be prepared for pushback and some compromise – for example, if France is keen to reduce their fines for not meeting their disability quota, they may not initially have the resource to also drive the LGBT agenda.
- Think carefully about the role of the person driving D&I locally and work with them to ensure they understand the principles of change management, are tenacious about their deliverables and can influence at all levels.
- Create some form of body that helps your key stakeholders to regularly connect, fuel the momentum and share their success stories.
- Make sure that what you are creating at 'head office' is something that your local leads actually need and can use. Engage them in your thinking from the outset.

part four

Reaping the rewards

Measuring impact and realising the benefits

Success requires first expanding ten units of effort to produce one unit of results. Your momentum will then produce ten units of results with each unit of effort.

CHARLES J. GIVENS, AUTHOR

We are now in the ultimate section of the STAR framework of 'reaping the rewards'. To truly operate at this level you will be embedding D&I into everything the business does as well as engaging employees as a normal way of doing things.

Measuring the impact of the work done in D&I is really important and one of the key areas that can be kept at too basic a level. For example, whilst it's good to track how many people attend networking events, you also need to assess the actual impact of the events.

In this chapter we take a look at creating the right trackable measures, the differences in targets and quotas and how to convert impact measures into business benefits.

Creating the right, trackable measures

When thinking about the right impact measures, this isn't just about reporting on the number of people you have at various levels within the company by diversity characteristic. That is an important part but take a look back at all the information we asked you to consider when assessing your current position in Part One (Starting out). How does that section help you think about the impact measures you would like to create? How does that help you create your own case for change over time, why this is so important and the positive contribution it brings to the wider business strategy?

There are a small number of golden rules to consider as you identify and create the right impact measures:

1. **Be clear on what is important for your organisation:** What you measure will depend on your organisation. This will be governed by what information is available and what you need to know to track progress against your strategy. There is a standard set of measures which are relevant for the majority of employers, such as:

   - employee demographics (by characteristic, level)
   - employee opinion survey data (by specific questions and perception gaps of different characteristics depending on question)
   - employee insights at different areas of the employee life cycle, such as exit interviews.

   Make sure you are tapping into what is important and of interest to both the organisation and the senior leaders. For example, if the organisation is reaching out to attract a wider consumer base, are you able to find the data that will tell you whether this is happening? If you don't have it, are you able to work with others to create the infrastructure to be able to find that information out over time?

2. **Measure diversity AND inclusion:** You need to gather demographic data and engagement information. Some organisations fall into the trap of stating that D&I is really important and then only measure the diversity. Ensure you are measuring the impact of all your actions on diversity AND inclusion.

3. **Different measures for different geographies:** The legislative and regulatory expectations and requirements are very different across the world. What we can ask in one country may be seen as culturally taboo in another and illegal elsewhere. When deciding what your impact measures are, consider what is possible in the different countries and jurisdictions you operate in. The majority of companies who measure impact in some way only have gender as the consistent measurement across multiple countries, and even then there can be data protection issues. That is fine; however, that should not limit or hinder what you can measure locally. Reviewing global impact is great, measuring the impact locally as broadly as possible is critical – global direction, local measurement.

4. **Personalise your measurement journey:** It has been mentioned earlier that it is important to measure what is important to your organisation. How this is reported and presented can be done in a number of ways. Some companies create their own 'balanced scorecard' which includes the key measures for their company. Put simply, a balanced scorecard is a strategic planning and measurement tool that has been used across many sectors and industries to align business activities to the vision and strategy of the organisation. For some, D&I measures may be included within the wider business balance scorecard or, for others, they may have created a specific scorecard purely for D&I.

Take Barclays, for example, when Charlotte was part of the Equality and Diversity team in the early 2000s, they were one of the first companies to include diversity measures across their whole business planning system. Fast-forward to 2015 and Barclays has a diversity measure within their whole business balanced scorecard. Figure 17.1 is an example of how D&I measures may be included within the business scorecard.

The challenge with the balanced scorecard is that this can be purely focused on the numbers. Yes, you can include aspects of engagement scores from employee opinion surveys that will give an indication of how inclusive the company is or how the culture is changing; however, that alone can hide a multitude of other important aspects.

Charlotte has worked closely with a number of companies to create their own version of the D&I roadmap. Figure 17.2 provides an overview that maps the progress made within specific areas or countries

Figure 17.1 Business scorecard including D&I measures

COMPANY	CUSTOMER
Increase return on equity year on year	Increase customer satisfaction
Improve conduct reputation as measured by stakeholders	Innovative products and services
COLLEAGUE	**COMMUNITY**
Increase percentage of women in leadership pipeline	Achieve a sustainable reduction in carbon emissions
Sustain employee engagement across all levels and disciplines	Increase funding and support to local charities

Figure 17.2 STAR – measuring progress

Clear **methodology and assessment** that will monitor progress on delivery and movement towards the ultimate goal of embedding into the 'way we do business'. This is appropriate for all areas of the business and wider than the colleague agenda i.e. including client and suppliers.

STARTING OUT	TAKE THE LEAP	ACHIEVING CHANGE	REAPING THE REWARDS
• Clearly understand the 'as is' and the impact on firm	• Appropriate resources in place to deliver against plan	• Data monitored by different 'groups' to identify trends and 'hot spots' within HR activity i.e. promotions, and appropriate action taken	• D&I thinking actively discussed and integrated at the start of any activity/project within the business
• Vision of 'where we want to be' in x timescale defined and articulated	• Awareness and understanding raised within region/country of subject matter including business rationale	• Data monitored and reviewed by business to assess activity and how to improve further i.e. client engagement	• Senior leaders take full responsibility for their performance on D&I and actively seek feedback
• Management/leadership commitment and accountability established	• Visible support from management/ leadership seen	• D&I thinking incorporated into all communications from leadership	• Authentic leadership seen from leaders at all levels across the firm
• Appropriate communications and engagement plan developed	• Leadership teams have a plan of how to embed D&I into their business priorities	• Inclusive leadership behaviours assessed within people processes and 360-degree feedback	• D&I naturally part of any business strategy and planning process

• Legal requirements in place and performance against them reviewed regularly	• Improvement in engagement and perception figures for 'different groups'	• D&I seen as a commercial opportunity to think about business issues and challenges differently
• Key policies and practices include D&I thinking	• Business issues and challenges reviewed looking through the 'D&I lens'	• Colleagues know how to, and do, embed D&I thinking into their day to day responsibilities
• Clear understanding of perception figures for 'different groups' and action required	• Reaches beyond the headquarter offices and culturally appropriate	• Engagement and perception figures of 'different groups' in line with 'majority' responses
	• D&I enhances the firm's brand and external profile	• All practices and processes incorporate D&I thinking (wider than HR, including client and supplier)
		• D&I central to the firm's brand and external profile

Each level is ongoing and builds from the previous one. Moving up to the next level can only be achieved by clearly delivering against all areas, unless business structure or rationale prevents that.

Ownership and sustainability will only be achieved by systematically delivering each level and embedding that activity/process before moving onto the next one.

of the organisation as well as across the overarching company to create a continual sense of progress made. It also includes barriers to continue to focus on as well as activity for the future. Figure 17.2 shows an overview of the measurement tool that supports the STAR framework as outlined in Chapter 1.

In this specific company the roadmap was used in each country and division to find out how individual progress was being made and then reported back to the steering group and executive committee of the company. What worked well was that each part of the business was measured against each other, which created a competitive edge as well as a very clear line of sight of what their delivery focus needed to be over the coming months. That said, as we touched on in point 3 above, be cautious when comparing across geographies. It may not always be a fair comparison.

Some organisations use an 'inclusion index' as a way to share a high-level overview of what progress is being made. In one organisation Charlotte created an index that consisted of 20 key questions from the employee opinion survey. The questions were pulled together to create an 'inclusion score' which was an overarching positive score of all 20 questions combined. This was also created for all diversity characteristics the organisation was able to measure to give an overview of how the 'inclusion score' changed depending on which group of employees were responding. Although the inclusion score was high level, it did create an overview of which employees felt more included and encouraged further detailed analysis to identify the issues and how to potentially overcome them.

EY in EMEIA has taken a two-pronged approach to measurement. They have a detailed template that is completed annually to inform strategy planning with a focus on gender. It focuses on measures such as retention, promotion, recruitment, engagement scores, participation on leadership programmes, scheduling of assignments and performance rankings against the three principles of:

- fair representation
- no dilution
- no regression.

They also ask all functions of the business to include a gender split in their regular reporting such as recruitment.

5. **What you measure is also a journey:** What you are able to measure at the beginning of this work may be less than what you will ultimately want to measure. Ensure you are clear on the data and information you would ultimately like to have in order to measure the impact, and add that into your wider delivery plan. Also ensure that others know why the data is important and how it will be used.

Individual measures

The above has mainly focused on the organisational metrics to measure the change that is taking place. However, what we haven't yet touched on is individual measures on D&I. Individual measures will focus the mind on the actions and behaviours at the micro level of the organisation, with each manager or individual employee. If this is a route that your organisation feels ready for, the development of the individual measures depends on the scope of the individual's role.

Some companies have responded to this by creating a performance management system that measures the 'whats' and the 'hows'. The 'whats' focus on what you have actually achieved, for example, the percentage of new hires who are female. The 'hows' focus on the behaviours, for example, were the new hires made to feel welcome and at ease throughout the process? To date, if organisations are measuring D&I progress at the micro level they have often focused this on the behaviours, the 'hows' of their activity. National Grid acknowledged this and has created a performance development system that focuses on the behaviours and values, where the 'whats' and the 'hows' have equal weighting in the regular performance discussions.

National Grid – P4G

National Grid[1] is an international organisation based in the United Kingdom with significant operations also in the United States. It is dedicated to being the world's premier network utility primarily focused on delivering energy safely, reliably and efficiently. They articulate their vision as 'connecting you to your energy today, trusted to help you meet your energy tomorrow'. They employ over 26,000 people worldwide.

National Grid created P4G (performance for growth) which is a performance management system which places equal importance on what their people do and how their people do it. By adhering to a '50%

(Continued)

what you do, 50% how you do it' framework, which applies to company's management population and non-operational staff, they have effected widespread, positive cultural change in a relatively short space of time. P4G is used globally and is communicated to their people annually as part of their 'line of sight' people framework enabling people to see how their personal objectives link back to the company vision.

Prior to implementing P4G, like most organisations, National Grid faced the challenge of placing too much emphasis on targets and not enough on behaviours.

If your organisation has either already implemented this way of measuring performance or is considering going down this route, it is important to consider the impact it can have on employees and the culture if implemented and delivered in the wrong way. Charlotte remembers working for one organisation that implemented the 'what and the how' style of performance management and then found themselves heavily criticised quite quickly afterwards. The challenge for the chief executive was that he publicly committed that the behaviours you displayed whilst delivering your targets were just as important as what you delivered. He then refused to dismiss one of his star traders who was clearly displaying bullying behaviours in order to reach his significant targets. This created the perception that what you delivered continued to be far more important than how you delivered it. As a result, the importance of behaviours in the workplace was never really taken seriously for the remaining tenure of that particular CEO.

When considering going down the route of individual measurement, it is important to consider the following:

- The maturity of the D&I activity – do you have a culture of measuring progress or will this be the first time?
- The culture of measurement – do individuals usually get measured on other aspects that are important to the company at a micro level?
- What is the role of the individual and what are they responsible for – it is important to ensure you are able to measure an individual on something they are responsible for, for example, a line manager may be responsible for the pay and recruitment decisions in their team – could they be measured on the level of diversity and inclusion in the process?

- Are you at a stage where individuals feel ownership and accountability for progress?
- Do you have a culture where the 'what and the how' are equally important? If not, how are you going to measure behaviours?

Again, one size will not fit all when it comes to individual measurement. What is important is to tailor any specific measures to the individual and the role. It is also important to consider when is the right time on your D&I journey to introduce this.

Targets versus quotas

It would be impossible for us to talk about measurement without discussing targets and quotas. Over the years targets and quotas have been hotly debated by numerous bodies across the world. Unfortunately the two words have also been used interchangeably without clear understanding, in some discussions, about the difference. We both favour using targets as you usually do for any other area of your business, but we are more cautious about quotas.

A target is a result or *situation* that you *intend* to *achieve*. Most businesses work to targets – for example, the turnover they want to achieve in a given month or year. It's a specific number or an upper limit on a specified subject which is usually set by an organisation at their own discretion. For example, with a target you might decide to try and improve the number of female graduates you recruit and set a target of aiming to get a 50 per cent split of male and female hires.

A quota is much more specific. For example, you agree that you are hiring ten people this year and six of them must be female. If you can't find six females you can only hire four men. Quotas are often mandatory and are often set externally by a body with authority to impose them on organisations.

The threat of imposed quotas for women on boards has been challenged by a number of countries including the United Kingdom who believe that they should be a last resort. Other governments, such as Norway, adopted quotas some years ago and at the time of writing this book, they continue to have the highest representation of women on boards across all European Union countries. That said, this hasn't translated to women at the executive level where they are still under-represented.

Some countries also have Government quotas for the number of disabled people they employ, and in the Middle East for nationals. Some carry with them fines for not meeting the quota, others are linked to the ease with which you can do business in that geography, for example how easy it is to obtain work permits for expats. EY's French business has worked hard over the past five years to successfully reduce the fine that they paid for not meeting their disability quotas. So, whilst it's not ideal to have such a stick, it certainly works in some cases.

That said, many organisations have made the decision to focus on creating targets within their companies for the areas in which they are wanting to progress. This isn't particularly new, although what is more recent is the number of organisations that are willing to go public with their targets. In the early 2000s when Charlotte was at Barclays, they created targets for the representation of women and ethnic minorities in senior positions. Again, fast-forward to the current day and companies such as PwC, Lloyds Banking Group and KPMG have publicly set very clear targets for the future demographic representation of senior levels within their companies.

As always, there are a number of elements to consider before jumping into creating targets for your organisation:

- What is the culture of the company? Is it target driven?
- Will creating a target encourage inappropriate behaviour? Will leaders aim to hit the target, whatever it takes or will they also consider the behaviours displayed to get there?
- Do your maths – what are the projections for the future if nothing else changes?
- Project longer term – what would you have to do over the next x years to hit the target, for example, how many new recruits into the organisation have to be from that particular group to hit the target?
- What would the ramifications be of not hitting the target? Public/ brand reputational issues? Financial losses for senior managers? Is the consequence big enough to drive change?
- Is the timing right? Do people within the organisation understand the importance of D&I? Do they understand why a target may be required? Timing, and communication, are everything.

If an organisation decides to go down the route of creating and communicating a target, it is important to do your homework first. A number of companies have failed at the first hurdle by creating a target that, once reviewed in more detail, is impossible to achieve taking into account their business objectives, their growth for the future and their recruitment projections. There is nothing more damaging to this agenda than creating a target and publicly promoting it when it can't stand up to the rigour and scrutiny of how it is actually going to be achieved.

Converting impact measures to business benefits

Realising the business benefits is about delivering what you said you would deliver and ensuring that it has the desired impact on the organisation. This is a critical time for the strategy. At this stage you are firstly sending a signal to the organisation about how all the hard work is having an impact on the areas of focus. You are setting an expectation of the future and making sure that you retain stakeholders' commitment to the work and the momentum – is the hard work to change the culture really worth it?

There are three key areas to consider when getting to the stage of realising the business benefits that we will look at in a little more detail:

- Gearing up to measuring the impact
- Measuring the impact and converting to business benefits
- Progressing further.

GEARING UP TO MEASURING THE IMPACT

Throughout the book we have highlighted the point that you can't do this alone. Sustainable culture change, regardless of the size of the organisation, isn't usually created by one person; it's rather a movement of people all going in the same direction, with the same vision.

When getting to the stage of measuring the impact, it is important to remind others of the measures that were agreed as well as the business benefits that were hoped to be realised. For example, the focus may have been on creating a more flexible workplace, so one of the measures may have been looking for improvement in the number of positive responses to specific questions within the employee opinion survey. The anticipated benefits may be increased productivity, increased employee morale and reduced travel expenses.

Figure 17.3 Realising benefits equation

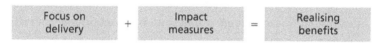

| Focus on delivery | + | Impact measures | = | Realising benefits |

It is also important to continue to hold people accountable for the commitments they have made and the part they agreed to play at the outset. We have both seen people not take their commitment to the delivery of the D&I plan as seriously as they have taken other aspects of their business delivery commitments. They have then struggled to meet deadlines and have not achieved the required level of impact to support converting action into benefits. Help where you can; however, don't take responsibility for other's commitments or inactions. If you do this once, they will continue to expect that in the future.

Make sure that the relevant departments/people who are helping you to pull the data and required information together, are aware of your deadlines and what you plan to do with the information. They may well be able to help you with the analysis and identify how much of the anticipated benefits have been realised.

Company x run their employee survey every other year (with a shorter people pulse in between) and within that there are some specific questions about inclusion. In addition they ask a number of demographic questions at the end of the survey. Depending on the geography, they may ask about a person's ethnicity, their gender, their sexual orientation and their religion. Most recently they have added a question asking employees whether they work flexibly (excluding contractually reduced hours). Not only has that given them a measure to track progress, they are able to link the level of engagement of employees with the amount of flexibility they have. They found that the people who responded to the flexibility questions favourably in the survey were more engaged than their counterparts who didn't.

MEASURING THE IMPACT AND CONVERTING TO BENEFITS

You're now at the stage where you are pulling the required information together and are able to convert that to show the impact the hard work and focus on this agenda has created. It may well be that you are unable to measure the impact of all aspects of your plan at the same time. For example, you may have agreed to deliver a pilot of a project to identify the benefits before rolling it out across the organisation, or your employee opinion survey is conducted once every year and has to be completed within a certain timescale. This isn't an issue; the main point here is that you are able to gain the information required, you are able to measure the impact and you are able to convert this into benefits. To be honest, staging the review of the impact and benefits will have a positive impact on the work that is being delivered as there will be regular drip-feeds of action, progress and impact within the organisation.

To do this effectively, first ensure you have the data available for the impact measures you are reviewing at this time. Don't forget, the initial measures and data you collected right at the very beginning of this process when assessing your current position will act as your benchmark data and will give you an overview of how you have progressed.

Review the information you are using as your benchmark data against the most recent data you have received and chart the difference. For example, if one of your measures was 'increase the percentage of candidate shortlists that are diverse', what was your benchmark data at the beginning and what does the data look like now?

Once you have that information, you will be able to see whether any change has taken place. Hopefully in this instance, you will see that the percentage of candidate shortlists that are diverse has significantly increased.

At this stage, it is time to convert that information into the business benefits. Ideally, this should be done with a number of people to discuss the benefits and ideally people who have been involved in this work. The benefit of doing this is that you have other people's perspectives who may well highlight something that you may not have considered.

If we continue with the example above, increasing the percentage of candidate shortlists that are diverse, the difference in results will enable you to consider some of the benefits below, for example:

- How many more talented 'diverse' individuals has the company interviewed that they may not have seen before?

- How many of those roles have been offered to 'diverse' individuals?
- How have the perceptions of the hiring managers changed by seeing, and interviewing, more diverse candidates?
- How many new relationships have you formed with potential candidates for the future?
- What impact has this had on the diversity of your talent pipeline?
- Can this be converted into a financial impact to the bottom line at this stage?
- What impact will this have had on the external perception of the organisation and your brand?

As you can see, the benefits will not all have a numerical response attached to them; however, it is important that you think about and articulate the benefits from as broad a range as possible. The wider the range of benefits and how you measure them, the more impactful this will be for your stakeholders.

To support your thinking on the business benefits and how they can be realised, take a look at some of the examples that large organisations have talked about:

Citi created a 'Maternity Programme' to up-skill line managers on how to support women on maternity leave. Their return-to-work rates increased from the industry average of 70 per cent to 97 per cent in a three-year period.

JP Morgan created a sponsorship programme for 56 ethnic minority employees. Over a six-month period 20 per cent of attendees improved their performance and 12 per cent were promoted.

PwC ensured all partners were educated in 'unconscious bias' before making partner promotion decisions. In 2014, 40 per cent of promotions to partner level were women compared to 21 per cent in 2012

IBM saved approximately $100 million a year on property costs through rolling out flexible working across the company

BT save, on average, 12 million litres of fuel per year through encouraging more conference and video calling than travel. This is both a cost saving and a benefit for their green credentials.

PROGRESSING FURTHER

Once you have completed the above exercise and started to see the impact and benefits of the work you are doing within D&I, it's important to maintain the momentum. This will be a combination of action, communications and a continued review of the impact the actions are having, as well as the business benefits for the organisation.

For some, however, the impact measures may not be moving in the right direction or the actions you had identified are not releasing the benefits you had intended. Don't take this as a defeat; take this as a learning opportunity and an opportunity to review what the next steps and focus will look like.

The following questions are an example of the questions you should ask yourself, and others, at this stage as an opportunity to reflect:

- Was the plan delivered as expected?
- Were the actions the right ones in the first place?
- Has anything changed within the organisation that may have had an impact on delivery?
- Were the impact measures/timescales for delivery too ambitious?
- Is the commitment really there from the organisation and the people who will influence the change?
- Is there anything we would do differently if we were to do this again?

The responses to the questions will help you identify what may need to change in the future to be able to realise the benefits you are committed to.

You may have also seen an increasing amount of focus on the 'return on investment' (ROI) element of D&I over recent years. For those who have a background in training and development, you will know how difficult it is in some cases to make direct links to the bottom line. For example, with leadership development, you know intuitively that it improves business outcomes. Sure, it is great if you can show that financial ROI and you will see this in a number of examples throughout this book. However, some of the links will be much more tenuous, for example, the impact of D&I awareness training beyond people attending and enjoying the session or the direct link to the bottom line from heightened morale.

As you can see, measuring the impact of the plan and the work the organisation decides to do on this agenda is a lot to think through. Many organisations do fall into the trap of thinking this isn't important or it will sort itself out as they start to deliver the plan. Our advice is to get your measures agreed at the outset.

Know what you are working towards and how you are going to measure it. How will you know how successful it has been and where the future focus is required if you're not measuring it. Taking the time to work through this at the start will reap dividends in the long run, and let's not forget the old adage, 'what gets measured, gets done'.

Five key takeaways from the chapter

- Be clear on how you are going to measure the impact of the D&I strategy from the start.
- Be flexible in how you measure impact in different locations – not all measures can be consistently applied across all countries.
- Consider how you can create individual measures for employees – how can you make them all accountable?
- Work with others to convert the progress made on your measures into tangible business benefits.
- Measure both the what and the how.

Strive for continuous improvement, instead of perfection. KIM COLLINS, ATHLETE

In this chapter we focus on continuous improvement and how to leverage your successes across the organisation. We will also consider the role that external awards and sponsorships play in embedding D&I into the culture.

Getting to the stage of embedding the D&I strategy into the culture is a clear indicator that a good level of progress has been made; the impact of the strategy will increasingly be clear to identify and you will be reaping the rewards. However, this is also the stage where some of that hard work can either be lost if not transitioned into the culture appropriately, or continue to be seen as an additional delivery plan rather than part of what the organisation stands for.

This is the stage where the work transforms from a programme to 'a way of life', where D&I becomes embedded into the day-to-day people and business processes and becomes a sustainable way for how the organisation operates and how it thinks about future plans for the business.

Building on the change and continuously improving

As we are all aware the world is constantly changing and constantly evolving. Business plans are regularly reviewed to ensure they are fit for purpose and will continue to deliver benefits for the organisation; this is no different for the D&I agenda.

Many organisations have spoken about their focus of embedding D&I into the fabric of the organisation and into all their practices and processes. This can be

easier said than done. Embedding D&I into your practices and processes do
mean that the job is done, and being diverse and inclusive will now natural
happen. What it does mean is that everyone within the organisation now has
responsibility in some way and is accountable for the part they play in ensuring
that D&I is continually embedded into what they do.

Ask yourself these questions to get a sense of whether D&I is embedded or on
track in your organisation:

- What are the behaviours you are seeing at a senior level? Has D&I
  influenced their behaviours? Are senior leaders behaving as inclusive
  role models or is further work required?

- Has D&I been integrated into existing business practices and
  processes, for example routine reporting? Can you clearly see where
  this has made a difference? If not, what would you have done
  differently?

- How are employees talking about equality, diversity and inclusion?
  Do they see this as an add-on or part of what they do on a day-to-day
  basis?

As well as reviewing what is already in place when embedding D&I into the
business for a continued, sustainable impact, it is important to consider how
this is going to be embedded into future business priorities:

- What are the new practices and processes within the business that
  require review to ensure that D&I thinking is embedded from the
  outset?

- What are the business priorities for the coming 12 months that you
  should be aware of and tapping into?

- Who are the leaders/stakeholders across the business you should
  continue to build a relationship with to ensure D&I thinking is
  embedded into all future activity?

Embedding into the business and culture of the organisation isn't a one-off
event. Continuously connecting with different groups and levels of employees
is critical to ensure that D&I remains front of mind, so that it is automatically
considered at the outset of any further change or adaptations, rather than
seen as an add-on which it may have been in the past.

One way that you can effectively embed D&I into the business is by creating a 'continuous improvement' mentality. One of the more popular methods being Kaizen.

Kaizen is an improvement process that can focus on a whole raft of business issues including quality, technology, processes, company culture, productivity, safety and leadership. Done right, it creates an opportunity to involve every employee in identifying and delivering ways to continually improve, thus increasing the level of employee engagement through the whole journey of D&I.

The principle behind the concept is that everyone is encouraged to identify small improvement suggestions on a regular basis. In most cases these are not ideas for major changes but small incremental changes that will create a much bigger impact over time.

Originating from Japan, the Kaizen philosophy is:

> 'Do it better, make it better, improve it even if it isn't broken, because if we don't, we can't compete with those who do.'

Today it is recognised worldwide as an important pillar of an organisation's long-term competitive strategy. Kaizen has a number of guiding principles, which include:

- Good processes bring good results
- Take action to contain and correct root causes of problems
- Work as a team
- Kaizen is everybody's business and everyone is involved in making improvements
- Big results can come from small changes accumulated over time.

When embedding into the business, as with the Kaizen principles, you can never truly say that you have finished; it becomes more of a way of life. Business and people practices and processes are constantly changing and this is where you need people to be aware of their role to ensure that you are continually embedding D&I into the fabric of the organisation and into everything they do.

Leveraging progress and celebrating successes across the organisation

With any culture change it does take time for the changes to become everyday activity. This does get easier to achieve when it starts to be embedded into day-to-day activities as discussed above. Another way of encouraging the continuous change is to recognise and celebrate successes and progress made.

There are a number of ways of doing this, whether publicly or privately, and the way that this is done really depends on how other areas of success are recognised within your organisation. From an internal perspective some organisations have included D&I within their own internal awards and other recognition schemes showing that it forms part of the daily expectation of good performance.

Some organisations recognise achievements through their performance management processes and this is discussed in more detail in the chapter on measuring impact (Chapter 17). We have both experienced organisations that incorporate D&I measures into individual performance reviews where people are either recognised or penalised for their contribution to the agenda.

Charlotte worked with one organisation where supporting the delivery of D&I was seen as part of everyone's role. If you were unable to prove the contribution you made to creating a more inclusive culture, your overall performance rating and bonus were reduced and feedback was included within your review. This continually sent the message that D&I was part of everyone's role regardless of job or level.

In contrast Fleur worked in one organisation where a significant 'bonus pot' was created and distributed to individuals that actively drove D&I, in addition to their 'day job', for example running an employee network. This sent the message that, although important and you would be rewarded for your contribution, it was in addition to your role and not quite embedded into what was expected from you on a day-to-day basis.

Leveraging progress and celebrating successes is also about sharing good practice across the organisation. In essence this can be achieved by bringing people together to share their learning points and experiences and encourage others to consider what they could either deliver or adapt to fit their part of the business. The key is to create an opportunity for employees to come together to share:

- what they have done
- the impact it has had
- if they were to do it again, what they would do differently.

Awards

One of the areas that is of great interest amongst organisations is how you can connect to the wider market through D&I. Many are keen to profile what they are doing and the positive impact this has had on their organisation. This also enables them to raise their profile as a progressive employer. This is a great way to increase the level of your knowledge about what others are doing. The challenge, however, is to achieve a fair balance between the market recognition/ how the outside world sees the organisation and what the individual actually experiences in their daily role within the organisation (see Figure 18.1).

Charlotte calls this the 'external perception versus internal reality gap'. The challenge for all organisations is to consider how the external perception of your organisation manifests itself in the day-to-day behaviours and actions that your employees see and feel. If an existing employee reads a copy of your promotional literature, would they recognise it as the same company they work for? If they read about you winning a high-profile D&I award for best practice, is this something that they have seen internally or even heard about?

Earlier (Chapter 6) we shared some perspectives on how you might recognise progress and successes from an external point of view via the benchmarks and charters that are available. Similar to benchmarks, the D&I-related awards have the potential to strengthen your brand and position your organisation as innovative and market leading. It can lead to increased motivation and heightened morale for your internal stakeholders, helping maintain momentum and keeping the spotlight on D&I.

At the time of writing this book, geographies such as New York and London are quite literally saturated with awards and there seems to be a new one launching on a regular basis. Some of the awards are classed as sector- or

Figure 18.1 External perception versus internal reality

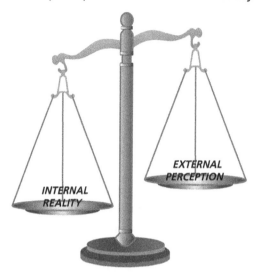

country-specific. They may be for a firm-wide initiative or recognising one role model or 'influential' person. Some have the word 'European' embossed in front of them, some are even heralded as 'global', but in our opinion some of them are of dubious quality, with a low and/or inconsistent level of rigour. The challenge for any organisation is that, if all of their competitors are winning awards, your own leadership team may well start to question why their brand is missing from the list.

The challenges with the quality of some of the awards tends to be: (i) the nominations process and (ii) the transparency of judging. We have both sat on a number of judging panels and have a good sense of what happens in the background. Take, for example, the Business in The Community (BiTC) awards in the United Kingdom. The process is professionally managed, with entries having to pass a number of stages including: (i) blind judging – where the judges have no idea who the nomination is from and (ii) the organisation/individual is invited to present to the judges or be interviewed.

The judging panel consists of three independent people, who have knowledge and experience in the field, and a formal observer whose role is to make sure that a consistent amount of time and questioning is given to each candidate. Each of the panellists have to rate the answers from each of the candidates using detailed guidance. Each panellist's ratings are then discussed, with the aim of coming to a group agreement on the winner. Feedback is later shared with all of the entrants, enabling them to learn from the whole experience.

At the other end of the scale, Fleur once judged an award where she didn't get to speak to any of the other judges. She was sent over 20 entries of varying levels of length and quality – some had clearly been written by the awards company themselves. She was told to score each of them on a scale of 1 to 20 and then didn't hear a word after she submitted her scores. It will come as no surprise that many of the genuine entrants left the awards evening very disillusioned, with the sense that there was a lot of 'inner circle' activity going on between sponsors and the awards organisers, with absolutely no transparency or fairness evident within the process.

Unfortunately, although a lot of this work is well intended, with the aim of raising the profile of people making an impact and being great role models, many of these lists can end up being thrown together and being judged by a group of 'mates'. This process undoubtedly increases the potential for bias to creep into the whole process, and people looking in could be forgiven for thinking that there is an element of 'I'll scratch your back if you will scratch mine' thrown into the mix.

A type of award that is starting to gain popularity, especially in the D&I field in the United Kingdom, is an award that people are asked to vote for. This is a great way to publicise the award nominations, increase the award brand visibility and drum up interest. However, if you are nominated for an award such as this, but don't have an extensive network to vote for you, or you are not the type of person that would go out and ask people to vote for you, then you are put at a disadvantage, regardless of how great you are.

We may be sounding a little cynical, but we have been immersed in this specialism for many years and we can usually identify the awards that are genuinely looking to recognise role models and share best practice that really does make a difference. Some are incredibly robust and are definitely worthwhile being associated with, but do your homework before getting involved.

Some of the areas to consider before you decide to get involved with a specific award are:

- Don't do anything that isn't evidence based. For the awards to be credible, you should be able to back up your submission with factual data and information.

- Will your employees recognise internally the work that is winning an external award?
- Consider the credibility of the awards organisation. Would it be seen as an accolade if they recognised you or your organisation or do they lack real knowledge in this area?
- Don't just follow the pack. How will getting involved with a particular award support the delivery of your overarching vision, D&I strategy and delivery plan? Would the recognition increase internal support and engagement, for example?
- How can you use involvement in an awards process to consider how you can continue to embed D&I into the culture of the company? For example, could you invite colleagues who are more cynical about the agenda to attend the awards event to better understand how well you are doing against your competitors?

Sponsorships

Another opportunity to increase your profile externally is with some form of sponsorship. These opportunities can come in many different guises, with many different price tags. Probably the first question you should be asking is how your involvement will ultimately support delivery of your vision, your D&I strategy and your delivery plan.

The vast majority of sponsorship opportunities will expect a financial payment. In some cases you might be able to offer them support for a project: for example, offering meeting room access in your building, printing the final report in-house, hosting a launch event or a training programme that gives you a couple of places on the course.

Not all D&I budgets have the flexibility to get involved in sponsorship opportunities, but where you do, this can be a difficult subject to make a decision on. There will be times when someone will approach you and the opportunity is a perfect match. For example, if you are a construction company and a consultancy wants to conduct some research into how to effectively attract women into the sector, which also happens to be your top priority. Another example might be an awards ceremony which has one particular award category devoted to 'Women in Retail' which is your sector and your key objective is to build your brand externally.

In our early days of D&I, we remember there was a vast amount of money spent on sponsorships – at times it felt like organisations found the easiest route to show their commitment to D&I was to write a big cheque. We saw (and still do see) multi-year sponsorships such as a three-year deal to sponsor a charities awards dinner, headline sponsors at a D&I conference, platinum members of a D&I not-for-profit organisation which then gives you a seat on the board. All of this is mutually beneficial, as long as you are clear about the motivators and are confident that the external perception you are creating mirrors the internal reality for your people.

A few areas to take into account when considering sponsorship include:

- Consider the credibility of the organisation you plan to sponsor. Would it be seen as a good partnership? Do their brand and the quality of their work have a good reputation?
- How will the sponsorship support the delivery of your overarching vision, D&I strategy and delivery plan? If there is no real benefit to any of these, then why are you considering it?
- If you were successful in gaining the sponsorship, what would that partnership say about what you are focused on achieving internally? Is it aligned? Would employees be surprised when they find out about the sponsorship? How could the partnership be perceived by other key stakeholders?
- Who else is a sponsor: for example, are you sponsoring alongside a competitor or can you gain exclusivity?
- How much influence do you have over the actions of the organisation you are sponsoring? For example, you wouldn't want to commit money and your name to a conference and find there is a lacklustre panel of speakers.
- What is the value for your brand and your people? For example, perhaps your CEO is invited to speak, your logo is included in the awards booklet or you are invited to be a judge.

Using your organisation's brand and your commitment to something externally via sponsorship is an important step to take. If you are unsure at any stage, talk to your colleagues and steering group, or other governance groups to gain their thoughts and perspectives. Regardless of how great the sponsorship opportunity may look, if you don't have the support to do this internally you will not realise the benefits that it could really give you.

Five key takeaways from this chapter

- Embedding D&I is more than a discrete one-off activity. You need to constantly be on the lookout for opportunities to embed into everyday business.

- Encourage others to consider how they can adopt the principles of continuous improvement when reviewing their areas of responsibility.

- Identify how you will be able to leverage successes across the organisation from the outset – how can you share and promote good practice and encourage others to consider how they may use this within their part of the organisation?

- Ensure D&I is integrated into internal reward mechanisms such as performance management or internal recognition awards and clearly articulate the success criteria.

- Think strategically about how you use award and sponsorship opportunities – how will they support delivery of your strategy and delivery plan as well as raising your profile internally?

Leveraging D&I in the market

The customer's perception is your reality. KATE ZABRISKIE,
BUSINESS CONSULTANT

When organisations start to leverage D&I in the market it is a prime indicator that they are truly seeing D&I as a business imperative rather than purely an important element of the talent management strategy. In this chapter we look at the role supplier diversity plays in the broader strategy, how to market to a diverse consumer base and how to think about creating appropriate products and services.

There are multiple reasons for you to turn your attention to what you are doing externally on D&I; it's just a question of timing which is important. You shouldn't really be out in the market talking about the value and impact of D&I and making demands of other organisations if your own programmes are in their infancy. Particularly, as discussed in the last chapter, if it means that your people will start to see you in the market, but what you are saying/doing doesn't resonate internally.

As we have covered in various chapters, you need to think about your brand – your attraction to customers, clients and potential employees. You need to develop products that appeal to the broadest customer base. It's always good to be recognised for the impact of your work, but as we say in the United Kingdom, don't try and run before you can walk. We have sat through too many conference presentations where we know that what the speaker is sharing is the vision, rather than the true reality in their organisation.

Something close to our hearts is being able to create opportunities to convene events for interested parties, to share best practice and, where possible, drive the agenda collectively. An example of this is when Fleur hosted a think tank in the summer of 2014. She invited a number of other organisations to spend half a day discussing the implications of taking the LGBT agenda global. From this, they produced a piece of thought leadership which identified eight ways to advance the global agenda from policy to practice. This was launched at a webcast that was run to mark IDAHOT day (International Day against Homophobia, Transphobia and Biphobia) which was attended by over 1,000 people globally.

Supplier diversity (driving inclusive procurement)

Supplier diversity is not usually high on the agenda for organisations to tackle in the early years of their D&I journey. That is, unless your organisation pitches for business where, increasingly, potential clients include supplier diversity questions in their business documents such as 'request for procurement' (RFPs). Fleur remembers attending a supplier diversity workshop at BT (British Telecommunications) a number of years ago and speaking to a man representing an engineering company. They had not focused on D&I at all, but had calculated that if they couldn't answer the relevant questions in their RFPs they would not be able to pitch for business, which could result in a potential loss of millions of pounds. For them, this was their initial, clear business case for a focus on D&I.

The aim of supplier diversity is to give companies owned and run by under-represented groups, the same opportunities to compete to supply quality goods and services alongside other, often larger, suppliers. This helps the organisation scale their procurement goals and supports a more sustainable future for their business as well as for economic growth. A minority-owned business is usually defined as being over 51 per cent owned and managed by a person/people recognised as a minority. In their 2011 research, the Environmental Information Management forum, EIM,[1] found that the top three aspects that SMEs (small- and medium-sized enterprises) are looking for are:

- Access to international customers
- Meeting customers/partners that otherwise they would have been unable to meet
- Increasing their knowledge on how to enter new markets.

There are a number of organisations who certify businesses as minority owned and will then introduce them to corporate members – organisations such as

WEConnect International[2] (United Kingdom, Canada, India, China), The National Minority Supplier Development Council[3] (Australia, Canada, China), National Gay & Lesbian Chamber of Commerce[4] (United States) and MSDUK[5] (United Kingdom) have all successfully done this.

For the SMEs, they conduct workshops on topics such as how to do business with multinational companies and effective use of social media. They also host forums to 'meet the buyer' and offer networking opportunities that all support the SMEs to be able to do business with larger organisations.

Maggie Berry, Executive Director for Europe, WEConnect International

'Supplier diversity is still in its infancy in Europe, but in the United States, it's firmly embedded in the business agenda. Our corporate members – mainly big US-based multinationals – want to replicate globally the way they're working with diverse owned businesses in America so that they can experience the same benefits across all of their operations.

'Essentially, it's about ensuring that diverse-owned businesses are properly represented in the supply chain. At WEConnect International, our focus is on businesses that are majority-owned, managed and controlled by women. Our role is to bridge the gap between those women-owned businesses and the corporates that are looking to procure a particular product or service.

'We believe that having a more diverse supplier base is a business imperative, in the same way as sustainability or protecting the environment. Put very simply, it fosters local economic development: if you invest in local businesses, you create jobs and wealth, which people can then spend on your products and services. Broadening out your supplier base also reduces risk, and encourages innovation and new ideas.

'Over the past few years, we've seen a move towards consolidation within procurement, going for one big supplier rather than several

(Continued)

smaller ones but now I think we're seeing the pendulum swinging back the other way. Companies want to know more about their suppliers – their credentials, their ethos, the way they do business.

'Of course they are also motivated to do the right thing and to be seen to be doing the right thing. Diversity isn't just about workforce diversity – responsible business practice means looking for opportunities to level the playing field in every area. Working with women-owned businesses ticks all of those boxes and more. It's a question of raising awareness, of making these suppliers more visible and making tender opportunities more accessible to them.

'For the potential suppliers, there are some barriers to be overcome. One is size: most SMEs (small- and medium-sized enterprises), including women-owned SMEs, are micro-businesses. That impacts on all sorts of things – their capacity for going out and winning new business, their readiness and ability to scale up to meet the demands of a larger contract and their preparedness for the corporate procurement process itself. We are able to provide that support, for example by connecting them with mentoring and networking opportunities. Often the corporate companies procuring will offer quite targeted training and support too.

'In future, I'd like to think that supplier diversity would be another aspect of business practice for which companies will be held properly accountable and on which they will need to report. We're some way away from that at the moment. At the same time, huge progress has already been made in other areas of corporate social responsibility. Now corporate organisations really should be asking themselves: What are we doing to support diverse businesses? Are we giving SMEs an opportunity to grow? Are we encouraging the economic empowerment of women?'

You may receive pushback when trying to introduce the concept of supplier diversity. The reason is generally that you are asking the functional owner of that specialism to potentially increase the number of companies they work with. This is usually in conflict with their strategy to reduce the preferred supplier list to a manageable minimum.

In our experience, it can be quite overwhelming to try and work out where to start on supplier diversity. Our advice is to start small by creating a pilot. The first step is to review all of your business functions and choose a small number that would be open to embracing the concept. They may be interested for a number of reasons, such as they are committed to this agenda and want to be more involved, or they see there are business benefits that could be quickly realised if they were to be one of the early adopters.

In Fleur's case she chose the business departments responsible for printing, recruitment and training. After gaining leadership buy-in, Fleur worked closely with WEConnect International and MSDUK to host events where the department heads could meet the SMEs who may be in a position to do business with them. The plan for the events was to:

- talk the SMEs through the firm's procurement process
- start to identify and understand the challenges the SMEs faced.

For example, as part of the procurement process, the SME is required to have a minimum annual financial turnover which is usually unrealistic for a small company.

Marketing to a diverse consumer base

Similar to the supplier diversity agenda, marketing doesn't always get to the top of the agenda when organisations focus on D&I. Unfortunately, for many this is a missed opportunity, as getting this right will have a positive impact not only on how potential consumers and clients perceive you but also on those who are your potential employees in the future.

Marketers that understand the impact of D&I know that they have to develop a mix of different communication approaches, different styles and channels in order to reach people in each of the diverse groups that make up their market. As in many other disciplines, not all marketing departments understand this.

Charlotte remembers working with the marketing team in a large organisation who stated 'our products are for the mass market so we don't have to tailor our commercials'. Charlotte has often wondered how much more impactful they could have been if they had been tailored for different consumer groups.

Organisations that include marketing in their wider D&I strategy generally do this for a number of reasons, including:

- They believe that how they are seen in the external market will have an impact on who they are able to attract and hire.
- They believe that D&I has a place in every part of the organisation as they aspire to embed it throughout all practices and processes.
- They are aware of the value of diverse groups: for example, the disposable income of the LGBT community called the 'pink pound', female breadwinners, and the 'silver dollar' of people over the age of 60.
- They know that supporting and promoting different communities can have a significant impact on their brand and increase the number of 'brand advocates' out in the market.

To engage your organisation in diversifying their marketing can initially be a challenge as it tends to cost more than marketing to the masses via one wider strategy. To do this effectively often requires additional research to identify which market segments are worth pursuing and why. They require the creation of more self-defined marketing materials to address each of those target segments in an appropriate and individual way. They also require a more tailored and far-reaching distribution process to promote the products and services to that market in an accessible and effective way.

There are a number of examples where organisations have taken the principles of D&I and placed them right in the centre of their marketing with obvious payback. Take for example, General Mills who aired a commercial in the United States for the cereal Cheerios. It featured a mixed-race family – white mum, black dad and mixed-race daughter. African-American audiences had an *overwhelmingly positive response* to the advert, which was popular among all viewers who were surveyed by television analytics firm Ace Metrix.[6] This is a classic example of an organisation taking the opportunity to engage with the people that are portrayed in their marketing. This incurred very little additional cost, as the marketing team looked at how they could embed D&I into the commercials they had already commissioned.

Another example is HSBC Bank, who we also referred to in the chapter on bias and unconscious bias training (see Chapter 10). For a number of years their marketing strapline 'The world's local bank' highlighted the cultural differences across the world. Many of their marketing campaigns have taken a prominent place in international airports as well as via their television campaigns. Their visual promotions, for a time, took the same format – showing the same picture two or three times with different captions under each of them highlighting the fact that we all have different perspectives of the world depending on our location and experiences.

Sadly, we still often see examples of stereotyping within marketing that clearly is not on the radar of the organisation. We regularly see retailers show pictures of girls playing with their toy kitchen and boys playing with their dumper trucks. Worse still, we see all-white families with Mum in an apron and Dad with a brief case, with nothing depicting some families as having two mums or two dads.

In late 2013, *The Guardian* reported on the progress that the pressure group, 'Let toys be toys' and customers were making to end gender-specific packaging and promotion of toys in shops.[7] One of their targets had been Marks & Spencer who had launched a range of toys called 'Boy's Stuff', which included planes, cars, dinosaurs and a pop-up fire station. The description on the latter said: 'This pop up fire station is perfect for little firemen everywhere', while the description of a watch in the same range read: 'The perfect wrist accessory no boy should be without', and a joke book read: 'Boys know the best jokes and here are 500 crackers to keep you ahead of the girls'. Marks & Spencer quickly responded by agreeing to make the packaging of all of its toys gender-neutral by spring 2014.

Whilst writing this book, Fleur found herself in a well-known children's toy and clothes shop and took a number of pictures of packaging. One was of a little boy playing with a wooden garage and the other was a little girl playing with her portable cleaning trolley – need we say more ...

We're sure there are other examples from across the world you could point to and show whether a company has or has not considered D&I within their marketing. Regardless of how much your organisation focuses on this from a marketing perspective, there are a number of next steps that we would recommend:

- Have an initial discussion with your marketing team, find out what their strategy is and how D&I is already considered and embedded throughout it.

- Review the demographics of your consumer/catchment audience. Work with your marketing teams to understand the future demographic trends. How can these influence the content of your marketing campaigns for the future?
- Consider how the organisation's key messages on D&I can influence the marketing campaigns.

Creating products and services for a diverse consumer base

Closely linked to the marketing element is how an organisation takes the insights and information that D&I can give them to directly benefit their bottom line via their commercial offering. This may be in the form of creating a new consumer product, an adaptation of what is already available or sourcing products that reflect the demography of your potential consumer base.

This is an important consideration for organisations when anticipating the on-going changes in demographics as well as the shift in the spending power and disposable income. The following shares a very small example of the spending power of different groups of consumers:

Women	Globally, women control approximately $28 trillion in annual consumer spending. Women represent a growth market twice the size of China and India combined. They make the decisions in the purchases of 94% of home furnishings, 92% of vacations, 91% of homes, 60% of cars and 51% of consumer electronics.[8]
Baby boomers (over 55 years)	In the next decade 66% of retail spending growth in the United Kingdom will come from shoppers aged 55 plus and it is predicted that the over-65s will account for £1 in every £4 of retail expenditure.[9]
BAME	In 2012 the spending power of the United Kingdom's black community was worth an estimated £300 billion.[10] Hispanic consumers in the United States commanded a $1.2 trillion market in 2013.[11]

LGBT	Globally, the annual spending power of the LGBT community is estimated at $3.7 trillion with Asia alone estimated to be $1.1 trillion.[12]
Disability	In the United Kingdom it is estimated that disabled people have a disposable spending power of over £80 billion; in the United States this is estimated to be $220 billion.[13]

As you can see from the above, if done right, the potential to tap into the disposable income of different consumer groups is significant. Many of these consumers are very discerning and will prefer to do business with companies that they believe understand them, their lifestyle and their requirements. Increasingly more organisations are taking this seriously and there are some good examples where organisations have got this right. Let's take a look at two here:

The Co-operative Funeralcare business in the United Kingdom was a very traditional business. As a result of increased life expectancy, they realised it needed to review its products as demand for its traditional services was stabilising. After reviewing the demographics across the United Kingdom, they decided to focus on broadening their customer base from a predominantly Christian one to include funeral services for other faiths. This marked a significant change in almost every aspect of how the business had traditionally operated. They systematically worked through the funeral and burial requirements of a number of faiths and what they needed to amend and change within their processes to deliver those requirements effectively and with respect: for example, they ensured that customers were aware they could ask for a person of the same sex to wash and dress their deceased loved one. They also focused on building relationships with the local communities to really understand their requirements during a time of mourning.

As a result of this work, Co-operative Funeralcare business benefited from a number of positive outcomes, including:

- Increased market share by 17.5 per cent
- Improved links with communities that the business serves
- Improved business profile with more people now knowing what Co-operative Funeralcare stands for

- Increased diversity within the workforce and an increase in business opportunities
- Stronger brand loyalty. Customer satisfaction spread through word of mouth and travelled quickly through some communities.

In 2014, Samsung Electronics opened a video call centre for the hearing impaired in Turkey, which is projected as being 3.5 million people. The campaign video 'Duyan Eller',[14] or the 'Hearing Hands Project' in English, shows how a customer with a hearing impairment reacts when all barriers are removed and is able to communicate effortlessly with the people around him. Samsung digitally provide a sign language service that can be accessed via a webpage via PC or mobile phone. At the other end of the service are a number of consultants who speak directly to the clients using sign language.

On the first day of the campaign video launching on Facebook it was viewed over two million times. By the end of the third day, views had increased to over seven million. There is little information available as to the impact this has had on attracting new clients or perceptions of customer service; however, the brand recognition alone with the video downloads will be significant.

The above was not intended to be fully comprehensive. Purely an exercise to whet your appetite with some examples of what some forward-thinking companies have done to build on their D&I strategy externally. Our key recommendation is for you to do some research into your market. Who are you trying to reach? What are their preferences in how they access information? What channels do they rate? What do they most value? Of course, you won't get one clean answer, but you will get a valuable insight into how and where you spend your investment 'dollars'.

Five key takeaways from this chapter

- Start small when introducing the concept of supplier diversity into your business – it can seem overwhelming.
- Spend your time wisely with your leadership teams to consider the impact of diversifying the supply chain – be armed with the case for change especially if their only motivating factor has been cost reduction.

- Work closely with your marketing department to share your knowledge and insights into the impact of non-diverse images – share examples of how they could make them more diverse.

- Arm yourself with the facts and figures of your market segment potential – be ready to sell the benefits of upfront investment.

- Spend time with the teams that create and develop the consumer products and services – how can you help them improve their knowledge and awareness of D&I?

Looking forward

Insanity is doing the same things time and time again and hoping for a different result. ALBERT EINSTEIN, THEORETICAL PHYSICIST

Throughout our book we have focused on how to deliver sustainable change to really create the diverse and inclusive organisations we are all striving for. However, what we are doing now will not necessarily be right for the future. A future that will see disruptive innovation continue to increase and potentially a whole new approach to work with various traditional roles displaced by technology. In EY's December 2015 report on transforming talent in the banking industry, they remind us that part of the technology innovation we will be seeing is the use of robots – now, that could drive an interesting conversation about D&I!

So much of this book has been about driving change, looking at the workplace differently, changing policies and processes, but none of this is a one-off activity. We need to be constantly looking ahead, assessing the landscape, thinking through the impact of pending legislation, changing demographics and technology innovation.

All that said, looking back on our journey to date, change on the whole has been slow in the D&I space and sometimes what we predict for the future can take time to evolve. Charlotte remembers making a public speech in 2001 about the 'ageing timebomb' in the United Kingdom, the impact it would have on companies in 2015 and what they should do to be prepared for it. She was asked to give a speech in 2015 on the same topic. Her opening comments were, 'Given that the pace of change in companies has been so slow to tackle the challenges of the ageing demographics, I have decided to share with you a speech I gave in 2001. The challenges we face and the actions we should take are exactly the same as then – it's just that we haven't done it.'

Earlier in the book we shared some of the mega trends that are emerging. In this chapter, we have taken some of that information into account as well as considering some of the trends we are seeing in forward-looking organisations. We won't go into any of these in great detail; however, this is food for thought and may well help you think about the challenges you face now a little differently.

Changing demographics

One topic that impacts many geographies is the changing demographics. What we mean by this is how the population is changing across the world as well as in the regions and countries in which you may operate. These changes will have an impact on every organisation in some shape or form from how they attract and retain future employees, right across to the products and services their client base may require.

As we write, we are in the middle of a refugee crisis with statistics telling us that EU member states received over 1.2 million first-time asylum applications in 2015, a number more than double that of the previous year. Germany, Hungary, Sweden and Austria received around two-thirds of the EU's asylum applications in 2015, with Hungary, Sweden and Austria being the top recipients of asylum applications per capita. Already companies are responding with programmes to help retrain and on-board new citizens, but the impact of these demographic shifts will be far reaching as we support the refugees to acclimatise to their new cultures and, in some cases, support our own people to welcome their new neighbours.

More broadly, a report published by PwC in 2015[1] stated that the global population is expected to increase by an additional one billion people by 2025, reaching eight billion, with the over-65-year-olds being the fastest growing group. Within that there are sharp regional variances; for example, Africa's population is projected to double by 2050, while Europe is expected to shrink.

Other projected changes to consider include:

- The number of people being assigned by their employers to roles outside their home country has increased by 25 per cent over the past decade. PwC has projected a further 50 per cent rise by 2020.
- Women in the G7 countries already control two-thirds of the household budget, the wage gap between men and women is

narrowing, and an estimated 865 million women are set to enter the workforce in the coming decade. So the purchasing power of women will continue to rise.

- The combination of rising life expectancy and – in some parts of the world – declining birth rates, will drive dependency ratios upwards. In 2050, the average age in Japan is set to be 53 years, compared to Nigeria where it is projected to be 21 years.

Demographics such as these will impact so much of what we do in the D&I space. In addition to still needing to attract and recruit the best talent, you will need to have a culture and people policies that support the diverse needs of that talent. For example, the global mobility of same-sex couples, an employee value proposition for an older employee with a portfolio career and more women on-ramping after their extended maternity leave.

With the changing demographics as a backdrop, here are some further thoughts on what may be on the horizon for us:

The need to connect with your mid-level managers

Throughout the book there has been reference to the role that senior leaders play in creating the right tone from the top and instigating change. Without exception, any change management expert will tell you that the commitment and drive for this agenda from senior levels is critical. However, we would argue that as much time, energy and resource, if not more, is needed from the mid level of an organisation – from the managers who are sometimes referred to as the 'permafrost'. This is the layer where great organisational vision often seems to get lost, forgotten about or stalled. In her research, Elisabeth Kelan[2] refers to this layer of management as the 'linchpin' who are 'reluctant to change because they are overwhelmed by their daily activities'. They are 'drowning in responsibilities with limited decision-making power, being under-trained and overworked, resistant to change'.

Looking to the future, there has to be far more focus on the mid-level managers and creating a case for change that they will buy in to. They are the ones that deliver what is expected from the top and deal with the challenges coming from those underneath them. They are the gatekeepers for the talent of the future and are a critical stakeholder in enabling organisations to build the talent pipeline required for sustainable change and growth. They are also in the frame for being the future leaders themselves; increasing their awareness and commitment now will stand the organisation in good stead for the future.

More emphasis will be required on supporting managers and leaders at all levels to effectively translate the vision and words of senior leaders on D&I into practical actions that are embedded into their day-to-day activities. Further focus will also be required into how managers and leaders are motivated to implement D&I which may be a result of how they are rewarded and the positive impact doing this right may have on their own career.

Put simply, the mid-level managers will be the deciding factor as to if and how sustainable change in creating a more diverse and inclusive organisation is actually achieved.

Small actions, big impact

Over the years, we have seen a lot of money in the D&I space being spent on sponsorships – conferences, awards, glittering dinners, publications and research. What we have concluded is that you can achieve just as much in a much more low-key way. It is often the smaller actions, what some call the 'nudges', that will have the biggest long-term impact.

We see this thinking taking shape with examples outlined in Margaret Heffernan's book *Beyond Measure – the big impact of small changes*.[3] In her book she reveals how organisations can make huge changes with surprisingly small steps. When a colleague says 'Just tell me what to do', you can be greeted with a look of surprise when the suggestions include active listening, the importance of reducing work hours and encouraging colleagues to share their views in meetings. These don't initially sound like the actions that will change a culture, but done by the majority the accumulation of small, everyday thoughts and habits can generate and sustain culture by strengthening social capital between workers.

Other examples of how small changes can make a big impact is the emerging profile that behavioural economics (BE) seems to be creating. BE is the study of psychology as it relates to the economic decision-making processes and choices of individuals and institutions. It looks at why and how people make irrational decisions and how behaviour does not follow predictions of economic models. Organisations such as the UK Government has used BE to influence small actions that will, ultimately, make a big impact. For example, they made a very simple amendment to their organ donor process by changing the usual 'opt in' opportunity to an 'opt out' one – instead of ticking the box to 'opt in', you had to tick the box to 'opt out'. As people generally left the box blank, it resulted in more people 'opting in' without changing their own behaviour.

Behavioural economics builds on the themes of bias that have been prevalent in the world of D&I over recent years. As this has been predominately used to influence behaviours and decisions around health and financial savings, it surely must only be a matter of time until this is considered and developed for other areas that require some form of behavioural change, such as creating more diverse and inclusive organisations.

Engaging men/allies as agents for change

In 2009, Catalyst introduced the notion of 'Men as agents for change' specifically focusing on the gender agenda. Since then the United Nations has created their #HeForShe campaign and the UK Government launched their programme of profiling prominent male business leaders and their support for gender equality. Many organisations that run awards have also started to include one that is specifically for men who are personally driving change in their organisation. The bottom line is that unless we are able to engage with the majority in leadership, which is often straight, white, men, we are not going to achieve the change that we want to see.

Although we have used 'engaging men' as an illustration, the LGBT community has leveraged the notion of engaging the majority group to support the cause of minority groups through the use of 'straight allies'. The principle behind this model is that people who are 'privileged' to be part of the majority group support the aims and aspirations of the minority group. Their focus is to raise the profile of equality, making it everyone's business and that we all have important roles to play in challenging cultural norms and stereotypes that hinder true equality.

The following is how EY describe the role of Allies:

Allies play a critical role in effecting culture change and making EY a place where our LGBT people feel safe and able to be out in the workplace. They can:

- Be heard! By openly challenging derogatory language and behaviour, we create a more inclusive work culture and productive work environment.
- Be involved! Stay informed of any internal or external client events and find out about activities in which your team can participate.
- Be inclusive! Foster an open environment by sharing family stories and ask about those of your colleagues in return.
- Be aware! Seek to understand the unique issues and challenges your LGBT colleagues face. Don't be afraid of saying the wrong thing or being rude – through mutual respect, your colleagues will appreciate the time you took to support an accepting work environment.
- Be seen! Display the available LGBT postcards or stickers at your desk. Create a safe place where LGBT colleagues can find support and understanding in the workplace.

Allies are needed at all levels of the organisation and the only qualifications required are that they care and people can relate to them.

Our prediction for the future is that more work will be done in this area with increased engagement of those who are in support of the various minority groups. We will not achieve sustainable change without the engagement of the majority of the people. Increased focus will be placed on inclusion and how the changes in the workplace for people deemed to be in 'minority groups' will positively impact and benefit the lives of everyone.

Multi-generational working

The demographic shift clearly articulates the impact that an ageing society will have on the workplace, as well as the challenges this will bring. For the first time in history, for the majority of countries, five different generations will soon be working together in the workplace – all at different life stages and all expecting a different proposition from their employer.

Some more enlightened organisations have started to focus on the impact that multi-generations will have both in the workplace and on business products and services. This focus will open up a real opportunity to engage every employee in D&I, given that everyone, of all ages, will be included.

Organisations will need to consider how they engage and retain employees in their late teens and early twenties as well as providing support to colleagues who believe that work contributes to their overall well-being well into their seventies.

Moving away from a focus on single strands to multiple strands

Difference is infinite and arguably you are setting yourself up to fail by dividing up your population and approaching inclusion and engagement through single strands. We have often heard researchers arguing that there are many more differences between women than there are between men and women. That said, you have to start somewhere and it is often the case that your burning platform is the turnover of your talented women and it is often the only metric that you can access.

We anticipate though that more and more companies will start to think about the multi-dimensional aspects of D&I. For example, how do you engage with your black lesbian population or how do you support your transgender graduate? Over the coming years more emphasis will be placed on understanding the impact of multi-dimensional characteristics of individuals and tailoring how organisations respond to this. D&I strategies and supporting actions will become more sophisticated and will focus more on how these dimensions enhance the drive to create more inclusive environments rather than hinder it.

We will start to see other areas of more sophisticated thinking, such as a move away from thinking about disability as just something you can see. Fleur was recently told by a people leader from a country with over 1,000 EY people that they had no disabled employees. What she meant was that there were no obviously disabled people in the office. Organisations focused on well-being are already doing a lot on mental health, looking at ways to proactively manage the challenges of job stress on individuals, before it impacts their health.

This will mean treating people truly as individuals rather than grouping everyone of a certain 'gender' or 'age' as being all the same with the same aspirations, needs and expectations. This will not be easy to deliver without a robust culture of openness and two-way communication.

Building the pipeline

As the number of women gaining boardroom seats increases in many geographies, there is a move in focus to ensure the pipeline of women coming up through the ranks is sustainable enough to feed these more senior positions. There is also a push to consider other strands of diversity. For example in the United Kingdom, there has been a debate about the lack of BAME non-exec directors and CEOs. In the United States there has been a recent call for a focus on getting more of the LGBT community in to leadership positions.

In EY's paper about the future of talent in banking,[4] they consider the question of how to change the culture of a very big and very old organisation so that employees can truly connect with customers of the future. They suggest that the key to achieving this is encouraging diversity of thought: 'The banking industry is still a long way from reflecting the makeup of society in terms of gender, ethnicity or background, at least at the senior levels of its workforce.' To change this, EY believes banks must 'change the way they make it possible for people to progress in their career: make their paths less siloed, foster flexibility and eliminate bias'.

We also predict that as organisations become comfortable on their D&I journey and in fact more confident, we will see more targets set for the pipeline: for example, with headhunters for the diversity of candidate lists, and these will be measurable and transparent. The debate about quotas versus targets will rumble on, but we both believe that, like any other part of your business, you set targets for what you want to achieve, so why not with D&I ... but don't forget the inclusion element in this.

Increased transparency

An emerging theme within corporate governance circles is the desire to increase transparency of what is happening within companies on a whole raft of issues – D&I increasingly becoming one of them. There has been equal pay legislation in many countries for decades – 1963 in the United States, 1970 in the United Kingdom and 1976 in Denmark to name a few, but the issue of the gender pay gap is a relatively new focus.

In the United Kingdom, in the last Conservative manifesto, they made a commitment to require companies with more than 250 employees to publish the difference between the average pay of their male and female employees. As David Cameron, their then Prime Minister said, 'You can't have true opportunity without real equality'. As we write, the government has announced that pay transparency reporting expectations will commence in 2018.

In the United States, President Obama announced new pay transparency rules for US companies arguing that 'women are not getting the fair shot that we believe every single American deserves' and, at the time of writing this book, California had just passed the Equal Pay Act which will provide for transparency in pay reporting starting September 2017.

Organisations have also started to share select parts of their demographic data via their corporate social responsibility (CSR) statements or annual reports and accounts (ARA) and some are comfortable publishing targets on their websites.

One sector that has become more transparent is the technology world. There was a media storm when the lack of diversity within Silicon Valley was branded across global news headlines. Since then companies such as Microsoft, Apple, Google and Facebook have started to share their demographic data and make public commitments to make significant improvements.

We expect the trend towards increased transparency will continue into all aspects of the diversity and inclusion agenda, ultimately resulting in nowhere to hide for organisations that do not take this seriously.

Heightened expectations of other stakeholders

Building on the previous area of transparency, we believe that there will be an increased interest from external stakeholders into what your organisation is doing and the potential impact your brand and reputation will have on theirs.

Stakeholders such as investors, pensions providers and sector-governing bodies will see D&I as an important agenda item when monitoring organisations. A survey conducted in 2015 found that only 23 per cent[5] of investors felt that D&I was important for them; however, they also felt that the level of importance would increase over the coming years.

Stakeholders will start to become more vocal on their thoughts of what organisations are and are not doing. They will increasingly feel confident to use their powers and challenge where they think progress is too slow and will increasingly start to vote with their feet, making organisations' lives challenging if this is not taken seriously.

Structuring the D&I function

Given the amount of change and our views of what the future may well have in store, it would be remiss of us to omit the thinking of where D&I will sit in the future and, indeed whether a dedicated D&I team will be required.

Historically D&I has usually sat within either HR/talent or CSR. Once or twice you might find it sitting under strategy or even reporting in to the CEO or chief administrative officer (CAO) office, but that is unusual. As we outlined earlier in the book, there is always a challenge with having too big a dedicated team leading D&I which can allow the business to think that they can just let them get on with it.

There is also the argument that, as you increase the sustainability of the changes delivered and continue to embed them into all practices and processes, the specialism is no longer required.

We would argue that access to the professional expertise and specialist knowledge of D&I is absolutely vital and required for all organisations. The level of complexity outlined throughout this book as well as the impact of a changing world and thoughts for the future clearly show that. However, how an organisation structures this is their choice; again, one size does not fit all.

The ideal scenario is to have a core specialist/s on hand to operate as in-house consultants who then work in partnership with the people on the ground who own the different functions/policies – for example, reward and recruitment. To deliver the impact that is usually sought requires a level of knowledge and experience that cannot be gained overnight. Our constant frustration is that this specialism is given to someone within the organisation that has 'a passion' for the subject but no skills, experience or knowledge – if this is really a business imperative, as so many leaders state it is, why would you give that responsibility to someone who is under-qualified?

Five key takeaways from this chapter

- Our world is ever-changing and our thinking about our talent has to be ahead of the game.
- Too many organisations are still spectators, which means they don't have a workforce that offers diversity of thought and the ability to really innovate.
- Employee engagement is key and it is critical to understand your people's motivators, particularly when you have four generations working together.
- Key to any real progress will be how to successfully engage your majority group in the conversation.
- Whilst culture change in the business should be owned and driven by the business, it needs strong support from a D&I specialist – passion alone is not enough.

Conclusion

I believe in the equality of men and women and I believe that we still have an awful lot of work to do to get there. What are you doing to change that configuration and draw out those extraordinary women who can be the leaders we need?. JUSTIN TRUDEAU, CANADIAN PRESIDENT

As the world continues to adapt and evolve, the level of diversity will both increase and become more complex. Diversity is a given; what we do with that diversity is an option – whether we focus on harnessing those differences and creating organisations where people can, and do, progress based purely on their skills, knowledge and expertise or whether we decide to do nothing in the hope that something will change naturally.

Throughout this book we have focused on how to create change within your organisation, from starting out on your journey to reaping the rewards with real progress. We have touched on the significant areas that are staples of the majority of D&I strategies as well as sharing our views of what may well be coming our way over the coming years. We have also focused on turning words into action, ensuring that every chapter includes some of our experience, as well as outlining pragmatic and tangible next steps for you to consider.

How we respond to our ever-changing world and workplaces is also evolving. Examples of good practice will continue to develop, research will continue to be published and new issues and challenges will continue to be identified. How we respond to all of this is critical – with an open, inquisitive mind and a desire to really want to get the best out of everyone. The constant in all of this will be the use of change methodology to create truly, sustainable change. This means moving away from initiatives and viewing D&I as a business imperative for the new age ... without this, organisations will not flourish.

As with all change, when it comes to D&I, the work is never finished. Following the guidance in this book you will, ultimately, get to the stage of reaping the rewards of creating an inclusive culture, but this doesn't mean that the journey is complete. Yes, it is important to celebrate your achievements along the way but don't think that it is done. There will always be something to do to ensure you and your organisation are continually improving and learning to maintain the sustainable change we are all aspiring to.

We wish you well on your continued journey. Do visit us at **www.diversity-andinclusiveleadership.com** to access further information and content that will support you to achieve that sustainable change. We welcome you to share your stories of how you have progressed in creating more diverse and inclusive organisations as well as the impact that this has created.

What did you think of this book?

We're really keen to hear from you about this book, so that we can make our publishing even better.

Please log on to the following website and leave us your feedback.

It will only take a few minutes and your thoughts are invaluable to us.

www.pearsoned.co.uk/bookfeedback

References

Introduction

1. http://vernamyersconsulting.com
2. 'Purchasing power of women' – http://www.fona.com/resource-center/blog/purchasing-power-women
3. http://www.mckinsey.com/business-functions/organization/our-insights/why-diversity-matters
4. http://www.ft.com/cms/s/0/4f4b3c8e-d521-11e3-9187-00144feabdc0.html#axzz43RSb5Akd
5. 'Women in business: The value of diversity' – http://www.grantthornton.global/globalassets/wib_value_of_diversity.pdf
6. The Peterson Institute for International Economics – *Is Gender Diversity Profitable? Evidence from a Global Study,* February 2016
7. 'World Population Ageing Report 2013' – http://www.un.org/en/development/desa/population/publications/pdf/ageing/WorldPopulationAgeing2013.pdf
8. http://reports.weforum.org/global-gender-gap-report-2015/
9. Open for Business (2015) – *The Economic and Business Case for Global LGB&T Inclusion 2015* by Jon Miller and Lucy Parker – www.open-for-business.org/wp-content/uploads/2016/01/Brunswick_Open_for_Business_full.pdf
10. World Health Organization – http://www.who.int/features/factfiles/disability/facts/en/index.html

Chapter 1

1. http://www.mckinsey.com/insights/organization/the_irrational_side_of_change_management
2. http://www.kotterinternational.com/the-8-step-process-for-leading-change/
3. http://www.heforshe.org/en

Chapter 2

1. *The Standard* (3 March, 2016) – 'Michael Dobson as chair may make it tough for Schroders to speak out' by Jim Armitage – www.standard.co.uk/business/jim-armitage-michael-dobson-as-chair-may-make-it-tough-for-schroders-to-speak-out-a3194881.html
2. http://www.qedconsulting.com/products/section2h.php

Chapter 3

1. http://www.talentinnovation.org/_private/assets/IDMG-ExecSummFINAL-CTI.pdf
2. https://publications.credit-suisse.com/tasks/render/file/index.cfm?fileid=8128F3C0-99BC-22E6-838E2A5B1E4366DF
3. http://www.ft.com/cms/s/0/60729d68-20bb-11e5-aa5a-398b2169cf79.html#axzz3rP65ZUD2

Chapter 5

1. www.conference-board.org

Chapter 6

1. www.creatinginclusivecultures.com

Chapter 8

1. http://www.cio.com/article/2915592/social-media/7-staggering-social-media-use-by-the-minute-stats.html#
2. http://extension.missouri.edu/extcouncil/documents/ecyl/Meet-the-generations.pdf

Chapter 9

1. https://implicit.harvard.edu/implicit/demo/takeatest.html
2. https://hbr.org/2015/08/what-facebooks-anti-bias-training-program-gets-right

Chapter 10

1. http://www.telegraph.co.uk/finance/newsbysector/banksandfinance/insurance/8370894/Tidjane-Thiam-the-man-from-the-Prus-beginnings-in-Ivory-Coast.html
2. http://leanin.org
3. 'How star women build portable skills', Boris Groysberg, *Harvard Business Review,* 2008
4. https://www.gov.uk/government/uploads/system/uploads/attachment_data/file/286342/bis-14-640-women-on-boards-voluntary-code-for-executive-search-firms-taking-the-next-step-march-2014.pdf
5. 'Off-ramps and on-ramps: Keeping talented women on the road to success,' Sylvia Ann Hewlett at the Centre for Talent Innovation (was the Centre for Work Life Policy), *Harvard Business Review,* March 2005
6. https://webaccess.berkeley.edu/resources/tips/web-accessibility
7. www.businessdisabilityforum.org.uk
8. R.B. Miller and S.E. Heiman, *The New Conceptual Selling: The Most Effective and Proven Method for Face-to-Face Sales Planning,* 2005
9. 'Orchestrating impartiality: The impact of "blind" auditions on female musician', by Claudia Goldin and Cecelia Rouse *American Economic Review,* September 2000
10. George T. Doran, There's a S.M.A.R.T. way to write management's goals and objectives, *Management Review,* vol. 70, p. 35.
11. http://www.fastcompany.com/3052988/the-future-of-work/heres-what-millennials-want-from-their-performance-reviews
12. *Ambition and Gender at Work,* Institute of Leadership and Management, 2011
13. 'Leadership in your midst: Tapping the hidden strengths of minority executive' Sylvia Ann Hewlett, Carolyn Buck Luce and Cornel West, *Harvard Business Review,* November 2005
14. Shifting the Needle – Increasing the number of Women in UK Partnerships, McKinsey and the 30% club 2012

Chapter 11

1. http://reports.weforum.org/global-gender-gap-report-2015/
2. http://ec.europa.eu/justice/gender-equality/files/gender_pay_gap/140319_gpg_en.pdf

3. http://www.theguardian.com/society/2016/feb/12/gender-pay-gap-reporting-big-firms-start-2018
4. 'Salary, gender and the social cost of haggling', *Washing Post* 30 July 2007
5. http://30percentclub.org
6. https://www.womenonboards.net/en-GB/Home

Chapter 13

1. 'Bringing equality to the workplace and cutting out the accidental manager' Interview with Anne Francke from CMI, Chris Blackwell, *Evening Standard,* 12 June 2015
2. 'Diversity training doesn't work', Peter Bregman, *Harvard Business Review* 12 March 2012
3. https://implicit.harvard.edu/implicit/education.html
4. http://www.aperianglobal.com/learning-solutions/online-learning-tools/globesmart/
5. 'The relationship between versatility and diversity among leaders' – a Tracom Group white paper
6. Sylvia Ann Hewlett, *Growing Global Executives: The New Competencies* A Vireo Book, Rare Bird Books, 29 October 2015 Stephen R. Covey, *The Speed of Trust*, FreePress, 2006
7. Catalyst report, 'The double-bind dilemma for women in leadership: Damned if you do, doomed if you don't' published in 2007 and updated in 2012
8. Women Matter, Gender Diversity in top Management, McKinsey 2013
9. https://hbr.org/2010/09/why-men-still-get-more-promotions-than-women
10. http://www.sylviaannhewlett.com/find-a-sponsor.html

Chapter 14

1. http://www.futureworkbook.com/
2. http://www.bbc.co.uk/news/technology-16314901
3. 'A study of flexibility in professional services workplaces', Luke Connoley, Head of Knowledge at UnWork, February 2012 – http://www.unwork.com/
4. http://www.myersbriggs.org/my-mbti-personality-type/mbti-basics/
5. https://hbr.org/2014/10/balancing-we-and-me-the-best-collaborative-spaces-also-support-solitude

6. https://hbr.org/2013/01/the-third-wave-of-virtual-work
7. Stephen R. Covey, *The Speed of Trust,* FreePress, 2006
8. Susanne Jacobs, The Positive Group – https://positivegroup.wordpress.com/2013/06/27/trust-the-real-currency-susanne-jacobs-programme-director-positive-group/

Chapter 15

1. http://www.isixsigma.com/tools-templates/cause-effect/determine-root-cause-5-whys/

Chapter 17

1. http://theapolloproject.net/apollo/wp-content/uploads/2014/05/1403-000076-National-Grid-V2.pdf

Chapter 19

1. The Environmental Information Management forum – EIM – https://eim.ecoinformatics.org/eim2011
2. WE Connect International (UK, Canada, India, China) – http://weconnectinternational.org/en/
3. The National Minority Supplier Development Council (Australia, Canada, China) – http://www.nmsdc.org/about-nmsdc/
4. National Gay & Lesbian Chamber of Commerce (US) – http://www.nglcc.org/
5. http://www.acemetrix.com/about-us/company-news/media-coverage/cheerios-interracial-ad-gets-high-viewer-marks/
6. https://www.theguardian.com/world/2013/dec/23/stores-agree-end-gendered-toys-displays-campaign
7. MSDUK (UK) – http://www.msduk.org.uk/
8. https://hbr.org/2009/09/the-female-economy
9. http://www.kpmg.com/uk/en/issuesandinsights/articlespublications/newsreleases/pages/how-will-demographic-trends-in-the-uk-affect-the-retail-sector.aspx
10. http://www.voice-online.co.uk/article/black-consumers-are-worth-£300-billion

11. http://www.terry.uga.edu/news/releases/minority-buying-power-grows-in-2013-according-to-selig-center-report
12. http://www.gaystarnews.com/article/global-lgbt-spending-power-estimated-to-be-3-7trillion/#gs.BW5CnXk
13. http://www.businessdisabilityforum.org.uk/customer-experience/the-evidence/
14. http://www.samsungvillage.com/blog/2015/03/26/hearing-hands-samsung-opens-a-video-call-center-for-the-hearing-impaired-in-turkey/

Chapter 20

1. http://www.pwc.com/gx/en/issues/megatrends/demographic-and-social-change-norbert-winkeljohann.html
2. 'Linchpin – men, middle managers and gender inclusive leadership', Elisabeth Kelan, Professor of Leadership at Cranfield University 2015
3. Margaret Heffernan, *Beyond Measure: The Big Impact of Small Changes*, 2015
4. 'Transforming talent: the banker of the future', published 8 December 2015 by EY Advisory
5. https://www.hermes-investment.com/wp-content/uploads/2015/10/Responsible-Capitalism-and-Diversity-Harriet-011015.pdf

Index